Unlock the Secrets of Unleashing Yahweh's Power Beyond 2044:

Fasting for Spiritual and Financial Breakthroughs

By

Dr. Jemilson Pierrelouis, Sr., PhD

Series 7, 63, 65, 66, 4, 24, 27, 28, MCPD, MCSD, MCAD, MCDBA, MCSE, AND MCSA, C.E.T

Hedge Consultants, LLC

Copyright © 2024 by Jemilson Pierrelouis. All rights reserved.

Published by Hedge Consultant, LLC, Dallas, Texas.

Please note that no part of this publication may be replicated and/or transmitted in any method or by any means (mechanical, electronic, recorded, photocopied, scanned, stored in any retrieval system, or otherwise) without the prior written permission of the publisher or authorization through payment of the appropriate per-copy fee to Hedge Consultants, LLC, jemilpierre@yahoo.com.

Requests for permission should be addressed to the Permissions Department, Hedge Consultants, LLC, online at www.hedgetradeuniversity.com

Limit of Liability/Disclaimer of Warranty: Although the publisher and author have used their best efforts in organizing this book, they make no representations or warranties with respect to the accuracy or wholeness of the contents of this book and precisely disclaim any implied warranties of merchantability or appropriateness for a particular purpose. No warranty may be created or extended by sales representatives or written sales materials.

Note: Nothing in this document or presentation should be taken as a recommendation to buy, hold, or sell certain securities or any other investment mentioned herein. Please know the author's opinion of a company's prospects should not be considered a guarantee of future events.

This document does not constitute an offer to sell or a solicitation of an offer to buy membership interests in any of the author's companies. All investors are reminded that there can be no assurance that past performance will continue and that a private company's current and future portfolio holdings are always subject to risk. The author will not make such an offer or solicitation prior to the delivery of a definitive offering memorandum and other materials relating to the matters herein.

All information provided herein is for informational purposes only and should not be deemed as a recommendation to buy or sell securities. All investments involve risk, including the loss of principal. You must know that no company can guarantee future performance, and past performance is not necessarily indicative of future results. Before making an investment decision with respect to the fund with any company, the author advises any potential investors of any company to carefully read the offering memorandum, the operating agreement, and the related subscription documents and to then consult with their tax, legal, and financial advisors.

There should be no assumption that any specific portfolio securities identified and described herein were or will be profitable. The guidance and strategies contained herein may not be appropriate for your situation. You should consult with a professional where suitable.

Neither the publisher nor author shall be liable for any loss of profit or any other commercial damages, including but not limited to special, incidental, consequential, significant, or other damages. This document may not be redistributed without the written consent of Hedge Consultants, LLC and does not constitute an offer to sell or the solicitation of an offer to purchase any security or investment product.

Hedge Consultants LLC also publishes its books in a variety of electronic formats. Some content that appears in print may not be available as an electronic book. For more information about Hedge Consultants, LLC products, visit our website at www.hedgetradeuniversity.com.

Library of Congress Cataloging-in-Publication Data:

Pierrelouis, Jemilson

Unlock the Secrets of Unleashing Yahweh's Power Beyond 2044: Fasting for Spiritual and Financial Breakthroughs / Jemilson Pierrelouis.

p. cm.

Includes index.

ISBN: 978-1-965052-99-0

Table of Contents

Unlock the Secrets of Unleashing Yahweh's Power Beyond 2044: 1

Fasting for Spiritual and Financial Breakthroughs 1

By 1

Table of Contents 4

Disclaimer 6

Acknowledgments 9

Preface: 11

Unlock the Secrets of Unleashing Yahweh's Power Beyond 2044: Fasting for Spiritual and Financial Breakthroughs 11

Introduction 19

About the Author 24

Chapter 1: 26

The Transformative Power of Fasting 26

Chapter 2: 35

Categories and Practices of Fasting 35

Chapter 3: 41

Prayer and Meditation: Deepening Spiritual Connection 41

Chapter 4: 57

The Significance of Praying through God's Names 57

Chapter 5: 80

The Aftermath: Sustaining Spiritual Growth 80

Chapter 6: 92

Fasting for Spiritual Clarity and Discernment 92

Chapter 7: 105

Fasting for Emotional Healing and Renewal 105

Chapter 8: 118

Fasting as a Catalyst for Social Justice and Compassion 118

Chapter 9: 130

Fasting for Physical Health and Wellness 130

Chapter 10: 142

How to Begin Your Fast and Awakening Your Potential 142

Chapter 11: 155

Important Strategies for Fasting: 40, 21, 14, 7, or 3 Days 155

Chapter 12: 174

In-Depth Overview of Different Fasting Approaches and Their Health Benefits .. 174

Chapter 13: 229

Praying for Financial Breakthrough: Seeking Yahweh's Provision 229

Chapter 14: 255

Importance of Using Proper Herbs When Fasting 255

Disclaimer

This book, "Unlock the Secrets of Unleashing Yahweh's Power Beyond 2044: Fasting for Spiritual and Financial Breakthroughs," authored by Dr. Jemilson Pierrelouis Dr. and published by Hedge Consultants, LLC, provides information and insights into the practice of fasting and its potential spiritual and financial benefits. The contents of this book are intended for educational and motivational purposes only. The author and publisher make no representations or warranties of any kind, express or implied, about the completeness, accuracy, reliability, suitability, or availability of the information contained herein.

The information presented in this book is not intended as a substitute for professional advice or treatment. Readers are advised to seek the guidance of qualified professionals regarding any medical, financial, legal, or other personal matters. The author and publisher expressly disclaim any liability or responsibility for any loss, damage, or inconvenience caused or alleged to be caused directly or indirectly as a result of the use of or reliance on any information contained in this book.

The views and opinions expressed in this book are those of the author and do not necessarily reflect the official policy or position of Hedge Consultants, LLC. References to specific individuals, organizations, products, or services are purely illustrative and do not imply endorsement or recommendation by the author or publisher unless explicitly stated.

All efforts have been made to ensure the accuracy of the information presented in this book at the time of publication. However, the author and publisher do not warrant that the information will be error-free or that defects will be corrected.

No part of this publication may be reproduced, stored in a retrieval system, or transmitted in any form or by any means—electronic, mechanical, photocopying, recording, or otherwise—without the prior written permission of the publisher, except as permitted under United States copyright law.

For permissions requests or inquiries, please contact Hedge Consultants, LLC.

The author and publisher acknowledge that fasting practices and spiritual pursuits may vary widely among individuals and cultures. Readers are encouraged to approach the concepts presented in this book with an open mind and to adapt any practices or recommendations to suit their personal beliefs and circumstances.

While every effort has been made to include accurate and up-to-date information, readers are advised to verify the information provided in this book with other sources and to exercise their own judgment when applying it to their lives. The author and publisher do not assume any responsibility for errors, inaccuracies, or omissions that may appear in this book.

This book may contain references to spiritual beliefs, practices, or rituals that some readers may find unfamiliar or challenging. Such references are intended to provide cultural and historical context and are not intended to promote or endorse any particular religious or spiritual beliefs.

Readers who choose to engage in fasting or other practices discussed in this book do so at their own risk. It is recommended that individuals consult with healthcare professionals, spiritual advisors, or other qualified experts before embarking on any fasting regimen, especially if they have pre-existing medical conditions or concerns.

By reading this book, you acknowledge and agree that the author and publisher are not responsible for any outcomes or consequences that may result from your interpretation or application of the information provided.

The author and publisher have taken utmost care in the preparation of this book, but make no representations or warranties of any kind, express or implied, about the suitability or applicability of the information contained herein for any purpose. The inclusion of specific prayers, affirmations, Psalms, or scripture references does not guarantee any specific spiritual or financial outcome, as individual results may vary based on personal beliefs, actions, and circumstances.

This book is protected by copyright laws and international treaties. Unauthorized reproduction or distribution of this book or any portion thereof may result in severe civil and criminal penalties and will be prosecuted to the maximum extent possible under the law.

Any references to financial strategies, investments, or market behaviors are purely educational and speculative in nature. Readers are advised to conduct their own research and consult with financial professionals before making any investment decisions.

The author and publisher reserve the right to revise and update the contents of this book as new information becomes available or as circumstances warrant. Such revisions will be made available in subsequent editions or updates, if applicable.

By reading this book, you agree to indemnify and hold harmless the author, publisher, and their respective agents, employees, and representatives from and against any claims, damages, losses, liabilities, costs, and expenses arising from your use of or reliance upon the information presented herein.

Acknowledgments

As you begin your transformative journey through the pages of "Unlock the Secrets of Unleashing Yahweh's Power Beyond 2044: Fasting for Spiritual and Financial Breakthroughs," I extend my deepest gratitude to all who have played a pivotal role in bringing this work to fruition. This book is a testament to the power of faith, fasting, and the unwavering support of those who believe in the boundless potential of Yahweh's blessings.

First and foremost, I offer heartfelt thanks to Yahweh Elohim, whose divine guidance and grace have illuminated the path to this endeavor. It is through His infinite wisdom and strength that this book seeks to empower you, dear reader, to accept spiritual clarity and financial abundance in your life.

To my beloved wife, your unwavering support and unwavering belief in the importance of this work have been my rock. Your encouragement has been a constant source of motivation, driving me to share Yahweh's light through the powerful practices of fasting and prayer. Together, we continue to walk hand in hand, fulfilling Yahweh's purpose for our lives.

To my son, your youthful enthusiasm and unwavering faith in our journey have inspired me beyond measure. Your encouragement has propelled me to strive for excellence and to envision greater possibilities. May you always walk in righteousness and continue to inspire others with your steadfast faith.

To my daughters, your belief in my abilities and your steadfast support have been a source of strength throughout this endeavor. Your love and encouragement have shaped this book into a beacon of hope and inspiration. May you continue to shine brightly, touching lives with your kindness and grace as you fulfill Yahweh's purpose for you.

I extend my heartfelt gratitude to every member of the Texas Financial Empowerment Future Millionaire Club. Your collective wisdom, shared experiences, and dedication to financial empowerment have enriched this book and made it stronger. Together, we are building a community where faith and financial stewardship go hand in hand.

Additionally, I extend my heartfelt gratitude to all the dedicated students of Hedge Trade University who are actively participating in our live Zoom classes. Your commitment to mastering the complexities of Stock Trading, Option Trading, Forex Trading, Cryptocurrency Trading, Commodities Trading, Future Trading, Real Estate Investment, and beyond is truly inspiring.

To each of you who diligently attends our sessions, asks insightful questions, and shares your perspectives, thank you for contributing to the vibrant learning environment of Hedge Trade University. Your enthusiasm and determination to excel in the financial markets are commendable.

I am grateful for the opportunity to guide and mentor such a motivated group of students. Together, we are not just learning the nuances of trading and investment strategies; we are shaping futures and paving the way for financial empowerment.

Special thanks to the entire Hedge Trade University team for their unwavering support and dedication to providing top-notch education and resources. Your efforts ensure that our students receive the best possible learning experience.

Lastly, I express my deepest appreciation to all our students for choosing Hedge Trade University as your educational partner. Your trust and commitment drive us to continuously innovate and deliver excellence in financial education.

And to you, dear reader, I thank you for boarding this journey with me. Your belief in yourself and in the power of Yahweh's provision is what drives the messages within these pages. May you find inspiration, guidance, and practical wisdom to unlock the doors to spiritual and financial abundance in your life.

In closing, remember that Yahweh has created you for greatness. Accept His promises, trust in His timing, and continue to walk in faith. May this book serve as a beacon of hope and a catalyst for your own spiritual and financial breakthroughs.

With gratitude and blessings,

Dr. Jemilson Pierrelouis Sr., PhD.

Preface:

Unlock the Secrets of Unleashing Yahweh's Power Beyond 2044: Fasting for Spiritual and Financial Breakthroughs

You hold in your hands a key to unlocking divine potential and experiencing profound transformation in your life. This book, "Unlock the Secrets of Unleashing Yahweh's Power Beyond 2044: Fasting for Spiritual and Financial Breakthroughs," is not merely a compilation of words but a roadmap to spiritual and financial liberation.

From the dawn of time, humanity has sought deeper connection with the divine, yearning for spiritual clarity, emotional healing, physical wellness, and financial abundance. Across cultures and faiths, fasting has been revered as a sacred practice—a gateway to unlocking spiritual truths and manifesting blessings. In the pages ahead, you will set off on an expedition of discovery and empowerment.

Revealing Your Divine Destiny

You are a masterpiece, intricately crafted by the Creator with unique talents and a divine destiny. Within your essence resides the power to conquer obstacles, accept greatness, and manifest blessings beyond imagination. This book serves as a testament to the truth that God has destined you for extraordinary achievements, threading through your very existence the ability to find profound spiritual fulfillment and abundant financial blessings.

Accepting the Power of Fasting

Fasting, as you will discover, goes beyond abstaining from food; it is a spiritual discipline that amplifies your prayers, purifies your intentions, and aligns your spirit with God's will. Through fasting, you will deepen your spiritual connection, gain clarity and discernment, and experience emotional healing and renewal. It serves as a catalyst for social justice, compassion, and personal growth—a transformative tool entrusted to the faithful.

Knowing the Promise of Abundance

Within the depths of your soul, Yahweh has planted seeds of greatness and promises of abundance. As you go on board this journey of fasting and spiritual awakening, remember that you are never alone. The God who parted seas and raised the dead walks with you, guiding every step and orchestrating divine encounters that shape your destiny.

Committing to Spiritual Discipline

Fasting transcends physical abstinence; it is a sacred act of surrender, a testament to your faith in God's provision and power. Through fasting, you align your desires with Yahweh's perfect will, inviting His transformative presence into every aspect of your life. In the crucible of fasting, weaknesses become strengths, doubts become unwavering faith, and trials become testimonies of His glory.

Unlocking the Mysteries of Prayer

In the chapters ahead, explore the profound connection between fasting and prayer—pillars of spiritual growth that strengthen your relationship with Yahweh. Through intimate communion with the Almighty, learn to pray with boldness and expectancy, unleashing supernatural breakthroughs in every area of your life. The names of God become your anthem of praise and declaration, resonating with power and authority as you speak them over your circumstances.

Nurturing Spiritual and Financial Health

Plunge into practical strategies and insights shared in this book, envisioning the holistic transformation taking place within you. From emotional healing and renewal to physical vitality and financial stewardship, each chapter is designed to equip you with the tools and wisdom needed to thrive in every season. Your journey toward spiritual clarity and discernment will lead to emotional freedom and financial empowerment, laying a foundation of stability and abundance for generations to come.

Leaving a Legacy of Faith

Your decision to get on this journey is not merely for personal benefit but also for the legacy you will leave behind. As you embrace the disciplines of fasting and prayer, you sow seeds of faith that will bear fruit in the lives of your loved ones and communities. Your commitment to spiritual growth and financial stewardship stands as a testament to Yahweh's faithfulness and provision, inspiring others to pursue their own paths of divine destiny.

Gratitude and Expectation

As we journey together through these pages, I am filled with gratitude for the privilege of sharing this transformative message with you. My prayer is that you will approach each chapter with an open heart and a spirit of expectation, knowing that Yahweh is faithful to fulfill His promises in your life. May this book ignite a passion for spiritual intimacy, financial wisdom, and unwavering faith in Yahweh's provision.

The Power of Transformation

As you immerse yourself in the teachings and practices outlined in this book, remember that transformation is not a one-time event but a continuous journey. Each chapter is a steppingstone towards greater spiritual clarity, emotional healing, and financial stewardship. Accept the process with patience and perseverance, knowing that every moment spent in fasting and prayer is an investment in your spiritual and financial future.

Divine Guidance and Revelation

Throughout history, Yahweh has spoken to His people through visions, dreams, and divine encounters. As you engage in fasting and spiritual disciplines, remain open to His voice and receptive to His guidance. The insights you gain will illuminate your path, empowering you to make decisions aligned with His perfect will and purpose for your life.

Community and Support

You are not alone on this journey. Surround yourself with fellow believers who share your commitment to spiritual growth and financial stewardship. Together, cultivate an environment of encouragement, accountability, and prayer. As you uplift one another in faith, you amplify the impact of your fasting and prayers, ushering in collective breakthroughs and blessings.

Stepping into Your Destiny

Beyond the practical tools and spiritual disciplines, this book invites you to step into the fullness of your divine destiny. You are destined for greatness, called to walk in authority and abundance as a child of the Highest God. Through fasting, prayer, and unwavering faith, you will experience spiritual breakthroughs that defy human understanding and financial blessings that surpass all expectations.

The Call to Divine Partnership

As you board on this journey of fasting and spiritual exploration, recognize it as a divine invitation to partner with Yahweh in co-creating your destiny. Your decision to dig into the depths of spiritual disciplines reflects your trust in His promises and your desire to align your life with His divine purpose. Through fasting, prayer, and deepening spiritual connection, you will forge a bond with Yahweh that transcends time and circumstance, unleashing His power to transform every area of your existence. I invite you to dive into these pages with an open mind and a spirit of expectancy. Allow the words to ignite a fire within you—a passion for seeking Yahweh's provision and experiencing His power in your life. Let this book be a beacon of hope and a guide to unleashing Yahweh's power beyond the confines of time and circumstance.

Illuminating the Path Ahead

Within the chapters of this book, you will discover practical insights and profound revelations that will illuminate your path towards spiritual clarity, emotional healing, and financial prosperity. Each chapter is designed not only to impart knowledge but to ignite a fire within you—a passion for seeking Yahweh's will and experiencing His abundant blessings. Whether you are beginning your journey or seeking deeper insights, may these teachings serve as a guiding light, leading you towards greater intimacy with Yahweh and profound breakthroughs in your life.

Cultivating a Heart of Gratitude

During your journey, cultivate a heart of gratitude for the blessings already bestowed upon you and the miracles yet to come. Celebrate each moment of spiritual growth, each answered prayer, and each instance of divine intervention as a testament to Yahweh's faithfulness and provision in your life. As you nurture a spirit of thanksgiving, you create an atmosphere conducive to receiving greater blessings and experiencing Yahweh's abundant grace in every season.

Divine Timing

Trust in Yahweh's perfect timing as you navigate the complexities of spiritual growth and financial stewardship. What may seem like delays or challenges are often divine appointments designed to refine your character, strengthen your faith, and prepare you for the abundant blessings ahead. Allow each season with faith and expectancy, knowing that Yahweh's plans for your life are good, filled with hope, and destined for prosperity beyond measure.

The life-changing impact of fasting

Chapter 1 begins your journey by unveiling the spiritual transformation through fasting. Beyond abstaining from food, fasting is a spiritual discipline that purifies your spirit, aligns your heart with Yahweh's will, and opens channels for His blessings to flow abundantly into your life. As you embrace fasting, you will experience a profound shift in your spiritual atmosphere, paving the way for miracles and breakthroughs.

Types and Methods of Fasting

Chapter 2 explores the various fasting styles and techniques, offering insights into how different forms of fasting—from intermittent fasting to extended periods of prayer and fasting—can deepen your spiritual connection and amplify your prayers. Each practice serves as a gateway to heightened spiritual awareness and divine revelation, preparing you to receive Yahweh's guidance and provision.

Deepening Spiritual Connection through Prayer and Meditation

In Chapter 3, you will delve into the art of prayer and meditation as essential tools for deepening your spiritual connection with Yahweh. Prayer transcends mere communication; it is communion with the Almighty, a sacred dialogue that strengthens your faith and fortifies your spirit. Through meditation, you will quiet the noise of the world and attune your heart to Yahweh's voice, receiving clarity and direction for your journey ahead.

The Meaningfulness of Praying with God's Names

Chapter 4 illuminates the impact of invoking God's names in prayer—a practice rooted in ancient tradition and biblical wisdom. Each name of God reveals a facet of His character and promises, offering a profound framework for declaring His power and sovereignty over every aspect of your life. As you invoke His names in prayer, you invite His presence to dwell richly within you, transforming challenges into opportunities and setbacks into divine appointments.

Sustaining Spiritual Growth: The Aftermath

Chapter 5 focuses on sustaining spiritual growth beyond moments of fasting and prayer. Spiritual maturity is cultivated through continuous seeking, learning, and applying biblical principles in daily life. This chapter provides practical guidance on nurturing a vibrant spiritual life, ensuring that your journey with Yahweh is marked by enduring faith, steadfast hope, and unwavering love.

Fasting for Clarity, Discernment, and Emotional Healing

Chapters 6 and 7 explore fasting as a means to attain clarity, discernment, and emotional healing. By surrendering physical desires, you create space for Yahweh to heal deep-seated wounds, clarify your purpose, and sharpen your spiritual discernment. These chapters offer a roadmap to emotional liberation and spiritual empowerment, equipping you to navigate life's challenges with grace and resilience.

Catalysts for Social Justice, Compassion, and Physical Wellness

Chapter 8 highlights fasting as a catalyst for social justice, compassion, and physical wellness. Your commitment to fasting extends beyond personal transformation; it ignites a passion for justice and compassion towards others. Moreover, fasting promotes physical health and vitality, aligning your body with Yahweh's design for holistic well-being. By stewarding your health, you honor Yahweh's temple and ensure longevity in fulfilling your sacred calling.

Unleashing Your Potential: Beginning Your Fast

Chapter 10 guides you in unlocking your potential through strategic fasting practices. Whether embarking on a 3-day, 7-day, 21-day, or 40-day fast, this chapter provides practical steps to prepare your heart, mind, and body for a transformative encounter with Yahweh. As you commit to fasting, you step into a season of divine alignment and empowerment, ready to receive Yahweh's abundant provision and breakthroughs.

Strategies and Benefits of Extended Fasting

Chapter 11 explores important strategies and benefits of extended fasting periods, offering insights into the spiritual, emotional, and physical benefits derived from longer periods of consecration. These strategies equip you to overcome spiritual obstacles, deepen your intimacy with Yahweh, and emerge strengthened in faith and resolve. Through extended fasting, you position yourself to receive supernatural intervention and divine acceleration in fulfilling your destiny.

Types of Fasting and Their Spiritual Significance

Chapter 12 delves into the various types of fasting and their spiritual significance. Whether engaging in water fasting, Daniel fasting, or corporate fasting, each type carries unique spiritual implications that align with Yahweh's purposes for your life. This chapter empowers you to discern the appropriate fasting method for specific seasons and circumstances, ensuring that your consecration yields maximum spiritual impact and divine favor.

Praying for Financial Breakthrough: Seeking Yahweh's Provision

Chapter 13 focuses on praying for financial breakthrough and seeking Yahweh's provision in every area of your life. As you align your financial goals with biblical principles and fervent prayer, you activate Yahweh's promises of prosperity and abundance. This chapter provides practical prayers, declarations, and strategies for financial stewardship, guiding you in sowing seeds of generosity and reaping a harvest of supernatural provision.

Harnessing the Power of Herbs in Fasting

Chapter 14 underscores the importance of using proper herbs during fasting to enhance spiritual clarity, physical health, and emotional well-being. From cleansing herbs to herbs that promote relaxation and focus, each botanical ally supports your journey of consecration and rejuvenation. This chapter offers insights into herbal remedies that complement fasting practices, ensuring holistic balance and vitality as you pursue Yahweh's purposes.

Closing Thoughts

In conclusion, I invite you to immerse yourself fully in the teachings and practices presented in this book. Allow the wisdom imparted to ignite a fire within you—a passion for seeking Yahweh's face, experiencing His presence, and unlocking His power for spiritual and financial breakthroughs. May your journey be marked by divine encounters, miraculous interventions, and a deepening relationship with the One who created you for greatness.

With faith as your shield and Yahweh's promises as your anchor, step boldly into the abundant life He has ordained for you. Let this book be your guide, your companion, and your testimony of Yahweh's surpassing goodness in the years to come.

Introduction

Enter the realm of Unlock the Secrets of Unleashing Yahweh's Power Beyond 2044: Fasting for Spiritual and Financial Breakthroughs. In this transformative journey, we delve deep into the profound practice of fasting, not just as a physical discipline but as a spiritual gateway to unlocking divine favor and financial prosperity. Fasting, an ancient practice revered across cultures and religions, holds within it the potential to transcend earthly limitations and connect us intimately with Yahweh, the source of all abundance.

Fasting is more than abstaining from food; it is a spiritual discipline that fosters humility, enhances prayer, and opens channels of divine communication. Throughout history, fasting has been a powerful tool used by spiritual giants to seek Yahweh's guidance, receive healing, and overcome spiritual strongholds. In today's fast-paced world, where materialism and distraction abound, fasting remains a potent antidote—a way to recalibrate our focus towards spiritual growth and financial breakthroughs.

In this comprehensive book, each chapter is meticulously crafted to not only inform but to inspire action. From understanding the different types of fasting and their benefits to exploring the intersection of prayer, meditation, and fasting, you will discover practical steps to integrate fasting into your spiritual routine. Whether you're seeking emotional healing, clarity in decision-making, or financial abundance, this book offers timeless wisdom and actionable strategies to help you achieve your goals.

Throughout the chapters, you will take the first step on a journey of self-discovery and spiritual empowerment. Each chapter is designed to deepen your understanding of fasting's transformative power and equip you with tools to navigate challenges and seize opportunities in your spiritual and financial life.

Join me on this journey as we unlock the secrets of *Unlock the Secrets of Unleashing Yahweh's Power Beyond 2044*, where fasting becomes not just a practice but a pathway to profound spiritual and financial liberation.

Chapter Summaries

Chapter 1: The Transformative Power of Fasting

Fasting is more than a physical discipline; it is a spiritual journey that transcends the mundane to touch the divine. In *Unlock the Secrets of Unleashing Yahweh's Power Beyond 2044*, we begin on a quest to understand the revitalizing impact of fasting. Through fasting, we open ourselves to Yahweh's presence, inviting His purification and guidance into our lives. This chapter explores how fasting can break chains of spiritual bondage, ignite spiritual fervor, and align us with Yahweh's purpose for our lives. Whether fasting for a day, a week, or longer, each moment of abstention becomes an opportunity for spiritual renewal and empowerment.

Chapter 2: Categories and Practices of Fasting

Fasting comes in various forms, each carrying unique spiritual and physical benefits. From intermittent fasting to water fasting and beyond, varieties and approaches to fasting, explores these methods in depth. Discover how different types of fasting can detoxify the body, enhance mental clarity, and deepen spiritual insight. Whether you're exploring fasting for health reasons or seeking deeper communion with Yahweh, this chapter provides guidance on choosing the right fasting practice to align with your spiritual goals.

Chapter 3: Prayer and Meditation: Deepening Spiritual Connection

At the heart of fasting lies prayer and meditation—essential tools for deepening our spiritual connection with Yahweh. *Prayer and Meditation* explores how fasting amplifies these practices, making us more receptive to Yahweh's voice and presence. Learn techniques to cultivate a prayerful spirit, enhance spiritual discernment, and sustain a vibrant dialogue with Yahweh throughout your fasting journey. This chapter empowers you to draw closer to Yahweh, fostering a relationship rooted in trust, intimacy, and divine guidance.

Chapter 4: The Significance of Praying through God's Names

Yahweh reveals Himself through many names, each reflecting a facet of His character and provision. *The power of prayer through divine names* explores how invoking these names enriches our prayers, aligning them with Yahweh's will and purposes. Discover the power of praying in Yahweh's authority, invoking His names of healer, provider, and protector. This chapter equips you with a deeper understanding of Yahweh's nature and invites you to experience His abundant blessings through personalized, name-based prayer.

Chapter 5: The Aftermath: Sustaining Spiritual Growth

After fasting, sustaining spiritual growth is essential for lasting transformation. *The Aftermath* explores how to carry the lessons and blessings of fasting into daily life. Learn practical strategies for maintaining spiritual momentum, integrating fasting's insights, and cultivating a lifestyle of spiritual discipline. This chapter guides you in navigating post-fast challenges with grace, ensuring that your spiritual journey continues to bear fruit long after the fast concludes.

Chapter 6: Fasting for Spiritual Clarity and Discernment

In moments of fasting, clarity and discernment become sharper as we silence the distractions of the world. *Fasting to Sharpen Spiritual Insight* explores how fasting heightens spiritual senses, enabling us to perceive Yahweh's guidance with clarity. Discover techniques to discern His voice amidst life's complexities, making decisions aligned with His divine will. This chapter empowers you to navigate spiritual challenges with wisdom and confidence gained through fasting.

Chapter 7: Fasting for Emotional Healing and Renewal

Emotional wounds and burdens can hinder spiritual growth and cloud our relationship with Yahweh. *Fasting for Emotional Healing and Renewal* examines how fasting becomes a catalyst for healing deep-seated emotional wounds. Explore methods to release past hurts, experience emotional restoration, and embrace Yahweh's healing touch. This chapter guides you in journeying towards emotional wholeness and spiritual renewal through the transformative influence of fasting.

Chapter 8: Fasting as a Catalyst for Social Justice and Compassion

Fasting extends beyond personal spiritual growth to impact societal issues. *Fasting as a Catalyst for Social Justice and Compassion* explores how fasting empowers us to advocate for justice and compassion. Learn how to channel fasting's energy into meaningful action, promoting Yahweh's righteousness and love in the world. This chapter inspires you to be a voice for the voiceless and a beacon of Yahweh's light through acts of social justice and compassion.

Chapter 9: Fasting for Physical Health and Wellness

Yahweh's design for fasting includes physical benefits that contribute to overall health and wellness. *Fasting for Optimal Physical Well-being* probes into the scientific and spiritual aspects of fasting's impact on the body. Discover how fasting promotes detoxification, enhances immune function, and supports longevity. This chapter equips you with knowledge to foster holistic well-being through Yahweh-inspired fasting practices.

Chapter 10: How to Begin Your Fast and Awakening Your Potential

Starting a fast effectively sets the stage for spiritual breakthroughs and personal growth. *How to Begin Your Fast* provides practical guidance on preparing physically, mentally, and spiritually for a successful fast. Learn rituals, prayers, and disciplines that awaken your potential and align your heart with Yahweh's purposes. This chapter empowers you to embark on each fast with confidence, expecting Yahweh to meet you in powerful and transformative ways.

Chapter 11: Important Strategies for Fasting: 40, 21, 14, 7, or 3 Days

Extended fasting periods require strategic preparation and spiritual resolve. *Important Strategies for Fasting* explores methods for safely and effectively undertaking 40, 21-, 14-, 7-, or 3-days fasts. Discover spiritual disciplines, nutritional considerations, and mental fortitude techniques to sustain you through prolonged abstention. This chapter equips you to embrace longer fasting periods with faith and perseverance, anticipating Yahweh's profound work in your life.

Chapter 12: In-Depth Overview of Different Fasting Approaches and Their Health Benefits

Different types of fasting yield varying spiritual and physical benefits. *In-Depth Overview of Different Fasting Approaches and Their Health Benefits* examines popular fasting methods such as intermittent fasting, juice fasting, and water fasting. Learn how each method detoxifies the body, enhances spiritual clarity, and aligns you with Yahweh's purposes. This chapter guides you in selecting the right fasting approach to achieve your spiritual and health goals effectively.

Chapter 13: Praying for Financial Breakthrough: Seeking Yahweh's Provision

Yahweh promises abundant provision to those who seek Him faithfully. *Praying for Financial Breakthrough* explores the spiritual dynamics of praying for financial abundance and stewardship. Learn principles of faith-based financial management and receive Yahweh's wisdom for achieving financial freedom and security. This chapter empowers you to trust in Yahweh's provision and align your financial decisions with His kingdom principles.

Chapter 14: Importance of Using Proper Herbs When Fasting

Herbs complement fasting by supporting detoxification and enhancing overall health. *Importance of Using Proper Herbs When Fasting* explores the role of herbs in fasting rituals and practices. Discover natural remedies that promote cleansing, strengthen immunity, and support holistic well-being during fasting periods. This chapter equips you with knowledge to enhance your fasting experience through Yahweh-inspired herbal remedies.

About the Author

Destiny has a peculiar way of revealing itself through the most unlikely of circumstances. For Dr. Jemilson Pierrelouis, this revelation came in the form of witnessing the devastating effects of poverty at a tender age. The struggles, the lack of necessities, and the overwhelming sense of despair etched themselves deep into his impressionable mind, igniting a flame of determination and resilience. This flame would not only drive him to overcome poverty but would also inspire him to empower others along the way.

At the age of eleven, Dr. Pierrelouis boarded a courageous journey, leaving behind his homeland to seek a better future in the United States. The promise of new opportunities and the pursuit of his dreams propelled him forward, despite the countless challenges he would face. Adapting to a new culture, learning a new language, and navigating the treacherous waters of financial hardship were just a few of the obstacles that awaited him. But rather than surrendering to adversity, he found the strength within to persevere.

Recognizing early on that education held the key to a brighter future, Dr. Jemilson Pierrelouis made a steadfast commitment to his studies. With unwavering determination, he pushed the boundaries of his intellect and expanded his horizons. Through the pursuit of knowledge, he began to unlock the secrets of success and empowerment.

Driven by an insatiable thirst for learning, Dr. Pierrelouis went on an impressive academic journey. His relentless pursuit of excellence led him to earn a doctoral degree—PhD—in his field of expertise. But he did not rest on his laurels. Instead, he became a lifelong learner, constantly seeking new opportunities for personal and professional growth.

Within the pages of "Unlock the Secrets of Unleashing Yahweh's Power Beyond 2044: Fasting for Spiritual and Financial Breakthroughs," you will discover the culmination of Dr. Pierrelouis's journey—a testament to the profound effects of fasting, spiritual growth, and financial success. Dr. Pierrelouis shares his most potent strategies for achieving personal and financial greatness, emphasizing the importance of faith, determination, and strategic thinking.

Today, Dr. Jemilson Pierrelouis stands as a testament to the power of determination, resilience, and unwavering belief in oneself. As the CEO of Hedge Consultants, LLC, Super Financial Trader Inc., and Hedge Methods Realty, LLC, he has solidified his position as a prominent and respected figure in the corporate world.

But Dr. Pierrelouis' success extends far beyond his entrepreneurial pursuits. He is not content with personal achievement alone; he feels a deep responsibility to uplift others and make a meaningful impact on society. Guided by his unwavering commitment to philanthropy, he has made it his mission to give back to his community and support those in need.

As a multifaceted entrepreneur and philanthropist, Dr. Jemilson Pierrelouis has not only excelled in the corporate world but has also pioneered new frontiers in technology and finance. His role as CEO of Hedge Consultants, LLC, and his expertise in information technology, security, and finance underscore his commitment to innovation and excellence.

Dr. Pierrelouis is a highly accomplished professional with a Ph.D. in Information Technology Management from AIU, based in Honolulu, Hawaii. His deep knowledge and proven track record in algorithmic trading systems, financial product development, and real-time Artificial Intelligence technology have positioned him as a trusted advisor and consultant in the financial industry.

With over 25 years of experience, Dr. Pierrelouis has developed high-frequency algorithmic trading systems and other financial products that optimize trading strategies and manage risk effectively. His certifications from Microsoft and extensive qualifications in the financial markets, including licensing with FINRA, highlight his expertise and proficiency in navigating the complexities of global finance.

Beyond his professional endeavors, Dr. Jemilson Pierrelouis remains grounded by his family values and a strong sense of community. He resides in Dallas, Texas, alongside his beloved wife, Natacha, and their four children. His commitment to family and community drives him to create a better future not only for his own family but for families worldwide.

Dr. Pierrelouis's journey is a testament to the revolutionary benefits of fasting, prayer, and strategic thinking. By accepting the principles outlined in this book, you can go on your own journey of spiritual and financial empowerment. Let Dr. Pierrelouis's wisdom and experience guide you as you unleash your inner greatness and fulfill your God-given potential.

Chapter 1:

The Transformative Power of Fasting

Fasting holds profound spiritual significance beyond its physical implications. It is a practice accepted by various faith traditions to deepen spiritual connection, seek divine guidance, and experience profound transformation. This chapter digs into the soul-renewing strength of fasting, exploring how abstaining from food for a set period can purify the soul, clarify spiritual insights, and open doors to spiritual and financial breakthroughs. By understanding and embracing fasting as a spiritual discipline, you go on an expedition of spiritual renewal, healing, and alignment with Yahweh's purpose for your life.

God has created you with the capacity to grow spiritually and experience His transformative power through fasting. As you embark on this journey, remember that fasting is not merely a physical act but a spiritual discipline that strengthens your faith and aligns your heart with Yahweh's will. By committing to fasting, you demonstrate your trust in Yahweh's provision and guidance, inviting His presence to transform your inner being and elevate your spiritual and financial life. Accept this opportunity to deepen your relationship with Yahweh and witness His miraculous work in every area of your life.

The decision to fast often arises from a desire for spiritual breakthroughs, personal renewal, or seeking divine guidance. It is a voluntary act of devotion, demonstrating one's commitment to spiritual growth and alignment with higher purposes. Fasting motivates individuals to prioritize their spiritual lives, setting aside temporal pleasures to pursue eternal truths and blessings.

Scripture Reference

"Yet when they were ill, I put on sackcloth and humbled myself with fasting. When my prayers returned to me unanswered, I went about mourning as though for my friend or brother. I bowed my head in grief as though weeping for my mother." — Psalm 35:13-14 (NIV)

This passage from Psalms illustrates fasting as a means of deepening prayer and seeking God's intervention in times of distress. It underscores fasting's role in expressing humility and urgency before God, acknowledging dependence on His mercy and grace.

Fasting transcends the physical realm, impacting emotional and spiritual dimensions profoundly. It cultivates spiritual discipline and strengthens faith, fostering resilience in the face of adversity. Through fasting, individuals experience inner healing, emotional clarity, and renewed purpose. It serves as a catalyst for personal transformation, breaking chains of spiritual bondage, and ushering in divine favor and breakthroughs.

Understanding the Gift of Fasting

Fasting is not merely abstaining from food; it is a spiritual discipline that transcends the physical realm. It is a conscious choice to set aside the comforts of the flesh to seek the treasures of the spirit. In your journey, God has woven a tapestry of purpose and destiny, and fasting serves as a catalyst to unlock the fullness of His plan for your life.

The Power of Purposeful Abstinence

When you begin a fast, you declare to the universe and to your inner being that there is something greater, something more significant than the immediate desires of the body. It is a declaration of faith, a testament to the belief that God has endowed you with the strength to conquer every obstacle and fulfill every divine mandate set before you.

Imagine standing on the precipice of your destiny, feeling the gentle breeze of God's favor whispering encouragement into your spirit. You are not alone in this journey; you are accompanied by angels dispatched to minister to your needs and to safeguard your steps. Fasting, therefore, becomes a symphony of surrender and empowerment—a melody where weakness transforms into strength, and doubt gives way to unwavering faith.

The Spiritual Dynamics of Fasting

Illuminating the Path to Spiritual Clarity

As you fast, clarity descends like the morning dew upon a parched land. The fog of confusion dissipates, revealing the road map of your purpose with crystalline clarity. Every moment of denial becomes a step closer to revelation, where the whispers of God become louder than the clamor of the world.

Strengthening Your Spiritual Resolve

Through the refining fire of fasting, your spiritual muscles are forged. Temptations lose their allure, and the transient pleasures of the world pale in comparison to the eternal joy found in communion with the Divine. Your resolve becomes unshakeable, anchored in the promises of God that declare you more than a conqueror through Christ who strengthens you.

Unlocking Supernatural Favor and Provision

God's promises are not empty words but living truths waiting to be activated through faith and fasting. As you fast, supernatural favor surrounds you like a protective shield, deflecting every arrow of adversity and opening doors that no man can shut. Provision flows abundantly, not just to meet your needs but to overflow into the lives of those around you, demonstrating the boundless generosity of your Heavenly Father.

Prayers for Seeking God's Guidance and Provision

Heavenly Father, I come before You in humility and gratitude, recognizing Your sovereignty over my life and finances. As I embark on this journey of fasting for financial breakthrough, I seek Your wisdom and guidance. Your Word says in James 1:5, "If any of you lacks wisdom, let him ask of God, who gives to all liberally and without reproach, and it will be given to him." Lord, grant me discernment and clarity in my financial decisions. Help me to align my desires with Your will, knowing that You have plans to prosper me and not to harm me, plans to give me hope and a future (Jeremiah 29:11). Amen.

Dear Lord, as I fast and seek Your face, I surrender all my financial worries and anxieties to You. Your Word assures me in Philippians 4:6-7, "Be anxious for nothing, but in everything by prayer and supplication, with thanksgiving, let your requests be made known to God; and the peace of God, which surpasses all understanding, will guard your hearts and minds through Christ Jesus." Grant me peace as I trust in Your provision and timing. Remove any barriers hindering my financial success and open doors of opportunity that only You can unlock. In Jesus' name, I pray. Amen.

Heavenly Father, I repent of any financial mismanagement or lack of faith in Your provision. Your Word teaches me in Malachi 3:10, "Bring all the tithes into the storehouse, that there may be food in My house, and try Me now in this," says the Lord of hosts, "if I will not open for you the windows of heaven and pour out for you such blessing that there will not be room enough to receive it." Lord, I commit to honoring

You with my finances and tithes. I trust in Your promise to bless me abundantly as I obey Your commands. Thank You for Your faithfulness and grace. In Jesus' name, I pray. Amen.

Dear God, as I fast for financial breakthrough, I pray for divine favor and supernatural provision in my life. Your Word assures me in Psalm 5:12, "For You, O Lord, will bless the righteous; with favor You will surround him as with a shield." Cover me with Your favor, Lord, in my career, business dealings, and financial investments. Remove any obstacles blocking my path to financial success and prosperity. Grant me opportunities to sow into Your kingdom and bless others abundantly. May my fasting be a catalyst for Your miraculous work in my life. In Jesus' name, I pray. Amen.

Lord Jesus, I surrender my financial burdens and struggles to You. Your Word promises in Matthew 11:28, "Come to Me, all you who labor and are heavy laden, and I will give you rest." Grant me rest and peace during my fasting time, as I deeply seek Your divine presence. Strengthen my faith and confidence in Your provision, knowing that You are Jehovah Jireh, my provider. Empower me to walk in financial freedom and abundance, breaking every chain of debt and lack in my life. Thank You, Lord, for hearing my prayers and for Your faithfulness. In Your mighty name, I pray. Amen.

Heavenly Father, I thank You for the transformative energy of fasting in my life. Your Word teaches me in Isaiah 58:6, "Is this not the fast that I have chosen: to loose the bonds of wickedness, to undo the heavy burdens, to let the oppressed go free, and that you break every yoke?" Lord, as I fast, break every yoke of financial bondage and oppression over my life. Release Your supernatural provision and abundance according to Your promises. May my fasting be a spiritual weapon against the enemy's schemes, bringing breakthrough and victory in my finances. In Jesus' name, I pray. Amen.

Dear Lord, I declare Your Word over my financial situation. Your Word says in Psalm 37:4, "Delight yourself also in the Lord, and He shall give you the desires of your heart." I delight myself in You, Lord, and I trust in Your perfect timing and provision. Grant me the desires of my heart for financial stability, prosperity, and generosity. May my fasting be a time of spiritual alignment with Your purposes and blessings. Thank You for hearing my prayers and for Your abundant grace. In Jesus' name, I pray. Amen.

Lord God, I lift up my financial goals and aspirations to You. Your Word declares in Proverbs 16:3, "Commit your works to the Lord, and your thoughts will be established." I commit my financial plans and endeavors to You, seeking Your guidance and wisdom. Align my thoughts and actions with Your will, that I may walk in financial success and prosperity according to Your divine plan. Thank You, Lord, for Your provision and faithfulness. In Jesus' name, I pray. Amen.

Heavenly Father, I pray for a breakthrough and restoration in my finances. Your Word promises in Joel 2:25-26, "So I will restore to you the years that the swarming locust has eaten, the crawling locust, the consuming locust, and the chewing locust, my great army which I sent among you. You shall eat in plenty and be satisfied, and praise the name of the Lord your God, who has dealt wondrously with you." Restore and multiply my financial resources, Lord, beyond what I can ask or imagine. Thank You for Your faithfulness and provision. In Jesus' name, I pray. Amen.

Prayers for Financial Breakthrough and Divine Intervention

Heavenly Father, I come before You with a heart full of gratitude and faith. I place my trust in Your unfailing love and provision. Your Word assures me in Philippians 4:19, "And my God shall supply all your need according to His riches in glory by Christ Jesus." Lord, I thank You for Your promise to meet all my needs abundantly. I surrender my financial worries and anxieties to You, knowing that You are my source and my strength. Grant me wisdom and discernment as I seek opportunities for financial growth and stability. In Jesus' name, I pray. Amen.

Lord Jesus, I acknowledge Your sovereignty over my finances. Your Word assures me in Matthew 6:26, "Look at the birds of the air, for they neither sow nor reap nor gather into barns; yet your heavenly Father feeds them. Are you not of more value than they?" Lord, I trust in Your provision and care for me. You know my needs before I even ask. As I fast, I surrender my financial concerns to You. Grant me peace and assurance that You are working all things together for my good and Your glory. Strengthen my faith and renew my spirit during this time of fasting. In Your precious name, I pray. Amen.

Heavenly Father, I declare Your promises over my life and finances. Your Word assures me in Jeremiah 29:11, "For I know the thoughts that I think toward you, says the Lord, thoughts of peace and not of evil, to give you a future and a hope." Lord, I trust in Your plans for my life, which are plans to prosper me and not to harm me. As I fast, align my heart with Your purposes and blessings. Grant me favor and divine opportunities that lead to financial breakthrough and abundance. Thank You for Your faithfulness and provision. In Jesus' name, I pray. Amen.

Lord Jesus, I come before You with a heart filled with gratitude and expectation. Your Word declares in Psalm 34:8, "Oh, taste and see that the Lord is good; blessed is the man who trusts in Him!" Lord, I taste and see Your goodness in my life, especially as I embark on this journey of fasting for financial breakthrough. You are a faithful God who provides for all my needs according to Your riches in glory. As I fast, increase my faith and deepen my trust in Your unfailing promises. Help me to lean not on my own understanding but to acknowledge You in all my ways, knowing that You will direct my paths (Proverbs 3:5-6). Thank You, Lord, for Your faithfulness and provision. In Jesus' name, I pray. Amen.

Heavenly Father, I lift up my financial concerns and challenges to You. Your Word assures me in Matthew 7:7-8, "Ask, and it will be given to you; seek, and you will find; knock, and it will be opened to you. For everyone who asks receives, and he who seeks finds, and to him who knocks it will be opened." Lord, I ask for Your divine intervention in my financial circumstances. Unlock pathways of opportunity beyond obstruction and provide for my needs abundantly. As I fast, grant me wisdom and discernment to make sound financial decisions that align with Your will. Thank You for hearing my prayers and for Your steadfast love. In Jesus' name, I pray. Amen.

Heavenly Father, I acknowledge You as the source of all my blessings, including financial provision. Your Word declares in James 1:17, "Every good gift and every perfect gift is from above, and comes down from the Father of lights, with whom there is no variation or shadow of turning." Lord, I thank You for the blessings You have bestowed upon me and my family. I ask for Your continued favor and grace in my life. Open doors of opportunity and prosperity that align with Your perfect will. Guide me in using my resources wisely and generously for Your kingdom's advancement. Thank You, Lord, for Your abundant blessings and provision. In Jesus' name, I pray. Amen.

Dear God, I come before You with a heart full of praise and thanksgiving. Your Word assures me in Psalm 103:1-5, "Bless the Lord, O my soul; and all that is within me, bless His holy name! Bless the Lord, O my soul, and forget not all His benefits: who forgives all your iniquities, who heals all your diseases, who redeems your life from destruction, who crowns you with lovingkindness and tender mercies, who satisfies your mouth with good things, so that your youth is renewed like the eagle's." Lord, I bless Your holy name and thank You for Your abundant blessings in my life. I ask for Your supernatural provision and favor. Remove any barriers or hindrances to my financial success and open doors that lead to prosperity and abundance. May my fasting be a time of spiritual growth and alignment with Your will for my life. Thank You, Lord, for Your faithfulness and grace. In Jesus' name, I pray. Amen.

Heavenly Father, I surrender my financial goals and aspirations to You. Your Word teaches me in Proverbs 3:9-10, "Honor the Lord with your possessions, and with the first fruits of all your increase; so, your barns will be filled with plenty, and your vats will overflow with new wine." Lord, I honor You with my finances and trust in Your promise to bless me abundantly. As I fast, grant me wisdom and discernment in managing my resources. Help me to sow seeds of generosity and kindness that honor Your kingdom. Thank You, Lord, for Your faithfulness and provision. In Jesus' name, I pray. Amen.

Dear God, I seek Your guidance and direction in my financial journey. Your Word assures me in Isaiah 58:11, "The Lord will guide you continually, and satisfy your soul in drought, and strengthen your bones; you shall be like a watered garden, and like a spring of water, whose waters do not fail." Lord, I thank You for Your promise to guide me and satisfy my needs abundantly. Grant me clarity and insight into Your will for my life. Remove any distractions or temptations that hinder my financial success. May my fasting be a time of spiritual refreshment and empowerment, aligning my heart with Your purposes and blessings. Thank You, Lord, in Jesus' name, I pray. Amen.

These prayers are crafted to align your heart with God's promises of provision, blessing, and breakthrough as you experience the powerful metamorphosis through fasting or financial success. Meditate on these prayers, personalize them, and continue to seek God's guidance and provision in every aspect of your financial journey.

Money Mindset Affirmations Through The healing power of fasting

I am abundantly blessed by the Lord, who promises in Psalm 84:11 that He will withhold no good things from those who walk uprightly.

I affirm that God is my provider, and as I fast and seek His face, He will supply all my needs according to His riches in glory by Christ Jesus, as stated in Philippians 4:19.

I declare that through fasting, I am aligning my heart with God's purposes, and He will direct my paths, as promised in Proverbs 3:5-6: "Trust in the Lord with all your heart and lean not on your own understanding; in all your ways acknowledge Him, and He shall direct your paths."

I affirm that God's plans for me are plans for prosperity and not for harm, to give me a future and a hope, as stated in Jeremiah 29:11.

I declare that through fasting, I am breaking free from financial strongholds and generational curses, and I am walking in the freedom and abundance that Christ has provided, as proclaimed in Galatians 5:1: "Stand fast therefore in the liberty by which Christ has made us free, and do not be entangled again with a yoke of bondage."

I declare that through fasting, I am renewing my mind and aligning my thoughts with God's promises of provision and abundance, as encouraged in Romans 12:2: "And do not be conformed to this world, but be transformed by the renewing of your mind, that you may prove what is that good and acceptable and perfect will of God."

I affirm that God has given me the power to create wealth, as stated in Deuteronomy 8:18: "And you shall remember the Lord your God, for it is He who gives you power to get wealth, that He may establish His covenant which He swore to your fathers, as it is this day."

I declare that through fasting, I am sowing seeds of faith and obedience, and I will reap a harvest of blessings and prosperity, as promised in Galatians 6:9: "And let us not grow weary while doing good, for in due season we shall reap if we do not lose heart."

I affirm that God is my shepherd, and I shall not lack any good thing, as proclaimed in Psalm 23:1: "The Lord is my shepherd; I shall not want."

I declare that through fasting, I am tapping into God's supernatural provision and favor, as stated in Ephesians 3:20: "Now to Him who is able to do exceedingly abundantly above all that we ask or think, according to the power that works in us."

I affirm that God's blessings are chasing me down and overtaking me as I obey His word and seek Him diligently through fasting, as promised in Deuteronomy 28:2: "You will experience an overflow of blessings, because you obey the voice of the Lord your God."

I declare that through fasting, I am sowing seeds of generosity and kindness, and God will multiply my seeds sown and increase the fruits of my righteousness, as stated in 2 Corinthians 9:10: "Now may He who supplies seed to the Sower, and bread for food, supply and multiply the seed you have sown and increase the fruits of your righteousness."

I affirm that God is faithful to His promises, and He will establish the work of my hands as I seek Him first through fasting and prayer, as promised in Psalm 90:17: "And let the beauty of the Lord our God be upon us and establish the work of our hands for us; yes, establish the work of our hands."

I declare that through fasting, I am breaking down spiritual barriers and hindrances to my financial success, and I am walking in the victory and authority that Christ has given me, as stated in Luke 10:19: "Behold, I give you the authority to trample on serpents and scorpions, and over all the power of the enemy, and nothing shall by any means hurt you."

I declare that through fasting, I am experiencing supernatural breakthroughs in my finances, and I am stepping into the fullness of God's blessings and provision, as promised in Isaiah 58:8: "Then your light shall break forth like the morning, your healing shall spring forth speedily, and your righteousness shall go before you; the glory of the Lord shall be your rear guard."

I declare that through fasting, I am renewing my strength and mounting up with wings like eagles, as stated in Isaiah 40:31: "But those who wait on the Lord shall renew their strength; they shall mount up with wings like eagles, they shall run and not be weary, they shall walk and not faint."

I affirm that through fasting, I am releasing any fear or anxiety about my financial future, knowing that God has not given me a spirit of fear, but of power, love, and a sound mind, as stated in 2 Timothy 1:7.

I declare that God is my refuge and strength, a very present help in times of financial trouble, as affirmed in Psalm 46:1: "God is our refuge and strength, a very present help in trouble."

I declare that God is faithful to His promises, and as I fast and seek His face, He will bless the work of my hands and make me prosperous, as stated in Deuteronomy 30:9: "Then the Lord your God will make you abound in all the work of your hand, in the fruit of your body, in the increase of your livestock, and in the produce of your land for good. For the Lord will again rejoice over you for good as He rejoiced over your fathers."

I declare that through fasting, I am breaking free from financial bondage and stepping into the freedom and abundance that Christ has provided for me, as affirmed in John 8:36: "Therefore if the Son makes you free, you shall be free indeed."

I affirm that God's word is a lamp to my feet and a light to my path, guiding me in every financial decision and leading me into prosperity, as stated in Psalm 119:105: Your Word illuminates my steps and guides my way.

These affirmations are designed to empower you as you align your heart and mind with God's promises of financial success through the transformative essence of fasting. Meditate on these affirmations, personalize them, and declare them over your life with faith and expectation, trusting in God's faithfulness and provision.

In summary of this section, the life-altering force of fasting lies in its ability to elevate the human spirit beyond earthly concerns, aligning it with divine purposes and blessings. It is a sacred journey of self-discovery, spiritual renewal, and communion with God. As believers embrace fasting with faith and sincerity, they open themselves to profound spiritual encounters and transformative experiences that transcend the ordinary and usher in the extraordinary.

Chapter 2:

Categories and Practices of Fasting

Fasting manifests in various forms across cultures and religious practices, each with its unique spiritual and physical benefits. This chapter explores the different fasting classifications and traditions, from water fasting to intermittent fasting, guiding you to choose methods that align with your spiritual goals and physical health. By understanding the diversity of fasting practices, you unlock pathways to spiritual clarity, physical rejuvenation, and divine intervention in your life. Accept these practices as tools to draw closer to Yahweh, renew your spirit, and experience supernatural breakthroughs.

Yahweh has appointed fasting as a means for you to experience His power and grace in profound ways. As you explore the various forms and practices of fasting, see them as opportunities to deepen your spiritual discipline and enhance your physical well-being. Each fasting practice has the potential to amplify your spiritual sensitivity, strengthen your faith, and align your life with Yahweh's divine purposes. Trust in His guidance as you embark on this journey, knowing that He will honor your commitment to seek Him through fasting and bless you with spiritual and financial abundance beyond measure.

Fasting emerges from a profound desire for spiritual purification, personal transformation, and divine communion. Motivated by a hunger for deeper spiritual experiences and a longing for divine intervention, individuals embark on fasting journeys to seek clarity, renewal, and alignment with higher spiritual truths. The motivation behind fasting lies in its capacity to elevate the soul, strengthen faith, and draw believers closer to God's presence and guidance.

Understanding the Special Power and Gift of Fasting

Fasting is a spiritual tool bestowed upon you to break chains, overcome obstacles, and receive divine guidance. It is a testament to your inner strength and faith in God's provision and promises. By abstaining from worldly comforts and focusing your heart on prayer and meditation, you open yourself to receive supernatural wisdom, healing, and breakthroughs that transcend human understanding.

The discipline of fasting empowers you to conquer spiritual strongholds, overcome adversity, and step into the fullness of God's blessings for your life. It teaches you patience, humility, and reliance on God's grace, guiding you towards a deeper intimacy with Him and a clearer vision of His purpose for your life.

Exploring Fasting Categories and Rituals

Fasting encompasses various practices and methods, each serving a unique purpose in your spiritual journey. Whether through intermittent fasting, water fasting, or partial fasting, each approach offers an opportunity to cultivate discipline, strengthen faith, and experience God's transformative power in your life.

Intermittent Fasting: This practice involves cycles of eating and fasting, aligning with natural bodily rhythms and promoting physical health while deepening spiritual awareness.

Water Fasting: By abstaining from solid food and consuming only water, you cleanse your body and soul, purifying your thoughts and renewing your spiritual vitality.

Partial Fasting: Restricting certain types of food or meals allows you to focus on specific spiritual goals, such as seeking wisdom, healing, or breakthrough in areas of need.

Prayers for Strength and Guidance

Heavenly Father, as I go on this journey of fasting, grant me the strength to overcome temptations and the clarity to discern Your will for my life.

Lord, fill me with Your Holy Spirit during this time of fasting, renewing my mind and empowering me to walk in obedience and faith.

Dear God, guide me through this period of fasting, granting me wisdom, healing, and breakthrough according to Your perfect plan and purpose.

Affirmations of Faith and Abundance

I am strengthened and empowered through fasting, aligning my spirit with God's divine purpose for my life.

My faith grows stronger as I fast, having faith in God's sufficiency and promises to lead me into abundant blessings and favor.

I declare breakthrough and transformation in every area of my life as I seek God through fasting and prayer.

Psalms for Protection and Financial Breakthrough

Psalms for Protection Part 1:

Psalm 91:11 - "For he will command his angels concerning you to guard you in all your ways."

Psalm 34:7 - "The angel of the Lord encamps around those who fear him, and he delivers them."

Psalm 121:8 - "The Lord will watch over your coming and going both now and forevermore."

Psalms for Financial Breakthrough Part 1:

Psalm 118:25 - "Lord, save us! Lord, grant us success!"

Psalm 23:1-2 - "The Lord is my shepherd, I lack nothing. He makes me lie down in green pastures; he leads me beside quiet waters."

Psalm 37:4 - "Take delight in the Lord, and he will give you the desires of your heart."

Scripture References

Isaiah 58:6-7 - "Is not this the kind of fasting I have chosen: to loose the chains of injustice and untie the cords of the yoke, to set the oppressed free and break every yoke? Is it not to share your food with the hungry and to provide the poor wanderer with shelter—when you see the naked, to clothe them, and not to turn away from your own flesh and blood?"

Matthew 6:16-18 - "When you fast, do not look somber as the hypocrites do, for they disfigure their faces to show others they are fasting. Truly I tell you, they have received their reward in full. But when you fast, put oil on your head and wash your face, so that it will not be obvious to others that you are fasting, but only to your Father, who is unseen; and your Father, who sees what is done in secret, will reward you."

James 4:8 - "Draw near to God, and he will draw near to you."

Scripture References

Psalm 35:13-14 - "Yet when they were ill, I put on sackcloth and humbled myself with fasting. When my prayers returned to me unanswered, I went about mourning as though for my friend or brother. I bowed my head in grief as though weeping for my mother."

Joel 2:12 - "Even now," declares the Lord, "return to me with all your heart, with fasting and weeping and mourning."

Luke 4:1-2 - "Jesus, full of the Holy Spirit, left the Jordan and was led by the Spirit into the wilderness, where for forty days he was tempted by the devil. He ate nothing during those days, and at the end of them he was hungry."

Benefits and Spiritual Insights from Fasting

Fasting, beyond its physical benefits, offers profound spiritual insights and blessings:

Spiritual Clarity and Focus: Fasting clears the mind and spirit, allowing for deeper communion with God and heightened sensitivity to His voice.

Breaking Strongholds: Fasting is a powerful tool to break spiritual strongholds, overcoming addictions, and renewing spiritual strength.

Divine Guidance and Direction: By humbling oneself through fasting, individuals open themselves to receive divine guidance and direction for life's decisions.

Healing and Restoration: Fasting can lead to emotional and spiritual healing, restoring brokenness and bringing wholeness.

Spiritual Warfare: Fasting strengthens spiritual defenses against spiritual attacks and prepares believers for spiritual warfare.

Practical Guidelines for Fasting

Seek God's Guidance: Before beginning a fast, seek God in prayer to discern the type and duration of fast suitable for your spiritual needs and health.

Start Gradually: If new to fasting, start with shorter fasts (e.g., skipping meals) and gradually extend the duration as guided by the Holy Spirit.

Stay Hydrated: During extended fasts, especially water fasts, ensure to drink plenty of water to maintain hydration and support bodily functions.

Spiritual Discipline: Combine fasting with prayer, meditation on scriptures, and worship to deepen spiritual experience and intimacy with God.

Break the Fast Wisely: After fasting, reintroduce food gradually to avoid digestive discomfort and continue in prayer and reflection.

Varieties of Fasting

Examine different types of fasting, including absolute, partial, intermittent fasting, and variations observed across religious traditions. Understand the nuances of each practice and their respective spiritual significance.

Practical Guidance

Provide practical guidance on preparing for and engaging in a fasting regimen. Address common challenges, such as physical discomfort and spiritual distractions, with strategies for overcoming obstacles and staying focused on spiritual goals.

Prayer

Heavenly Father, I thank You for the gift of fasting, a spiritual discipline that draws us closer to Your heart and aligns us with Your spiritual mission. As I go on this journey of fasting, I humbly submit myself to Your will and seek Your guidance and presence in every moment. Grant me strength, wisdom, and discernment as I fast and pray, and may Your Holy Spirit empower me to walk in obedience and faith. I declare breakthroughs, healing, and supernatural provision over our lives as I trust in Your unfailing love and promises. In Jesus' name, Amen.

Fasting is a sacred practice that spans across cultures and religions, uniting believers in a journey of spiritual growth, renewal, and alignment with God's divine purpose. As you embark on this transformative journey of fasting, may you experience the profound blessings and spiritual insights that come from seeking God with a humble and contrite heart. May your faith be strengthened, your spirit renewed, and your life transformed as you draw closer to God through the discipline of fasting.

In accepting fasting as a spiritual discipline, you position yourself to receive divine wisdom, healing, breakthroughs, and supernatural provisions that exceed your expectations. Let your fasting be an expression of faith and trust in God's sovereignty and loving care for your life. As you surrender your desires and needs to Him through fasting, may His abundant blessings and favor overflow in every area of your life, bringing glory and honor to His name.

In closing of this section, fasting Varieties and disciplines reflect humanity's quest for spiritual transcendence and divine connection. Whether intermittent, partial, absolute, or seasonal, fasting serves as a conduit for personal and communal renewal. It embodies self-discipline, strengthens faith, and aligns believers with spiritual truths and moral imperatives. As individuals engage in fasting with sincerity and reverence, they unlock spiritual depths, experience transformative growth, and embody the virtues of compassion, justice, and humility.

Chapter 3:

Prayer and Meditation: Deepening Spiritual Connection

Prayer and meditation are foundational disciplines that enrich your spiritual journey and deepen your connection with Yahweh. This chapter explores the profound impact of prayer and meditation in cultivating spiritual intimacy, discerning divine guidance, and fostering inner peace. By engaging in regular communion with Yahweh through prayer and meditation, you open channels for His wisdom, comfort, and provision to flow into your life. Embrace these practices as essential tools for spiritual growth, empowerment, and alignment with Yahweh's divine will.

Your journey with Yahweh is nurtured through prayer and meditation, as these disciplines open your heart to receive His love, guidance, and transformative power. As you dedicate time to prayer and meditation, remember that Yahweh desires to commune with you intimately and reveal His plans for your spiritual and financial well-being. Accept these moments of spiritual connection as opportunities to surrender your cares, seek His direction, and experience His peace that surpasses all understanding. Trust in Yahweh's faithfulness as you deepen your prayer life and meditation practice, knowing that He is ever-present and ready to lead you into paths of righteousness and prosperity.

Prayer, a conversation with the divine, encompasses various forms—adoration, confession, thanksgiving, and supplication—each reflecting different facets of spiritual communication. It serves as a pathway to express gratitude, seek forgiveness, present petitions, and offer praise to God. Through prayer, individuals open their hearts to receive divine wisdom, comfort, and strength, deepening their faith and surrendering their concerns to God's care.

Meditation complements prayer by cultivating inner stillness and mindfulness. It involves contemplative practices that quiet the mind, center the soul, and attune the spirit to divine presence. Techniques like focused breathing, mantra repetition, or reflection on sacred texts facilitate a profound sense of awareness and receptivity to spiritual insights. Meditation enables individuals to transcend external distractions, quiet internal chatter, and enter a state of profound peace and spiritual clarity.

The Power Within You

Within you lies a reservoir of untapped potential, a spiritual power bestowed upon you by the Creator Himself. You are not merely a product of chance but a deliberate creation, fashioned with purpose and imbued with the capacity to manifest greatness. It is through prayer and meditation that you unlock this potential, harnessing the divine energy that flows through every fiber of your being.

Your Divine Purpose

God has intricately designed you with a unique purpose, a calling that resonates with the essence of your soul. Through prayer, you align yourself with His divine will, seeking guidance and clarity amidst the tumultuous currents of life. Meditation becomes the vessel through which you commune with the sacred, quieting the noise of the world to hear the whisper of the divine within.

Cultivating the soul's growth

In the stillness of prayer and the depth of meditation, you launch into a quest of spiritual growth and enlightenment. Like a tender shoot reaching towards the sun, your soul stretches towards spiritual maturity and deeper understanding. Each moment of communion with the divine nurtures your inner landscape, cultivating virtues of faith, patience, and wisdom.

The Metamorphic Influence Power

Prayer and meditation are not mere rituals but transformative practices that shape your character and destiny. They soften the hardened edges of your heart, fostering compassion and empathy towards others. Through these practices, you accept humility, recognizing your place in the grand tapestry of humanity.

Strengthening Your Faith

Faith is the cornerstone of your spiritual journey, the unwavering belief that God's promises are true and His love unconditional. Through prayer, you express your trust in

His providence, surrendering your fears and anxieties at His feet. Meditation strengthens this faith, grounding you in the certainty that His guidance will light your path.

Illuminating Your Path

As you examine deeper into prayer and meditation, the murky waters of uncertainty begin to clear, revealing a path illuminated by divine grace. You gain clarity of purpose and direction, discerning the steps you must take towards fulfilling your divine destiny. Each moment spent in communion with God becomes a beacon of light, guiding you through life's challenges and triumphs.

Your Spiritual Arsenal

In your journey of spiritual empowerment, prayer and meditation serve as your most potent weapons. They shield you from spiritual attacks and fortify your soul against adversity. Through prayer, you invoke divine protection, surrounding yourself with the angelic hosts that stand guard over your life. Meditation becomes a fortress of peace, a sanctuary where you retreat to replenish your spirit and recharge your soul.

Invoking Divine Presence

The act of prayer draws you into the presence of the Almighty, where His glory envelops you like a warm hug. It is here, in the sacred sanctuary of His love, that you find solace and strength. Through meditation, you open channels of divine communication, listening intently to the still, small voice that speaks words of comfort and guidance into your heart.

Manifesting Abundance

God desires abundance for His children, not only in material blessings but also in spiritual fulfillment and emotional well-being. Through prayer, you align your desires with His divine purpose, invoking His favor and provision over every area of your life. Meditation deepens this alignment, quieting the noise of doubt and fear, and amplifying your faith in His promises.

The Gift of Intimacy

At the heart of prayer and meditation lies the gift of intimacy with God—a sacred communion that transcends words and thoughts. It is in the quiet moments of reflection and surrender that you draw near to His heart, experiencing His love in its purest form.

Through these practices, you cultivate a deeper understanding of His character and a profound sense of belonging in His presence.

Your Journey Begins Here

Dear reader, as you undertake this journey of prayer and meditation, know that you are going on a path of transformation and spiritual awakening. God has intricately crafted you with purpose and intention, and He beckons you to explore the depths of His love and the richness of His grace. Embrace the power within you, nurture your faith, and allow His presence to illuminate every step of your path.

The Role of Prayer

Explore the inseparable relationship between fasting and prayer. Understand how fasting amplifies the power of prayer, heightens spiritual sensitivity, and facilitates intimate communion with the divine.

Guided Prayers

Present a collection of guided prayers tailored for different stages of the fasting journey. These prayers encompass petitions for spiritual guidance, healing, deliverance, and divine favor, providing a framework for personal and collective spiritual encounters.

Prayers of Invocations for Prosperity

Prayer for Divine Provision

"Heavenly Father, I come before You with gratitude in my heart for Your abundant blessings in my life. You are the provider of all good things, and I trust in Your divine provision. As I seek financial success, guide my steps and open doors of opportunity. Grant me wisdom to make sound decisions and discernment to recognize Your leading. May Your favor surround me like a shield, and may Your blessings overflow in my life. Thank You, Lord, for Your faithfulness and for meeting all my needs according to Your riches in glory. Amen."

Scripture Reference:

Philippians 4:19: "And my God will meet all your needs according to the riches of his glory in Christ Jesus."

Prayer for Wisdom in Financial Matters

"Gracious God, Your wisdom surpasses all understanding, and I seek Your guidance in all financial matters. Grant me discernment to manage resources wisely, to invest prudently, and to steward Your blessings faithfully. Help me to prioritize Your kingdom and seek first Your righteousness in all financial decisions. May Your wisdom fill my heart and mind, guiding me towards prosperity that honors You. Thank You, Lord, for Your provision and for equipping me with everything I need for success. In Jesus' name, Amen."

Scripture Reference:

James 1:5: "If any of you lacks wisdom, you should ask God, who gives generously to all without finding fault, and it will be given to you."

Prayer for God's Favor in Business and Career

"Dear Lord, I humbly ask for Your favor to be upon my business/career endeavors. Unlock opportunities that are impervious to closure and grant me success in all my endeavors. May Your favor go before me and surround me like a shield, bringing prosperity and growth. I commit my plans and ambitions to You, trusting that You will establish them for Your glory. Thank You, Lord, for Your abundant blessings and for guiding me towards financial success. In Jesus' name, Amen."

Scripture Reference:

Psalm 90:17: "May the favor of the Lord our God rest on us; establish the work of our hands for us— yes, establish the work of our hands."

Prayer for Debt Freedom and Financial Freedom

"Gracious Father, I lift up my financial burdens to You and ask for Your help in achieving debt freedom and financial freedom. Give me wisdom to manage my finances responsibly and provide opportunities to increase my income and reduce my debts. Grant me strength and perseverance during times of financial challenge, and fill my heart with hope and confidence in Your provision. Thank You, Lord, for Your promise to supply all my needs according to Your glorious riches. I trust in Your timing and Your perfect plan for my financial success. In Jesus' name, Amen."

Scripture Reference:

Psalm 37:5: "Commit your way to the Lord; trust in him and he will do this."

Prayer for Trusting God's Timing

"Lord, I surrender my financial goals and desires into Your hands. Help me to trust Your timing and Your plans for my life. Give me patience and perseverance as I wait upon You. Strengthen my faith, Lord, and remind me that Your ways are higher than my ways. May I find peace in knowing that You are working all things together for my good and Your glory. Thank You, Lord, for Your faithfulness and for the assurance that You will never leave me nor forsake me. In Jesus' name, Amen."

Scripture Reference:

Psalm 27:14: "Wait for the Lord; be strong and take heart and wait for the Lord."

Prayer for Gratitude and Contentment

"Father, I thank You for the blessings of life, health, and provision. Help me to cultivate a heart of gratitude and contentment in every circumstance. Teach me to be faithful with the resources You have entrusted to me and to use them wisely for Your kingdom. Guard my heart against the love of money and the pursuit of worldly gain. May I find true joy and satisfaction in You alone, knowing that You are my greatest treasure. Thank You, Lord, for Your abundant grace and for Your commitment to fulfill all my necessities from Your boundless riches. In Jesus' name, Amen."

Scripture Reference:

1 Timothy 6:6: "But godliness with contentment is great gain."

Prayer for Overcoming Financial Challenges

"Dear God, I come to You with my financial struggles and challenges. You are my provider, and I trust in Your ability to meet my needs. Strengthen me in times of difficulty and grant me wisdom to overcome financial obstacles. Help me to see opportunities where others see limitations and guide me towards solutions that honor You. I declare Your promises of abundance and prosperity over my life, knowing that You are faithful to fulfill Your word. Thank You, Lord, for Your unfailing love and for Your grace that sustains me. In Jesus' name, Amen."

Scripture Reference:

Philippians 4:13: "I can do all this through him who gives me strength."

Prayer for Wise Financial Planning

"Heavenly Father, I seek Your wisdom as I plan for my financial future. Help me to set goals that align with Your will and to make decisions that honor You. Guide me in budgeting, saving, and investing, so that I may be a good steward of the resources You have entrusted to me. Grant me discernment to distinguish between wise investments and risky ventures. May my financial planning reflect Your priorities and contribute to Your kingdom purposes. Thank You, Lord, for Your guidance and provision in every area of my life. In Jesus' name, Amen."

Scripture Reference:

Proverbs 16:3: "Commit to the Lord whatever you do, and he will establish your plans."

Prayer for Abundance and Overflow

"Lord, You are the God of abundance, and I thank You for Your promise to bless me abundantly. Pour out Your blessings upon me, Lord, so that I may overflow with Your goodness. Open the windows of heaven and pour out blessings that I cannot contain. May Your abundance in my life be a testimony of Your faithfulness and provision. I receive Your blessings with gratitude and praise, knowing that You are a generous and loving Father. Thank You, Lord, for Your unending grace and for Your provision that exceeds all expectations. In Jesus' name, Amen."

Scripture Reference:

Malachi 3:10: "Bring the whole tithe into the storehouse, that there may be food in my house. Test me in this," says the Lord Almighty, "and see if I will not throw open the floodgates of heaven and pour out so much blessing that there will not be room enough to store it."

Prayer for God's Guidance in Career and Business

"Dear Lord, I come before You seeking Your guidance and direction in my career/business. You know the desires of my heart and the talents You have entrusted to me. Lead me to opportunities that align with Your will and purpose for my life. Grant me wisdom and insight to make decisions that honor You and bless others. May my work glorify Your name and be a source of blessing and provision. Thank You, Lord, for Your faithfulness and for the assurance that You go before me. In Jesus' name, Amen."

Scripture Reference:

Proverbs 3:5-6: "Trust in the Lord with all your heart and lean not on your own understanding; in all your ways submit to him, and he will make your paths straight."

Prayer for Financial Wisdom and Discernment

"Gracious God, I come to You seeking Your wisdom and discernment in financial matters. You are the source of all wisdom, and I trust in Your guidance. Help me to manage my finances wisely, to make sound investments, and to honor You with my resources. Grant me clarity of mind and heart as I seek Your will in budgeting, saving, and giving. May Your wisdom lead me on paths of prosperity and blessing, aligning my desires with Your perfect plan. Thank You, Lord, for Your provision and for Your faithfulness in all things. In Jesus' name, Amen."

Scripture Reference:

Proverbs 2:6: "For the Lord gives wisdom; from his mouth come knowledge and understanding."

Prayer for Faith in God's Provision

"Lord, I confess my worries and anxieties about finances. Help me to trust in Your provision and to have faith that You will meet all my needs according to Your glorious riches. Strengthen my faith, Lord, and remind me of Your faithfulness throughout history. I choose to rely on Your promises rather than my circumstances. Thank You, Lord, for being my provider and my protector. In Jesus' name, Amen."

Scripture Reference:

Matthew 6:31-33: "So do not worry, saying, 'What shall we eat?' or 'What shall we drink?' or 'What shall we wear?' For the pagans run after all these things, and your heavenly Father knows that you need them. But seek first his kingdom and his righteousness, and all these things will be given to you as well."

Prayer for Philanthropy and Spiritual Influence

"Heavenly Father, You have blessed me abundantly, and I thank You for Your goodness. Help me to be a faithful steward of the resources You have entrusted to me. Show me opportunities to bless others and to advance Your kingdom on earth. May my generosity reflect Your love and grace, and may it bring glory to Your name. Use me as a channel of Your blessings, Lord, and help me to make a lasting impact in the lives of those around me. Thank You, Lord, for Your provision and for Your unwavering love. In Jesus' name, Amen."

Scripture Reference:

2 Corinthians 9:11: "You will be enriched in every way so that you can be generous on every occasion, and through us your generosity will result in thanksgiving to God."

Prayer for Humility and Wisdom in Prosperity

"Heavenly Father, as You bless me with financial prosperity, guard my heart against pride and selfishness. Grant me humility to acknowledge that all good things come from You. Help me to use my resources wisely and to bless others generously. May my prosperity be a testimony of Your goodness and grace, reflecting Your love to a world in need. Thank You, Lord, for Your abundant blessings and for Your faithfulness in every season of life. In Jesus' name, Amen."

Scripture Reference:

James 4:10: "Humble yourselves before the Lord, and he will lift you up."

Prayer for God's Guidance in Investments

"Dear Lord, I seek Your guidance and wisdom as I make investment decisions. You are the source of all wisdom, and I trust in Your perfect plan for my financial future. Help me to discern between wise investments and risky ventures. Grant me peace and confidence in Your provision, knowing that You hold my future in Your hands. May my investments honor You and contribute to Your kingdom purposes. Thank You, Lord, for Your guidance and for Your faithfulness in all things. In Jesus' name, Amen."

Scripture Reference:

Proverbs 3:9-10: "Honor the Lord with your wealth, with the first fruits of all your crops; then your barns will be filled to overflowing, and your vats will brim over with new wine."

Prayer for Strength and Resilience in Financial Challenges

"Heavenly Father, I lift up to You my financial challenges and difficulties. You are my refuge and strength, an ever-present help in times of trouble. Grant me the strength and resilience to endure hardships and to overcome obstacles. Fill me with Your peace that surpasses all understanding, knowing that You are in control of every situation. Provide for all my needs according to Your glorious riches in Christ Jesus. Thank You, Lord, for Your unfailing love and for Your promise to never leave me nor forsake me. In Jesus' name, Amen."

Scripture Reference:

Psalm 46:1: "God is our refuge and strength, an ever-present help in trouble."

Invocation for Economic Liberation and Debt Relief

"Dear God, I come to You with a heart burdened by financial obligations and debts. You are the God of freedom and deliverance, and I trust in Your power to release me from financial bondage. Grant me wisdom and discipline to manage my finances wisely. Provide opportunities for increased income and financial breakthroughs. Help me to be a good steward of the resources You have entrusted to me. Thank You, Lord, for Your promise to supply all my needs according to Your riches in glory. I place my trust in You, knowing that You are faithful to fulfill Your word. In Jesus' name, Amen."

Scripture Reference:

Psalm 34:17: "The righteous cry out, and the Lord hears them; he delivers them from all their troubles."

Prayer for Supernatural Increase and Overflow

"Lord, I thank You for Your promise of supernatural increase and overflow in my life. You are the God of abundance, and I believe in Your power to bless me exceedingly and abundantly. Open the floodgates of heaven and pour out blessings that I cannot contain. Ensure my needs are met from your bountiful treasures. May Your favor rest upon me, and may Your goodness and mercy follow me all the days of my life. Thank You, Lord, for Your faithfulness and for Your provision that exceeds all expectations. In Jesus' name, Amen."

Scripture Reference:

Ephesians 3:20: "Now to him who is able to do immeasurably more than all we ask or imagine, according to his power that is at work within us."

These prayers are crafted to deepen your spiritual connection and strengthen your faith in God's provision for financial success. May they inspire and uplift you as you walk in faith and trust in His abundant blessings.

Affirmations for Financial Success

Affirmation of God's Favor in Financial Matters

"I am blessed and highly favored by God in all my financial endeavors. His favor surrounds me like a shield, opening doors of opportunity and prosperity."

Scripture Reference:

Psalm 5:12: "Surely, Lord, you bless the righteous; you surround them with your favor as with a shield."

Declaration of Economic Independence and Debt-Free Living

"I am financially free and debt-free, as God's blessings enable me to live a life of abundance and generosity."

Scripture Reference:

Romans 13:8: "Let no debt remain outstanding, except the continuing debt to love one another, for whoever loves others has fulfilled the law."

Affirmation of Gratitude for Financial Blessings

"I am grateful for God's abundant blessings in my financial life. I receive His blessings with thanksgiving and use them to bless others."

Scripture Reference:

Psalm 118:1: "Give thanks to the Lord, for he is good; his love endures forever."

Affirmation of Financial Stability and Security

"I am financially stable and secure, believing in God's generosity and His promise to care for all my needs."

Scripture Reference:

Psalm 34:10: "The lions may grow weak and hungry, but those who seek the Lord lack no good thing."

Affirmation of Faith in God's Promises for Prosperity

"I have unwavering faith in God's promises for prosperity and success in every area of my life, including my finances."

Scripture Reference:

Jeremiah 29:11: "For I know the plans I have for you," declares the Lord, "plans to prosper you and not to harm you, plans to give you hope and a future."

Affirmation of Divine Provision in Times of Need

"God's provision meets all my financial needs according to His glorious riches. I trust in His timely provision in every circumstance."

Scripture Reference:

Philippians 4:6: "Do not be anxious about anything, but in every situation, by prayer and petition, with thanksgiving, present your requests to God."

Affirmation of Faithfulness in Financial Stewardship

"I am a faithful steward of God's blessings and resources. I manage my finances wisely and honor God with my financial decisions."

Scripture Reference:

1 Corinthians 4:2: "Now it is required that those who have been given a trust must prove faithful."

Affirmation of Strength and Resilience in Financial Challenges

"I am strong and resilient in the face of financial challenges. God's strength empowers me to overcome obstacles and emerge victorious."

Scripture Reference:

Isaiah 40:31: "But those who hope in the Lord will renew their strength. They will soar on wings like eagles; they will run and not grow weary, they will walk and not be faint."

Affirmation of God's Promises for Prosperity and Success

"I claim God's promises for prosperity and success in my life. His word is true, and His blessings follow me wherever I go."

Scripture Reference:

Joshua 1:8: "Keep this Book of the Law always on your lips; meditate on it day and night, so that you may be careful to do everything written in it. Then you will be prosperous and successful."

Affirmation of Peace and Confidence in Financial Planning

"I am filled with peace and confidence in my financial planning. God's peace guards my heart and mind as I trust in His provision."

Scripture Reference:

Philippians 4:7: "And the peace of God, which transcends all understanding, will guard your hearts and your minds in Christ Jesus."

Affirmation of Joy and Thankfulness in Financial Blessings

"I rejoice and give thanks for God's financial blessings in my life. His goodness and mercy follow me, and I am grateful for His provision."

Scripture Reference:

Psalm 100:4: "Enter his gates with thanksgiving and his courts with praise; give thanks to him and praise his name."

Affirmation of God's Faithfulness in Financial Seasons

"God is faithful in every season of my financial life. His faithfulness endures forever, and I trust in His unfailing love and provision."

Scripture Reference:

Lamentations 3:22-23: "Because of the Lord's great love we are not consumed, for his compassions never fail. They are new every morning; great is your faithfulness."

Affirmation of God's Guidance in Career Advancement

"I am guided by God's wisdom and favor in my career. He opens doors of opportunity for promotion and advancement, leading me to success."

Scripture Reference:

Proverbs 16:9: "In their hearts humans plan their course, but the Lord establishes their steps."

Affirmation of Abundant Blessings and Overflowing Prosperity

"I am blessed with abundant blessings and overflowing prosperity from God. His goodness and mercy follow me all the days of my life."

Scripture Reference:

Psalm 23:6: "Surely your goodness and love will follow me all the days of my life, and I will dwell in the house of the Lord forever."

Affirmation of Trust in God's Timing for Financial Breakthroughs

"I trust in God's perfect timing for financial breakthroughs. He makes all things beautiful in His time, and I patiently await His blessings."

Scripture Reference:

Ecclesiastes 3:11: "He has made everything beautiful in its time. He has also set eternity in the human heart; yet no one can fathom what God has done from beginning to end."

Affirmation of Gratitude for Financial Abundance

"I am grateful for the financial abundance that flows into my life. God's blessings exceed my expectations, and I receive them with a thankful heart."

Scripture Reference:

1 Thessalonians 5:18: "Give thanks in all circumstances; for this is God's will for you in Christ Jesus."

Affirmation of Abundance and Generosity

"I am abundantly blessed by God to bless others generously. His blessings flow through me to impact lives and advance His kingdom."

Scripture Reference:

2 Corinthians 9:8: "And God is able to bless you abundantly, so that in all things at all times, having all that you need, you will abound in every good work."

Affirmation of Divine Order and Prosperity

"Divine order and prosperity manifest in every area of my life, including my finances. God's blessings align with His perfect plan for my life."

Scripture Reference:

1 Corinthians 14:40: "But everything should be done in a fitting and orderly way."

Affirmation of Trust in God's Sovereignty over Finances

"I trust in God's sovereignty over my finances. He is my provider and sustainer, and I rest in His provision for all my needs."

Scripture Reference:

Psalm 145:15-16**:** "The eyes of all look to you, and you give them their food at the proper time. You open your hand and satisfy the desires of every living thing."

Affirmation of Peace and Confidence in Financial Stability

"I am filled with peace and confidence in my financial stability. God's provision sustains me, and His faithfulness ensures my financial security."

Scripture Reference:

Isaiah 26:3: "You will keep in perfect peace those whose minds are steadfast, because they trust in you."

These affirmations are designed to strengthen your faith and align your thoughts with God's promises for financial success. May they inspire you to trust in His provision and experience His abundant blessings in every area of your life.

In inference of this section, prayer and meditation are essential spiritual disciplines that enrich believers' lives by deepening their connection with the divine. Through heartfelt prayer and intentional meditation, individuals experience spiritual renewal, receive divine guidance, and cultivate a profound sense of peace and purpose. These practices transcend mere rituals, becoming transformative journeys that align hearts with God's will and empower believers to live authentically and faithfully. As individuals commit to regular prayer and meditation, they cultivate spiritual resilience, deepen their understanding of divine truths, and embody the virtues of compassion, humility, and steadfast faith.

Chapter 4:

The Significance of Praying through God's Names

The names of God hold profound significance, revealing His nature, attributes, and promises to His people. This chapter explores the life-altering force of praying through God's names, guiding you to invoke His character and authority in your prayers. By understanding and proclaiming Yahweh's names—such as Jehovah-Jireh (The Lord Will Provide) and El Shaddai (God Almighty)—you align your petitions with His divine will and open doors to supernatural provision, protection, and favor. Embrace the richness of God's names as keys to deeper spiritual insight, divine connection, and financial breakthroughs in your life.

Yahweh's names are not merely titles but declarations of His sovereignty, love, and provision over your life. As you pray through God's names, declare His promises and embrace His character, you activate His power and authority in your circumstances. Each name carries the assurance of Yahweh's faithfulness and commitment to bless you abundantly according to His riches in glory. Trust in His names as you intercede for spiritual and financial breakthroughs, knowing that Yahweh delights in revealing Himself to those who earnestly seek Him. Let your prayers through His names be a testament to His goodness and a catalyst for miracles and blessings in every area of your life.

Praying the names of God holds profound importance in our spiritual journey. It allows us to invoke the very essence of God into our prayers, affirming His character and proclaiming His supremacy in our lives. This practice becomes crucial as it aligns our hearts with His truth, serving as a potent weapon in spiritual warfare (Ephesians 6:12).

In moments of challenge and uncertainty, we are reminded of the greatness of our God. Declaring His goodness, faithfulness, and justice reinforces His active presence amidst life's adversities. Even when circumstances seem bleak, praying the names of God serves as a beacon of hope, affirming His sovereignty over every situation (Psalm 27:1).

The names of God revealed in Scripture unveil His very nature and attributes, guiding us to deeper intimacy with Him. Each name carries profound meaning, reflecting facets of His divine character that offer strength, comfort, and assurance (Isaiah 40:28).

Prayer becomes our lifeline to God, essential in both turbulent times and moments of joy. Through fervent prayer, especially invoking the names of God, we express our trust that He hears and responds to our petitions (1 John 5:14).

How to Pray the Names of God with Impact

Praying the names of God with power begins with understanding their significance and applying them intentionally in our prayers. Each name signifies a unique aspect of God's majesty and authority over creation (Psalm 145:3). By comprehending these names, we can confidently incorporate them into our prayers, declaring their truths over our circumstances (Jeremiah 32:27).

Here are some names of God along with their meanings and scriptural references:

Yahweh Elohim – The LORD God (Genesis 2:4)

Yahweh Elohim means "The LORD God." This name combines Yahweh, the personal name of God, with Elohim, the generic Hebrew word for God. It emphasizes God's identity as the supreme, sovereign, and personal God who created the heavens and the earth (Genesis 1:1).

Understanding God as Yahweh Elohim motivates us to recognize His authority and lordship over all creation. He is the one true God, worthy of our worship and obedience. This name reminds us of God's power to create, sustain, and redeem us through His Son, Jesus Christ.

Scripture Reference: Genesis 2:4 – "This is the account of the heavens and the earth when they were created, when Yahweh Elohim made the earth and the heavens."

Prayer: Yahweh Elohim, The LORD God, I praise you for your sovereignty and power as the Creator of all things. Help me to trust in your wisdom and to submit to your lordship in my life. Thank you for revealing yourself to us through your Word and through Jesus Christ. Amen.

Affirmation: I affirm that Yahweh is my God. Yahweh Elohim reigns supreme over all creation and in my life. I acknowledge His authority and submit to His will, knowing that He is faithful and trustworthy. I worship Him as my Creator and Redeemer. Amen.

Prayer: Heavenly Father, Yahweh Elohim, I come before You in awe of Your majesty and power. You are the Creator of all things, the sustainer of life, and the source of my strength. I worship You for Your faithfulness and love that endures forever. As I seek Your presence, I pray for wisdom and discernment in every decision I make. Guide my steps according to Your perfect will and let Your light shine brightly through me. Amen.

Affirmation: I declare that Yahweh Elohim is my refuge and fortress, my rock and my salvation. In Him, I find courage and peace, knowing that He goes before me in every situation. His promises are true, and His Word is my foundation. I am secure in His love and provision, confident that nothing can separate me from His presence. I walk in faith, knowing that Jehovah Elohim is with me, leading me into abundant life. Amen.

Yahweh Elohim reveals Himself as the all-powerful God who created the universe and everything in it. He is not only the Creator but also the sustainer of all life. Meditating on His attributes can fill us with awe and reverence, reminding us of His sovereignty and love for His creation. Understanding Yahweh Elohim's nature strengthens our faith and encourages us to trust His plans for our lives.

Scripture Reference: Genesis 1:1 - "In the beginning, God created the heavens and the earth."

Yahweh Adonai – The LORD Master (Genesis 15:2)

Yahweh Adonai means "The LORD Master." Adonai signifies God's authority and ownership over His people. In Genesis 15:2, Abraham addresses Yahweh as Adonai, acknowledging Him as his sovereign Lord and Master.

Understanding God as Yahweh Adonai motivates us to surrender our lives fully to His authority and guidance. He is not only our Creator but also our Master who directs our steps and cares for us. This name reminds us to trust in His sovereignty and to serve Him wholeheartedly.

Scripture Reference: Genesis 15:2 – "But Abram said, 'Sovereign LORD [Adonai Yahweh], what can you give me since I remain childless and the one who will inherit my estate is Eliezer of Damascus?'"

Prayer: Yahweh Adonai, The LORD Master, I humbly submit myself to your authority and lordship. Guide my steps and lead me in your paths of righteousness. Help me to trust in your provision and to serve you faithfully with all my heart. Amen.

Affirmation: I affirm that Yahweh is my Master. Yahweh Adonai rules over my life with wisdom and love. I surrender to His authority and follow His guidance, knowing that He cares for me and leads me in paths of righteousness. I serve Him with joy and obedience. Amen.

Yahweh Rapha – The LORD Who Heals (Exodus 15:26)

Yahweh Rapha means "The LORD Who Heals." This name emphasizes God's role as our healer, both physically and spiritually. In Exodus 15:26, God reveals Himself to Israel as Yahweh Rapha, promising healing and health to those who obey Him.

Understanding God as Yahweh Rapha motivates us to seek His healing power in our lives and to trust in His ability to restore and renew us. He is the source of all healing, offering wholeness and restoration through His Son, Jesus Christ. This name reminds us to approach God with faith for healing in every area of our lives.

Scripture Reference: Exodus 15:26 – "He said, 'If you listen carefully to the LORD [Yahweh] your God and do what is right in his eyes, if you pay attention to his commands and keep all his decrees, I will not bring on you any of the diseases I brought on the Egyptians, for I am the LORD [Yahweh], who heals you.'"

Prayer: Yahweh Rapha, The LORD Who Heals, I come to you in faith, believing in your power to heal and restore. Touch my life with your healing hand, both physically and spiritually. May your healing presence bring wholeness and renewal to every part of my being. Amen.

Prayer: Gracious Yahweh Rapha, my Healer, I come before You with a humble heart, acknowledging Your power to heal and restore. You are the God who heals all my diseases and binds up my wounds. I surrender my health into Your loving hands, trusting in Your divine healing touch. May Your peace and comfort surround me as I wait upon You for restoration. Amen.

Prayer: Healing God, Yahweh Rapha, I come before You with my heart open to Your healing touch. You are the God who restores and heals all wounds. I surrender my sickness and pain to You, trusting in Your power to bring wholeness to my body, mind, and spirit. Strengthen my faith and grant me patience as I wait upon Your healing. May Your name be glorified through my restoration. Amen.

Affirmation: I affirm that Yahweh is my Healer. Yahweh Rapha brings healing and restoration to my body, mind, and soul. I trust in His promise to heal me according to His will and timing. I receive His healing touch with faith and gratitude. Amen.

Affirmation: I declare that Yahweh Rapha is my healer, and by His wounds, I am healed. I walk in faith, knowing that His healing power flows through me, restoring health and wholeness. I receive His healing touch and embrace His promise of abundant life. Amen.

Affirmation: I declare that Yahweh Rapha is my Healer, and His healing power flows through me. I am restored and renewed by His grace. I walk in faith, knowing that His healing touch brings wholeness to my life. I receive His healing with thanksgiving and praise. Amen.

Yahweh Rapha reveals Himself as the God who heals physically, emotionally, and spiritually. His healing is comprehensive, addressing every aspect of our being. Meditating on His healing nature brings comfort and assurance, encouraging us to believe in His ability to restore and renew us.

Scripture Reference: Exodus 15:26 - "...for I am the Lord who heals you."

Yahweh Rapha is the compassionate Healer who restores us to health and wholeness. His healing touch brings comfort and hope, inspiring us to trust in His ability to heal all our afflictions. Meditating on His healing power motivates us to believe in His promises and to seek His restoration in every area of our lives.

Scripture Reference: Exodus 15:26 - "He said, 'If you listen carefully to the Lord your God and do what is right in his eyes, if you pay attention to his commands and keep all his decrees, I will not bring on you any of the diseases I brought on the Egyptians, for I am the Lord, who heals you.'"

Yahweh Nissi – The LORD Is My Banner (Exodus 17:15)

Yahweh Nissi means "The LORD Is My Banner." This name signifies God's victory and protection over His people. In Exodus 17:15, Moses builds an altar and names it Yahweh Nissi after God grants Israel victory over their enemies.

Understanding God as Yahweh Nissi motivates us to trust in His protection and to proclaim His victory in our lives. He fights our battles and leads us to triumph over every obstacle and enemy. This name reminds us to stand firm in faith, knowing that God goes before us as our banner of victory.

Scripture Reference: Exodus 17:15 – "Moses built an altar and called it The LORD [Yahweh] Is My Banner [Nissi]."

Prayer: Yahweh Nissi, The LORD Is My Banner, I thank you for your protection and victory in my life. You go before me and fight my battles. I declare your victory over every challenge and obstacle I face. May your banner of love and triumph be lifted high in my life. Amen.

Prayer: Victorious God, Yahweh Nissi, I come before You acknowledging Your victory in my life. You are the God who fights for me and leads me to triumph. I surrender my battles to You, trusting in Your banner of love and protection over me. Strengthen my resolve and grant me courage to face every challenge with faith. May Your name be exalted as I proclaim Your victory. Amen.

Prayer: Heavenly Father, Yahweh Nissi, I come before You with praise and thanksgiving. You are my victorious banner, the One who leads me into battle and grants me triumph over my enemies. I surrender my fears and weaknesses to You, knowing that Your banner over me is love and protection. Strengthen me with Your courage and empower me to walk boldly in Your victory. Amen.

Affirmation: I affirm that Yahweh is my Banner. Yahweh Nissi leads me in triumph and victory. I trust in His protection and guidance, knowing that He goes before me to secure my path. I declare His victory over every area of my life. Amen.

Affirmation: I declare that Yahweh Nissi goes before me in every battle, and His banner over me is love and victory. I am more than a conqueror through Him who loves me. I stand firm in His strength, knowing that He fights for me and leads me into triumphant living. Amen.

Yahweh Nissi is revealed as the God who leads His people to victory. His banner signifies His presence and protection over us. Reflecting on His role as our banner encourages us to trust in His guidance and to live boldly in His victory, knowing that He equips us for every challenge we face.

Yahweh Nissi, the Lord Is My Banner, is the victorious God who leads us to triumph over every adversity. Reflecting on His banner of love and protection inspires us to face our battles with confidence and faith. Meditating on His victory motivates us to trust in His leadership and to declare His triumph in our lives.

Yahweh Shalom – The LORD Is Peace (Judges 6:24)

Yahweh Shalom means "The LORD Is Peace." This name emphasizes God's role in bringing peace and wholeness to His people. In Judges 6:24, Gideon builds an altar to Yahweh and calls Him Yahweh Shalom after experiencing God's peace and reassurance.

Understanding God as Yahweh Shalom motivates us to seek His peace in every circumstance of life. His peace surpasses understanding and guards our hearts and minds (Philippians 4:7). This name reminds us that true peace is found in relationship with God, who calms our fears and brings harmony to our lives.

Scripture Reference: Judges 6:24 – "So Gideon built an altar to the LORD [Yahweh] there and called it The LORD [Yahweh] Is Peace [Shalom]. To this day it stands in Ophrah of the Abiezrites."

Prayer: Yahweh Shalom, The LORD Is Peace, I come to you seeking your peace that transcends all understanding. During turmoil and uncertainty, calm my heart with your presence. Fill me with your peace that brings wholeness and harmony to my life. Thank you for being my source of true peace. Amen.

Affirmation: I affirm that Yahweh is my Peace. Yahweh Shalom fills me with His peace that surpasses understanding. His peace guards my heart and mind in Christ Jesus (Philippians 4:7). I trust in His faithfulness to bring peace to every area of my life. Amen.

Yahweh Tsidkenu – The LORD Our Righteousness (Jeremiah 23:6)

Yahweh Tsidkenu means "The LORD Our Righteousness." This name emphasizes God's role as the source of our righteousness and justification. In Jeremiah 23:6, the prophet speaks of a future king who will reign wisely and do what is just and right, and he will be called Yahweh Tsidkenu. This points to Jesus Christ, who fulfills this prophecy as our righteousness.

Understanding God as Yahweh Tsidkenu motivates us to live in righteousness and holiness before Him. He provides the righteousness we need through faith in Jesus Christ (Romans 3:22), enabling us to stand blameless before Him. This name reminds us of God's justice and His provision for our salvation.

Scripture Reference: Jeremiah 23:6 – "In his days Judah will be saved and Israel will live in safety. This is the name by which he will be called: The LORD [Yahweh] Our Righteous Savior [Tsidkenu]."

Prayer: Yahweh Tsidkenu, The LORD Our Righteousness, I praise you for providing righteousness through Jesus Christ. Thank you for making me righteous before you and enabling me to live a holy life. Help me to walk in obedience and righteousness according to your will. Amen.

Affirmation: I affirm that Yahweh is my Righteousness. Yahweh Tsidkenu clothes me in His righteousness and enables me to live a blameless life. In Christ, I am justified and declared righteous before God (Romans 5:1). I trust in His righteousness to guide my steps and shape my character. Amen.

Yahweh Jireh – The LORD Will Provide (Genesis 22:14)

Yahweh Jireh means "The LORD Will Provide." This name emphasizes God's provision for His people's needs. In Genesis 22:14, Abraham names the place where God provides a ram for sacrifice as Yahweh Jireh, acknowledging God's faithfulness and provision. Throughout Scripture, God demonstrates His provision in miraculous ways.

Understanding God as Yahweh Jireh motivates us to trust in His provision for every aspect of our lives—spiritual, emotional, and physical. He is our provider who meets our needs according to His riches in glory (Philippians 4:19). This name reminds us to rely on God's faithfulness and to seek first His kingdom and righteousness (Matthew 6:33).

Scripture Reference: Genesis 22:14 – "So Abraham called that place The LORD [Yahweh] Will Provide [Jireh]. And to this day it is said, 'On the mountain of the LORD [Yahweh] it will be provided.'"

Prayer: Yahweh Jireh, The LORD Will Provide, I thank you for your faithfulness in providing for all my needs. You are my provider and my upholder, and I trust in your provision for my life. Help me to seek you first and to trust in your abundant provision. Amen.

Affirmation: I affirm that Yahweh is my Provider. Yahweh Jireh supplies all my needs according to His riches in glory (Philippians 4:19). I rely on His provision for every area of my life and trust in His timing and abundance. I declare His faithfulness to provide for me as I seek Him first. Amen.

Yahweh Rohi – The LORD Is My Shepherd (Psalm 23:1)

Yahweh Rohi means "The LORD Is My Shepherd." This name emphasizes God's role as our caring and attentive Shepherd. In Psalm 23:1, David declares Yahweh as his Shepherd who provides, guides, and protects His flock.

Understanding God as Yahweh Rohi motivates us to trust in His guidance and provision in our lives. He leads us beside still waters and restores our souls (Psalm 23:2-3). This name reminds us of God's intimate care and His commitment to lead us in paths of righteousness.

Scripture Reference: Psalm 23:1 – "The LORD [Yahweh] is my shepherd [Rohi], I lack nothing."

Prayer: Yahweh Rohi, The LORD Is My Shepherd, I thank you for your loving care and guidance in my life. Lead me beside still waters and restore my soul. Help me to follow you faithfully and to trust in your provision and protection. May I rest in your presence and follow your lead. Amen.

Affirmation: I affirm that Yahweh is my Shepherd. Yahweh Rohi leads me with love and wisdom. I trust in His guidance and provision, knowing that He cares for me deeply. I follow Him faithfully and find rest in His presence. Amen.

Yahweh Sabaoth – The LORD of Hosts (1 Samuel 1:3)

Yahweh Sabaoth means "The LORD of Hosts" or "The LORD of Armies." This name emphasizes God's sovereign rule over all angelic armies and earthly powers. In 1 Samuel 1:3, Hannah prays to Yahweh Sabaoth, recognizing His supreme authority and power.

Understanding God as Yahweh Sabaoth motivates us to trust in His ultimate authority and to recognize His power over all circumstances. He commands angelic armies and fights on behalf of His people (Psalm 46:7). This name reminds us that God is our mighty defender and protector.

Scripture Reference: 1 Samuel 1:3 – "And this man went up out of his city yearly to worship and to sacrifice unto the LORD [Yahweh] of hosts [Sabaoth] in Shiloh. And the two sons of Eli, Hophni and Phinehas, the priests of the LORD [Yahweh], were there."

Prayer: Yahweh Sabaoth, The LORD of Hosts, I praise you for your sovereign rule and mighty power. You are the commander of angelic armies and the defender of your people. Protect me from spiritual and earthly foes and fight battles on my behalf. I trust in your victory and authority. Amen.

Affirmation: I affirm that Yahweh is the LORD of Hosts. Yahweh Sabaoth commands angelic armies and fights for me. I trust in His sovereign rule and power, knowing that He is my defender and protector. I stand firm in His strength and victory. Amen.

Yahweh Shammah – The LORD Is There (Ezekiel 48:35)

Yahweh Shammah means "The LORD Is There." This name emphasizes God's presence among His people. In Ezekiel 48:35, the prophet describes the future city of Jerusalem, which will be named Yahweh Shammah, signifying God's eternal presence with His redeemed people.

Understanding God as Yahweh Shammah motivates us to seek His presence in our lives and to worship Him with reverence and awe. He promises to be with us always, even to the end of the age (Matthew 28:20). This name reminds us of God's abiding presence and His faithfulness to never leave us nor forsake us.

Scripture Reference: Ezekiel 48:35 – "The distance all around will be 18,000 cubits. And the name of the city from that time on will be: THE LORD [Yahweh] IS THERE [Shammah]."

Prayer: Yahweh Shammah, The LORD Is There, I thank you for your abiding presence in my life. You are with me in every season and circumstance. Help me to recognize and cherish your presence daily. May I worship you with reverence and joy, knowing that you are always near. Amen.

Affirmation: I affirm that Yahweh is always with me. Yahweh Shammah dwells in my midst and walks with me daily. I rejoice in His presence and trust in His faithfulness. I worship Him with awe and gratitude, knowing that He is with me wherever I go. Amen.

These names of Yahweh reveal His character, attributes, and promises to His people. They are a testament to His love, power, and faithfulness throughout history and in our lives today.

Yahweh Raah: The Lord is My Shepherd

Yahweh Raah, meaning "The Lord is My Shepherd," is a name of God found in Psalm 23:1. It reflects the intimate care and guidance that God provides for His people, likened to a shepherd caring for his flock. In ancient Israel, shepherding was a familiar metaphor for leadership and provision, highlighting God's role as the protector and provider for His people.

The imagery of Yahweh Raah as the Shepherd motivates believers to trust in God's guidance and provision. Just as a shepherd knows his sheep and leads them to green pastures, God intimately knows and cares for each of His children. This name encourages reliance on God's wisdom and direction in navigating life's challenges.

Scripture Reference: Psalm 23:1 - "The Lord is my shepherd; I shall not want."

Prayer and Affirmation: Prayer: "Yahweh Raah, my Shepherd, I thank You for leading me beside quiet waters and restoring my soul. You are my provider and protector, guiding me with Your gentle hand. Help me to follow Your lead and trust in Your provision in all circumstances. Amen."

Affirmation: "I declare that Yahweh Raah, the Lord my Shepherd, watches over me with love and care. He leads me in the paths of righteousness and provides for all my needs. I will fear no evil, for He is with me, comforting and guiding me through every valley."

El Elyon: The Most High God

El Elyon, meaning "The Most High God," is a name used to denote God's supreme sovereignty and authority over all creation. The title emphasizes God's transcendence above all other gods and powers. It first appears in Genesis 14:18-20 when Melchizedek, the king of Salem and priest of God Most High, blesses Abraham. This encounter highlights God's authority and provision in blessing Abraham after his victory in battle.

The name El Elyon motivates believers to acknowledge and submit to God's supreme authority in their lives. It inspires awe and reverence for His power and wisdom, reassuring us that nothing in this world is beyond His control. Knowing that God is the Most High instills confidence in His ability to guide and protect us through every circumstance.

Scripture Reference: Genesis 14:19-20 - "And he blessed him and said, 'Blessed be Abram by God Most High, Possessor of heaven and earth; and blessed be God Most High, who has delivered your enemies into your hand!' And Abram gave him a tenth of everything."

Prayer and Affirmation: Prayer: "El Elyon, Most High God, I worship You for Your sovereignty and authority over all creation. You alone are worthy of all praise and honor. Help me to surrender every aspect of my life to Your divine will, trusting in Your wisdom and guidance. May Your kingdom come, and Your will be done on earth as it is in heaven. Amen."

Affirmation: "I declare that El Elyon, the Most High God, reigns over my life and circumstances. His authority is absolute, and His plans for me are good. I will trust in His power and submit to His guidance, knowing that He is faithful to fulfill His promises and lead me into His perfect will."

El Roi: The God Who Sees

El Roi, which means "The God Who Sees," is a profound name given to God in Genesis 16:13. It originates from the story of Hagar, the Egyptian maidservant of Sarah, Abraham's wife. When Hagar fled into the wilderness, distressed and alone, after being mistreated by Sarah, the Angel of the Lord appeared to her and comforted her. Hagar then called God El Roi, saying, "You are the God who sees me," for she realized that God saw her affliction and cared for her welfare despite her circumstances.

The name El Roi inspires deep comfort and assurance that God sees and understands our struggles, even in the most difficult situations. It motivates believers to trust in God's omniscience and compassion, knowing that He is intimately aware of every aspect of our lives. This awareness encourages us to open our hearts to God in vulnerability and seek His guidance and comfort.

Scripture Reference: Genesis 16:13 - "She gave this name to the Lord who spoke to her: 'You are the God who sees me,' for she said, 'I have now seen the One who sees me.'"

Prayer and Affirmation: Prayer: "El Roi, the God Who Sees, I praise You for Your unwavering attention to my life. Thank You for seeing me in every circumstance, understanding my joys and struggles. Help me to trust in Your perfect vision and guidance, knowing that You care deeply for me. May Your presence surround me always. Amen."

Affirmation: "I declare that El Roi, the God Who Sees, watches over me with love and compassion. He sees beyond my outward appearance and understands the depths of my heart. I trust in His perfect vision and rest in His care, knowing that He is attentive to my needs and will never leave me. I am comforted by His presence and guided by His wisdom."

El Shaddai: God Almighty

El Shaddai, often translated as "God Almighty," is a name used for God in the Old Testament. It first appears in Genesis 17:1 when God appears to Abram (later called Abraham) and says, "I am God Almighty; walk before me faithfully and be blameless." The name El Shaddai emphasizes God's sovereign power and might. It is derived from the Hebrew word "shad," which means "breast" or "mountain," symbolizing God's sufficiency and nurturing provision as a mighty mountain provides protection and sustenance.

The name El Shaddai inspires awe and reverence for God's omnipotence and provision. It motivates believers to trust in God's ability to fulfill His promises and to rely on His strength in times of need. It signifies that God is more than able to meet every need and overcome every obstacle, reinforcing faith in His power and care.

Scripture Reference: Genesis 17:1 - "When Abram was ninety-nine years old, the Lord appeared to him and said, 'I am God Almighty; walk before me faithfully and be blameless.'"

Prayer and Affirmation: Prayer: "El Shaddai, Almighty God, I come before You with reverence and gratitude for Your mighty power and provision in my life. Thank You for being my sufficiency and strength. Help me to walk faithfully before You, trusting in Your promises and relying on Your unfailing love. May Your name be glorified in all I do. Amen."

Affirmation: "I affirm that El Shaddai, God Almighty, is my refuge and strength. In His presence, I find security and peace. His power sustains me through every challenge, and His provision meets all my needs. I rest in His sovereignty, knowing that He is able to do exceedingly abundantly above all that I ask or think. I am confident in His mighty hand that guides and protects me."

Abba: Father

The term "Abba" is an Aramaic word for "father" or "daddy," conveying an intimate and affectionate relationship. Jesus used this term to address God the Father in prayer, revealing a profound closeness and trust between Father and Son (Mark 14:36). In the New Testament, believers are encouraged to approach God with the same intimate familiarity and trust, recognizing Him as their loving Father who cares deeply for them (Romans 8:15, Galatians 4:6).

The name "Abba" inspires believers to approach God with childlike trust and openness, knowing that He loves them unconditionally as a perfect Father. It motivates them to cultivate a deep, personal relationship with God, characterized by trust, intimacy, and dependency on His care and guidance.

Scripture Reference: Mark 14:36 - "And he said, 'Abba, Father, all things are possible for you. Remove this cup from me. Yet not what I will, but what you will.'"

Prayer: "Abba Father, I come to You with gratitude and love, acknowledging You as my Heavenly Father. Thank You for adopting me into Your family through Christ, and for Your unconditional love and care. Help me to trust You completely and to seek Your will above all else. May Your fatherly guidance and provision be evident in my life every day. Amen."

Affirmation: "I affirm that God is my Abba Father, who loves me deeply and cares for me intimately. In His presence, I find security and peace. I trust His perfect plans for my life, knowing that His love for me is unfailing. I rest in His embrace, knowing that I am His beloved child, and He delights in me. I am grateful for His fatherly care and guidance, which lead me on paths of righteousness. Thank You, Abba Father, for Your boundless love and grace."

Sar Shalom: Prince of Peace

"Sar Shalom" is a Hebrew title meaning "Prince of Peace." This name of God is prominently prophesied in Isaiah 9:6, where it describes the Messiah, Jesus Christ, as the one who brings everlasting peace and reconciliation between God and humanity. The title "Sar Shalom" signifies Jesus' role as the ultimate ruler and authority over peace, both in the spiritual and earthly realms.

The name "Sar Shalom" inspires believers to trust in Jesus Christ as the source of true peace. It motivates them to seek reconciliation with God and others, knowing that Jesus has provided the means for peace through His sacrificial death and resurrection. This name encourages believers to live in harmony with others and to pursue peace in their relationships, communities, and the world.

Scripture Reference: Isaiah 9:6 - "For to us a child is born, to us a son is given; and the government shall be upon his shoulder, and his name shall be called Wonderful Counselor, Mighty God, Everlasting Father, Prince of Peace."

Prayer: "Sar Shalom, Prince of Peace, I thank You for bringing peace into my life through Your sacrifice. Help me to experience Your peace in every aspect of my life — in my relationships, my work, and my daily challenges. May Your peace reign in my heart, calming every fear and anxiety. Grant me wisdom and grace to be a peacemaker, reflecting Your love and reconciliation to others. Amen."

Affirmation: "I affirm that Jesus Christ is my Sar Shalom, the Prince of Peace. In Him, I find true peace and reconciliation with God and others. His peace guards my heart and mind, enabling me to live fearlessly and joyfully. I embrace His peace, which surpasses all understanding, and I extend His peace to those around me. I am grateful for His presence, which brings harmony and unity in every situation. Thank You, Sar Shalom, for Your everlasting peace."

Yahweh Hoshiah–O LORD Save (Psalm 20:9)

Yahweh Hoshiah, derived from Psalm 20:9 which states "O LORD, save the king! May he answer us when we call," emphasizes God's role as the ultimate Savior and Deliverer. The name Yahweh Hoshiah encapsulates the plea for divine salvation and intervention in times of distress, both individually and collectively. It reflects the biblical understanding of God's sovereignty over all circumstances and His willingness to respond to the cries of His people for deliverance.

Prayer: "Yahweh Hoshiah, O LORD, save us! We call upon Your name, knowing that You are our ultimate Deliverer. In times of trouble, we seek Your intervention, trusting in Your unfailing love and power to rescue us from every trial. May Your salvation be our strength and our hope, now and forevermore. Amen."

Affirmation: "I affirm that Yahweh Hoshiah hears my cries for help. His saving power is at work in my life, bringing deliverance and victory over every challenge. I declare His sovereignty over every situation, confident that His salvation is near to those who call upon Him in faith."

Yahweh Hoshiah inspires deep faith and trust in God's ability to save and deliver His people. It motivates believers to turn to God in times of trouble, knowing that He is faithful to answer prayers for salvation. This name encourages a reliance on God's sovereignty and His promise to hear and respond to the pleas of His children.

In Psalm 20:9, the cry "O LORD, save!" expresses the profound trust of the psalmist in God's ability to rescue and deliver. It signifies a plea for divine intervention in times of distress or danger, acknowledging God's supreme authority and His role as Savior. The history of Yahweh Hoshiah is rooted in the biblical narrative of God's consistent deliverance of His people throughout history, reinforcing the belief that God is the source of ultimate salvation.

Scripture Reference: Psalm 20:9 (ESV) - "O LORD, save the king! May he answer us when we call."

This name of God, Yahweh Hoshiah, reminds us that God is our ever-present help in times of need, ready to save and rescue those who call upon Him in faith.

Yahweh El Emeth–LORD God of Truth (Psalm 31:5)

In the Hebrew Bible, "El Emeth" is a descriptive term used to emphasize God's attributes of truthfulness, faithfulness, and reliability. It underscores God's character as the ultimate source of truth and the one who fulfills His promises without fail. This name signifies God's unwavering commitment to truth and righteousness in all His dealings with humanity.

Prayer: "God of Truth, Yahweh El Emeth, I come before You with gratitude for Your unwavering faithfulness and truthfulness. Your promises are sure, and Your word stands forever. Help me to walk in Your truth and to trust in Your faithfulness in every aspect of my life. Let Your truth guides me, and Your faithfulness sustain me through all circumstances. Amen."

Affirmation: "I affirm that Yahweh El Emeth is the God of truth and faithfulness. His words are my foundation, and His promises are my assurance. I trust in His unfailing truth to lead me and His steadfast faithfulness to uphold me."

Yahweh El Emeth inspires confidence and trust in God's reliability and truthfulness. It motivates believers to anchor their lives on the unchanging truth of God's word and to rely on His faithfulness in every situation. This name encourages a deepening of faith and a commitment to living according to God's truth.

The concept of "El Emeth" is deeply rooted in the Hebrew understanding of God as the ultimate standard of truth and reliability. It reflects God's character as revealed throughout the biblical narrative, where His faithfulness and truthfulness are consistently demonstrated in His interactions with His people.

Scripture Reference: Psalm 31:5 (NIV) - "Into your hands I commit my spirit; deliver me, LORD, my faithful God."

While "Yahweh El Emeth" may not be a specific compound name found in the Bible, the attributes of truth and faithfulness associated with "El Emeth" are foundational to understanding God's character as Yahweh, the LORD.

Yahweh Gibbor Milchamah–The LORD Mighty in Battle (Psalm 24:8)

Detail Description and History:

"Yahweh Gibbor Milchamah" translates to "The LORD Mighty in Battle" in Hebrew. This name emphasizes God's supreme power and authority over all conflicts and battles, whether physical, spiritual, or emotional. It denotes God as the ultimate warrior who fights on behalf of His people and ensures victory over every adversary.

The term "Gibbor" signifies strength, might, and bravery in battle, while "Milchamah" refers specifically to warfare or battle. Together, "Yahweh Gibbor Milchamah" underscores God's role as the champion and defender of His people in times of struggle and conflict.

Prayer: "Mighty God in Battle, Yahweh Gibbor Milchamah, I humbly come before You acknowledging Your sovereignty and power over every battle I face. Strengthen me with Your might, and fight on my behalf against the spiritual forces of darkness and every challenge in my life. Thank You for Your assurance of victory and protection. Amen."

Affirmation: "I affirm that Yahweh Gibbor Milchamah is my strength and defender in every battle. His power is greater than any adversary, and His victory is assured. I trust in His mighty hand to deliver me and bring triumph in every circumstance."

Yahweh Gibbor Milchamah inspires believers to rely on God's strength and authority in times of struggle. It motivates courage and confidence in facing challenges, knowing that God fights alongside His people and ensures triumph over adversity. This name encourages steadfast faith and reliance on God's power to overcome every obstacle.

The title "Yahweh Gibbor Milchamah" appears in Isaiah 42:13 (NIV), where it emphasizes God's role as the warrior who will go forth like a mighty man, stirring up zeal like a soldier. This passage underscores God's proactive engagement in battles, ensuring justice and deliverance for His people. Throughout the Old Testament, God demonstrates His power in various conflicts, illustrating His supremacy and faithfulness in protecting His chosen ones.

Scripture Reference:

Isaiah 42:13 (NIV) - "The Lord will march out like a champion, like a warrior he will stir up his zeal; with a shout he will raise the battle cry and will triumph over his enemies."

Yahweh Gibbor Milchamah reassures believers that God is not only powerful but actively intervenes on their behalf in times of struggle. It invites individuals to trust in God's unfailing strength and to draw courage from His promises of victory.

El Simchath Gili–God My Exceeding Joy (Psalm 43:4)

El Simchath Gili, if interpreted as "God my exceeding joy," would imply a name reflecting God's nature as the source of profound joy and delight for His people. This concept aligns with biblical themes of joy and rejoicing in the presence and blessings of God.

Prayer: Almighty God, El Simchath Gili, I come before You with gratitude and reverence. You are my exceeding joy, the source of all delight and happiness in my life. In Your presence, there is fullness of joy, and I find true contentment. Fill my heart with Your joy that surpasses all understanding, even in times of trial and uncertainty. May Your joy be my strength, lifting my spirit and renewing my hope each day. Thank You for the joy of salvation and the assurance of Your unfailing love. Amen.

Affirmation: I declare that God is my exceeding joy, El Simchath Gili. His joy strengthens me, His presence comforts me, and His love fills my life with purpose and peace. I rejoice in His goodness and faithfulness, knowing that His joy is my strength in every circumstance.

The name El Simchath Gili reminds us that God desires His people to experience deep, lasting joy in Him. This joy is not dependent on external circumstances but is rooted in His eternal presence and love. As we embrace God as our exceeding joy, we discover that true happiness flows from knowing Him intimately and trusting in His promises.

Scripture affirms the concept of God as our joy:

- Psalm 16:11: "You make known to me the path of life; in your presence there is fullness of joy; at your right hand are pleasures forevermore."
- Nehemiah 8:10: "And do not be grieved, for the joy of the LORD is your strength."

These verses emphasize that God Himself is the source of joy and strength for His people. El Simchath Gili encapsulates this truth, inviting believers to find ultimate fulfillment and delight in their relationship with God.

El Sali–God my Rock (2 Samuel 22:47)

El Sali, translated as "God my Rock," is a profound name of God found in 2 Samuel 22:47 (also Psalm 18:46). In Hebrew, "Sali" signifies rock or cliff, denoting strength, stability, and refuge. This name emphasizes God's unshakeable nature as a firm foundation and stronghold for His people. Throughout biblical narratives, God is depicted as a Rock, symbolizing His reliability, protection, and immutability amidst life's storms.

Prayer: Mighty God, El Sali, You are my Rock and my fortress. In You, I find unwavering strength and security. When the trials of life threaten to overwhelm me, I take refuge in Your steadfast presence. Thank You for being my shelter in the storm and my sure foundation. Help me to trust in Your unfailing protection and to stand firm on Your promises. Amen.

Affirmation: I declare that God is my Rock, El Sali. He is my refuge and my strength, a present help in times of trouble. I anchor my faith in His unchanging character and find peace in His steadfast love.

The name El Sali inspires confidence and trust in God's enduring faithfulness. Like a solid rock that withstands every storm, God remains constant and dependable. He invites us to build our lives upon Him, knowing that His strength is more than sufficient for all our needs.

The metaphor of God as a Rock is prevalent in Scripture:

Psalm 18:2: "The LORD is my rock and my fortress and my deliverer, my God, my rock, in whom I take refuge, my shield, and the horn of my salvation, my stronghold."

Psalm 62:6: "He only is my rock and my salvation, my fortress; I shall not be shaken."

These verses underscore God's role as a source of protection, stability, and salvation. El Sali encapsulates these attributes, reminding us to place our trust in Him as our Rock and stronghold.

Elohim Ozer Li–God My Helper (Psalm 54:4)

Elohim Ozer Li, meaning "God My Helper," is a comforting name of God found in Psalm 54:4. The term "Ozer" denotes assistance, support, and aid, emphasizing God's role as the Helper of His people. This name highlights God's readiness to come to our aid in times of need, offering strength, guidance, and provision.

Prayer: Heavenly Father, Elohim Ozer Li, You are my Helper and my strength. In every trial and challenge, I rely on Your unfailing assistance. Thank You for Your faithfulness and for being a constant source of support in my life. I humbly ask for Your help today and trust in Your sovereign care over every circumstance. Amen.

Affirmation: I declare that God is my Helper, Elohim Ozer Li. His guidance and provision sustain me, and His presence gives me courage. I lean on His strength and trust in His unfailing assistance.

Elohim Ozer Li inspires us to lean on God's strength and seek His guidance in all aspects of life. Knowing that God is our Helper encourages us to approach challenges with confidence, knowing that He will provide the wisdom and strength needed.

The concept of God as our Helper is affirmed throughout Scripture:

Psalm 121:1-2: "I lift up my eyes to the hills. From where does my help come? My help comes from the LORD, who made heaven and earth."

Hebrews 13:6: "So we can confidently say, 'The Lord is my helper; I will not fear; what can man do to me?'"

These verses highlight God's willingness and ability to assist His people. Elohim Ozer Li reflects His compassionate nature as the One who comes alongside us in every circumstance.

El Olam—The Everlasting God (Isaiah 26:4)

El Olam, which translates to "The Everlasting God," is a profound name used in Scripture to describe God's eternal nature and unchanging character. The term "Olam" signifies eternity or forever, emphasizing God's timeless existence and His presence throughout all generations. This name appears in Isaiah 26:4, where it says, "Trust in the LORD forever, for the LORD GOD is an everlasting rock."

The name El Olam first appears in Genesis 21:33, where Abraham plants a tamarisk tree in Beersheba and calls on the name of El Olam, the Everlasting God. This act signifies Abraham's acknowledgment of God's enduring faithfulness and sovereignty. Throughout the Old Testament, El Olam is invoked in contexts that underscore God's permanence, faithfulness, and enduring love for His people.

El Olam inspires confidence and trust in God's unchanging nature and eternal presence. It encourages believers to rely on His steadfastness and to find comfort in His eternal promises. In times of uncertainty and change, meditating on El Olam reminds us that God's love and faithfulness endure forever.

Prayer: Dear El Olam, Everlasting God, I praise You for Your eternal nature and Your unchanging love. You are the Alpha and Omega, the beginning and the end, and in You, there is no shadow of turning.

Affirmation: I affirm my trust in Your promises, knowing that You are my rock and my refuge in every season of life. Help me to lean on Your everlasting arms and to find peace in Your enduring presence.

Scripture Reference:

Genesis 21:33: "Abraham planted a tamarisk tree in Beersheba, and there he called on the name of the LORD, the Eternal God."

Isaiah 26:4: "Trust in the LORD forever, for the LORD GOD is an everlasting rock."

El Olam encapsulates the concept of God's eternity in both directions—past and future. It signifies that God existed before time began and will continue to exist beyond the end of time. This eternal nature of God assures believers that His promises are not bound by temporal constraints but are rooted in His everlasting nature. It underscores His immutability, meaning He does not change, providing a stable foundation for faith and trust.

Prayer: Heavenly Father, El Olam, I come before You with awe and reverence for Your eternal nature. You are the Everlasting God, from everlasting to everlasting, and Your faithfulness endures forever.

Affirmation: Today, I affirm my trust in You, knowing that Your plans for me are eternal and filled with hope. Help me to rest in Your unchanging love and to find peace in Your eternal presence. May Your everlasting arms uphold me in every circumstance, and may Your eternal truth guide my steps.

Scripture Reference:

Psalm 90:2: "Before the mountains were born or you brought forth the whole world, from everlasting to everlasting you are God."

Isaiah 40:28: "Do you not know? Have you not heard? The LORD is the everlasting God, the Creator of the ends of the earth. He will not grow tired or weary, and his understanding no one can fathom."

Reflecting on El Olam inspires believers to adopt an eternal perspective in their daily lives. It encourages them to prioritize spiritual values and eternal truths over temporary concerns. Knowing that God is eternal provides comfort during trials, reminding us that His purposes are far-reaching and ultimately good. Embracing El Olam deepens our faith, enabling us to navigate life with confidence and hope in His everlasting presence.

Yahweh Mekoddishkem–The Lord Who Sanctifies You (Leviticus 20:8)

Yahweh Mekoddishkem, or "The Lord Who Sanctifies You," emphasizes God's role in sanctifying His people. The name is derived from Leviticus 20:8: "Keep my decrees and follow them. I am the Lord who makes you holy." This name highlights God's attribute as the One who sets apart His people for sacred purposes, purifying them from sin and consecrating them for His service.

In the context of Leviticus, God gave specific laws to Israel, instructing them to live holy lives separate from the practices of other nations. By obeying these laws, Israel would demonstrate their commitment to Yahweh as their sanctifier. Through obedience, they acknowledged Yahweh's authority and His role in sanctifying them.

Prayer: "Yahweh Mekoddishkem, I come before You acknowledging Your holiness and Your desire for me to live a sanctified life. Purify my heart and cleanse me from all unrighteousness. Help me to honor You in everything I do, that my life may reflect Your holiness to the world. May I walk in obedience to Your commands, knowing that You are the One who sanctifies me."

Affirmation: "I am sanctified by Yahweh Mekoddishkem. I am set apart for His purposes and His glory. My life is a testament to His holiness, and through His sanctifying work, I am empowered to live in obedience and righteousness."

Understanding Yahweh Mekoddishkem inspires a deeper commitment to holiness and obedience. It reminds believers that sanctification is not just a personal act but a divine work initiated by God Himself. It motivates believers to pursue purity and righteousness, knowing that God sanctifies His people to reflect His glory.

Scripture Reference:

Leviticus 20:8 - "Keep my decrees and follow them. I am the Lord who makes you holy."

This name of God encourages believers to embrace a life of consecration and obedience, recognizing God's role as the sanctifier who empowers His people to live holy lives.

Beyond their individual meanings, the names of Yahweh collectively reflect His relational nature with humanity. They serve as portals through which believers experience intimate communion with the Creator of the universe. Whether seeking healing, provision, or peace, these names invite us to approach God with confidence, knowing He hears our prayers and responds according to His perfect will. Moreover, they emphasize the significance of cultivating a deep, personal relationship with God, one that transcends mere rituals and embraces genuine encounters with the living God.

In closing of this section, the names of Yahweh are not mere titles but windows into profound truths about God's character, His promises, and His unwavering commitment to His people. From Yahweh Rapha's healing touch to Yahweh Jireh's abundant provision and Yahweh Shalom's calming presence, each name beckons believers into a transformative journey of faith and reliance on God's sovereignty. As we contemplate these names, may our hearts be stirred with gratitude and awe, recognizing that we serve a God who intimately knows us and delights in revealing Himself to us in ways that transcend human understanding. Thus, let us accept the names of Yahweh as beacons of hope and assurance, guiding us through life's challenges and victories, and drawing us closer to the One who reigns supreme for all eternity.

Chapter 5:
The Aftermath: Sustaining Spiritual Growth

The aftermath of fasting extends far beyond the period of abstaining. It encompasses the ongoing spiritual growth, renewal, and alignment with Yahweh's purpose that continues long after the fast concludes. This chapter explores how sustained spiritual growth is nurtured through fasting, guiding you to cultivate habits, disciplines, and mindsets that foster lasting transformation. By embracing the aftermath of fasting, you position yourself to maintain spiritual vitality, deepen your relationship with Yahweh, and experience enduring spiritual and financial blessings.

Your journey of spiritual growth doesn't end with the completion of a fast—it is a continuous, lifelong pursuit of intimacy with Yahweh and alignment with His will. Accept the aftermath of fasting as a season of consolidation and growth, where you build upon the spiritual foundations laid during your fasting. Allow Yahweh to shape your character, renew your mind, and empower you to walk in His purposes each day. As you commit to sustaining spiritual growth, remember that Yahweh's grace and favor accompany you, guiding you toward greater spiritual maturity and financial prosperity.

Sustaining spiritual growth is a lifelong journey marked by phases of transformation, challenges, and divine guidance. It encompasses the aftermath of spiritual milestones, where initial fervor and revelations meet the realities of everyday life. This phase is critical, as it tests the depth of one's commitment and resilience in spiritual practices.

Understanding Spiritual Growth

Spiritual growth is not a linear path but a dynamic process where individuals deepen their connection with the divine. It involves cultivating virtues, embracing spiritual disciplines, and aligning one's life with divine principles. The aftermath of initial spiritual experiences often brings challenges such as doubt, complacency, or external pressures that threaten newfound faith.

Challenges in Sustaining Spiritual Growth

Maintaining spiritual growth requires perseverance amidst distractions and worldly temptations. The aftermath may include periods of spiritual dryness or testing, where faith is refined through trials. Challenges may arise from internal struggles with sin, external opposition, or the mundane demands of life that detract from spiritual focus.

Strategies for Sustaining Spiritual Growth

1. **Commitment to Spiritual Disciplines:** Regular prayer, meditation, study of scripture, and fellowship with believers and nurture spiritual growth. These disciplines create a foundation for intimacy with the divine and provide strength during trials (James 1:2-4).
2. **Accountability and Community:** Surrounding oneself with supportive believers fosters accountability and encouragement in the journey of faith. Sharing experiences and praying together builds resilience and deepens understanding of God's grace (Hebrews 10:24-25).
3. **Accepting Divine Guidance:** Seeking God's guidance through prayer and discernment is essential. Surrendering personal desires and aligning with God's will fosters spiritual growth and ensures alignment with divine purposes (Proverbs 3:5-6).
4. **Perseverance in Adversity:** Enduring trials with faith strengthens spiritual muscles and deepens trust in God's sovereignty. Adversity refines character and prepares believers for greater responsibilities in God's kingdom (Romans 5:3-5).

The journey of sustaining spiritual growth is motivated by the promise of eternal rewards and intimate communion with God. It is inspired by the examples of biblical figures who persevered through trials and experienced profound spiritual transformation (Hebrews 12:1-2).

The Special Power Within You

Within you resides a special power, a gift bestowed upon you by the Almighty. This power transcends earthly limitations, enabling you to overcome obstacles, break through barriers, and impact the world around you with divine love and truth. It is a power rooted in faith, nurtured by prayer, and strengthened through your unwavering commitment to walk in alignment with God's will.

Nurturing Spiritual Growth

Sustaining spiritual growth requires intentional nurturing. Just as a plant needs water and sunlight to flourish, your spirit requires nourishment from the Word of God, fellowship with believers, and moments of solitude in His presence. This nurturing process involves:

- **Daily Devotion**: Committing time each day to seek God through prayer and meditation.

- **Scripture Study**: Delving into the Bible to gain wisdom and insight into God's promises and His plan for your life.

- **Community Engagement**: Building relationships with fellow believers who can support and encourage you on your spiritual journey.

Motivation to Persevere

In moments of doubt or weariness, remember that God has equipped you with everything you need to persevere. He is your strength when you are weak, your comforter in times of sorrow, and your provider in moments of need. Your journey is a testimony of His faithfulness, a narrative of how He turns brokenness into beauty and trials into triumphs.

Inspiration for Transformation

Your life is a canvas upon which God paints His masterpiece of redemption and restoration. Every experience, whether joyful or challenging, contributes to the tapestry of His grace unfolding in your life. Be inspired by the transmutative potential of God's love, knowing that He who began a good work in you will carry it on to completion.

Prayers of Blessings for Wealth

Gratitude in Financial Blessings

Gracious God, I thank You for the financial blessings You have bestowed upon me. You are the source of all blessings, and I acknowledge Your hand in every provision and increase in my life. Help me to always be grateful and generous with what You have entrusted to me, knowing that You bless those who give cheerfully and abundantly.

Scripture Reference: 2 Corinthians 9:7
"Each of you should give what you have decided in your heart to give, not reluctantly or under compulsion, for God loves a cheerful giver."

Abundant Harvest of Blessings

Lord of the harvest, I pray for an abundant harvest of blessings in my life. May every seed sown in faith and obedience yield a bountiful return, spiritually and materially. Bless the work of my hands and the fruits of my labor, that I may experience Your faithfulness and provision in greater measure each day.

Scripture Reference: Galatians 6:9
"Let us not become weary in doing good, for at the proper time we will reap a harvest if we do not give up."

Blessing in Career and Business

Heavenly Father, I lift up my career/business before You, asking for Your divine favor and blessing. Guide me in making wise decisions that align with Your purpose for my life. Open doors of opportunity and grant me success in all my endeavors. May my work bring glory to Your name and be a testimony of Your faithfulness and provision.

Scripture Reference: Proverbs 22:29
"Do you see someone skilled in their work? They will serve before kings; they will not serve before officials of low rank."

Generosity and Kingdom Impact

Gracious God, teach me the joy of generosity and the impact of giving according to Your Word. Help me to be a cheerful giver, knowing that You bless those who bless others. Use my resources to advance Your kingdom on earth and to bring hope and transformation to those in need. May my giving be a reflection of Your love and grace in my life.

Scripture Reference: Luke 6:38
"Give, and it will be given to you. A good measure, pressed down, shaken together and running over, will be poured into your lap. For with the measure you use, it will be measured to you."

Guidance in Financial Planning

Holy Spirit, guide me in creating and executing a sound financial plan that aligns with Your wisdom and principles. Give me clarity of mind and discernment to make wise investments, save diligently, and plan for the future. May my financial decisions honor You and reflect Your kingdom values.

Scripture Reference: Proverbs 24:3-4
"By wisdom a house is built, and through understanding it is established; through knowledge its rooms are filled with rare and beautiful treasures."

Protection from Greed and Temptation

Lord Jesus, protect me from the lure of greed and materialism that can lead me away from Your will. Keep my heart focused on eternal treasures rather than temporary wealth. Help me to use my resources wisely and to be a good steward of all that You have entrusted to me.

Scripture Reference: Matthew 6:19-21
"Do not store up for yourselves treasures on earth, where moths and vermin destroy, and where thieves break in and steal. But store up for yourselves treasures in heaven, where moths and vermin do not destroy, and where thieves do not break in and steal. For where your treasure is, there your heart will be also."

Patience in Financial Waiting

Heavenly Father, grant me patience and perseverance as I wait upon Your timing for financial breakthroughs. Help me to trust Your perfect timing and to remain steadfast in faith, believing You are weaving all things together for my betterment. Strengthen my resolve to continue believing and hoping in You.

Scripture Reference: Hebrews 10:36
"You need to persevere so that when you have done the will of God, you will receive what he has promised."

Surrendering Financial Worries

Lord, I surrender all my financial worries and anxieties into Your loving hands. Replace my fears with faith and my uncertainties with trust in Your provision. Help me to cast all my cares upon You, knowing that You care deeply for every detail of my life, including my financial well-being.

Scripture Reference: 1 Peter 5:7
"Cast all your anxiety on him because he cares for you."

Confidence in God's Promises

Heavenly Father, I come to You with confidence in Your promises regarding my financial success. Your Word declares that You desire to prosper Your children and bless them abundantly. I claim these promises over my life, trusting in Your faithfulness to fulfill them according to Your will.

Scripture Reference: Jeremiah 29:11
"'For I know the plans I have for you,' declares the Lord, 'plans to prosper you and not to harm you, plans to give you hope and a future.'"

Guidance in Career and Financial Goals

Lord God, I seek Your guidance and direction in my career and financial goals. Lead me in paths of righteousness and prosperity, according to Your perfect plan for my life. Grant me clarity of mind to set achievable goals and the perseverance to pursue them diligently.

Scripture Reference: Psalm 37:4
"Take delight in the Lord, and he will give you the desires of your heart."

Breakthrough in Financial Stagnation

Lord Jesus, I lift up to You my financial situation that feels stagnant and unchanging. You are the God of breakthroughs and miracles. I pray for Your divine intervention to break through every barrier and limitation hindering my financial progress. Open new doors of opportunity and bring forth abundant blessings in unexpected ways.

Scripture Reference: Isaiah 43:19
"See, I am doing a new thing! Now it springs up; do you not perceive it? I am making a way in the wilderness and streams in the wasteland."

Protection from Financial Temptations

Lord, protect me from the allure of financial temptations that may lead me away from Your will. Shield me from greed, dishonest gain, and the love of money. Help me to prioritize Your kingdom and righteousness in all my financial decisions and to use my resources for Your glory.

Scripture Reference: 1 Timothy 6:9-10
"Those who want to get rich fall into temptation and a trap and into many foolish and harmful desires that plunge people into ruin and destruction. For the love of money is a root of all kinds of evil. Some people, eager for money, have wandered from the faith and pierced themselves with many griefs."

Provision in Times of Economic Uncertainty

Heavenly Father, I place my trust in You during times of economic uncertainty. You are my rock and fortress, a refuge in times of trouble. Provide for my needs and grant me peace amidst financial challenges. May Your faithfulness shine brightly in my life as a testimony of Your care and provision.

Scripture Reference: Psalm 62:5-8
"Yes, my soul, find rest in God; my hope comes from him. Truly he is my rock and my salvation; he is my fortress; I will not be shaken. My salvation and my honor depend on God; he is my mighty rock, my refuge. Trust in him at all times, you people; pour out your hearts to him, for God is our refuge."

Faithfulness in Financial Stewardship

Lord God, help me to be a faithful steward of the finances You have entrusted to me. Teach me to manage my resources wisely and to honor You with my financial decisions. May I be a good steward of Your blessings, using them to bless others and advance Your kingdom on earth.

Scripture Reference: Luke 16:10-11
"Whoever can be trusted with very little can also be trusted with much, and whoever is dishonest with very little will also be dishonest with much. So if you have not been trustworthy in handling worldly wealth, who will trust you with true riches?"

These petitions prayers for abundance are offered in faith and humility, acknowledging God's sovereignty and provision in every aspect of our lives. As you pray these prayers and meditate on God's Word, may you experience His guidance, protection, and abundant blessings in your financial journey. Trust in His promises, seek His wisdom, and continue to walk in faith, knowing that He is faithful to fulfill His purposes in your life.

Declarations for Prosperity

Affirmations are powerful declarations of truth and faith that reinforce positive beliefs and attitudes. By speaking these affirmations daily, you can align your thoughts with God's promises and cultivate a mindset of abundance and stewardship in your financial journey.

Financial Freedom and Abundance

"I declare financial freedom and abundance over my life. God's blessings make me rich, and He adds no sorrow with it."

Scripture Reference: Proverbs 10:22
"The blessing of the Lord makes one rich, and He adds no sorrow with it."

Confidence in God's Timing

"I trust in God's perfect timing for financial blessings. As I wait upon Him with patience and faith, He fulfills His promises in my life."

Scripture Reference: Habakkuk 2:3
"For the vision is yet for an appointed time; but at the end it will speak, and it will not lie. Though it tarries, wait for it; because it will surely come, it will not tarry."

Protection from Financial Challenges

"I am protected from financial challenges and uncertainties. God is my refuge and strength, a very present help in trouble."

Scripture Reference: Psalm 46:1
"God is our refuge and strength, a very present help in trouble."

Patience and Perseverance in Financial Goals

"I am patient and perseverant in pursuing my financial goals. I trust in God's guidance and provision every step of the way."

Scripture Reference: Hebrews 10:36
"For you have need of endurance, so that after you have done the will of God, you may receive the promise."

Financial Integrity and Honesty

"I conduct my financial affairs with integrity and honesty. God's favor rests upon the righteous, and He blesses the work of my hands."

Scripture Reference: Proverbs 11:3
"The integrity of the upright will guide them, but the perversity of the unfaithful will destroy them."

Confidence in God's Blessings

"I am confident in God's blessings over my life. He delights in the prosperity of His servants, and He crowns my efforts with success."

Scripture Reference: Psalm 35:27
"Let them shout for joy and be glad, who favor my righteous cause; and let them say continually, 'Let the Lord be magnified, who has pleasure in the prosperity of His servant.'"

Focused and Purposeful Financial Planning

"I am focused and purposeful in my financial planning. God directs my steps and leads me in paths of righteousness for His name's sake."

Scripture Reference: Psalm 23:3
"He restores my soul; He leads me in the paths of righteousness for His name's sake."

Abundance and Overflow in Finances

"I declare abundance and overflow in my finances. God blesses me so that I can be a blessing to others and fulfill His purposes."

Peace and Security in Financial Matters

"I have peace and security in my financial matters. God's peace guards my heart and mind, reassuring me of His presence and provision."

Favor and Success in Financial Endeavors

"I walk in God's favor and success in all my financial endeavors. His favor opens doors of opportunity and brings success to my efforts."

Diligence and Success in Work

"I am diligent and successful in my work and endeavors. God's hand of favor rests upon the work of my hands, and He prospers me in all that I do."

Scripture Reference: Proverbs 12:24
"The hand of the diligent will rule, but the lazy man will be put to forced labor."

Wisdom in Financial Management

"I walk in wisdom and discernment in managing my finances. God's wisdom guides my decisions, and I steward His resources with integrity and prudence."

Scripture Reference: Proverbs 3:13
"Happy is the man who finds wisdom, and the man who gains understanding."

Faithful Stewardship of Resources

"I am a faithful steward of God's resources entrusted to me. I honor Him with my finances, giving generously and managing wisely for His kingdom purposes."

Scripture Reference: 1 Corinthians 4:2
"Moreover, it is required in stewards that one be found faithful."

Prosperity in Soul and Spirit

"I prosper in my soul and spirit, aligning with God's purposes for my life. His peace and joy overflow in me, impacting every area, including my finances."

Scripture Reference: 3 John 1:2
"Beloved, I pray that you may prosper in all things and be in health, just as your soul prospers."

God's Guidance in Financial Decisions

"I seek God's guidance in every financial decision I make. His Spirit leads me in paths of righteousness and prosperity, according to His perfect will."

Abundance of Opportunities and Blessings

"I attract an abundance of opportunities and blessings into my life. God opens doors that no one can shut, and He leads me into paths of prosperity and success."

Overflowing Joy and Generosity

"I experience overflowing joy and generosity in my financial life. As I give, it is given to me—pressed down, shaken together, and running over."

God's Promise of Provision

"I trust in God's promise of provision in every season. He supplies all my needs according to His riches in glory, and I lack no good thing."

Divine Protection and Financial Security

"I am divinely protected and secure in my finances. God's angels encamp around me, guarding me against financial pitfalls and securing my prosperity."

Scripture Reference: Psalm 91:11
"For He shall give His angels charge over you, to keep you in all your ways."

Wealth and Riches in Righteousness

"I am blessed with wealth and riches in righteousness. God's blessings bring me prosperity, and I use His abundance to bless others and advance His kingdom."

Scripture Reference: Proverbs 8:18
"Riches and honor are with me, enduring riches and righteousness."

Financial Wisdom and Prosperity

"I am blessed with financial wisdom and prosperity. God's Spirit guides me in making wise financial decisions that lead to abundance and blessings."

Scripture Reference: Proverbs 3:16
"Length of days is in her right hand, in her left-hand riches and honor."

Strength and Courage in Financial Challenges

"I am strong and courageous in financial challenges. God's strength upholds me, and I overcome every obstacle with His wisdom and guidance."

These positive Statements for wealth are designed to inspire and empower you to align your thoughts and beliefs with God's promises and purposes for your life. As you speak these affirmations daily, meditate on the accompanying Scriptures, and cultivate a mindset of faith and abundance, may you experience God's provision, wisdom, and blessings in every area of your financial journey. Trust in His faithfulness, seek His guidance, and continue to walk in obedience and stewardship as you pursue sustained spiritual growth and financial prosperity in His kingdom.

Sustaining spiritual growth requires intentional effort, reliance on God's strength, and commitment to spiritual disciplines. Through prayer, affirmation, and reliance on God's Word, believers can navigate challenges, experience transformation, and deepen their relationship with God. May these prayers and affirmations strengthen your faith journey and inspire you to pursue God's will with passion and perseverance.

Chapter 6:
Fasting for Spiritual Clarity and Discernment

Fasting serves as a catalyst for achieving spiritual clarity and discernment during life's challenges and decisions. This chapter explores how fasting sharpens your spiritual senses, enhances your ability to discern Yahweh's voice, and aligns your decisions with His perfect will. By dedicating time to seek Yahweh's wisdom through fasting, you gain clarity on spiritual matters, receive divine direction, and experience breakthroughs in areas requiring discernment. Adopt fasting as a powerful tool for spiritual discernment and empowerment in navigating life's complexities with divine insight and confidence.

Yahweh has ordained fasting as a pathway to clarity and discernment, enabling you to perceive His guidance and make decisions aligned with His perfect plan for your life. As you engage in fasting for spiritual clarity, surrender your concerns and uncertainties to Yahweh, trusting in His faithfulness to illuminate your path and lead you into greater understanding. Incorporate this opportunity to deepen your spiritual discernment, knowing that Yahweh equips you with wisdom and discernment to navigate every season and circumstance with divine insight and assurance.

Grasping the Distinct Power and Grace of Fasting

Fasting involves more than simply skipping meals; it is a sacred act of surrender and devotion. It is a deliberate choice to set aside the physical to focus on the spiritual, recognizing that true sustenance comes from God alone. Throughout history, fasting has been a catalyst for spiritual breakthroughs, clarity in decision-making, and profound encounters with the divine.

As you start on this journey of fasting for enhanced spiritual understanding, remember that God has created you for greatness. He has placed within you the capacity to hear His voice clearly, to discern His will accurately, and to walk in His divine wisdom. Your decision to fast is an affirmation of your hunger for more of God, for deeper intimacy with Him, and for a clearer vision of His plans for your life.

You Are Created for Great Things

God's Word declares that you are fearfully and wonderfully made (Psalm 139:14). He has fashioned you with purpose and intentionality, equipping you with spiritual gifts and talents to fulfill His divine calling. As you fast, you are positioning yourself to receive clarity regarding the path God has laid out for you. Whether you are seeking direction in your career, guidance in relationships, or clarity in your spiritual walk, fasting opens the door for God to speak directly to your heart.

Accepting the Gift of Spiritual Clarity

Imagine standing on the precipice of a decision, uncertain of which path to take. In those moments, fasting becomes a spiritual weapon, enabling you to discern God's voice amidst the clamor of conflicting voices. It is in the stillness of fasting that God often speaks loudest, unraveling the complexities of life and illuminating the next steps on your journey.

Fasting not only affects your spiritual life but also permeates into every aspect of your being. It purifies your motives, strengthens your resolve, and deepens your reliance on God's grace. Through fasting, you cultivate a spirit of humility and dependence, acknowledging that true wisdom comes from above (James 3:17). It is through this process of self-denial that you open yourself up to receive the fullness of God's blessings and breakthroughs in your life.

As you investigate into the discipline of fasting to deepen spiritual perception, anticipate moments of revelation and renewal. Each day of fasting is an opportunity to draw closer to God, to lay bare your heart before Him, and to experience His transformative presence. Just as Moses fasted on Mount Sinai to receive the commandments (Exodus 34:28) and Jesus fasted in the wilderness to prepare for His ministry (Matthew 4:2), your fasting journey holds the potential to usher in profound spiritual encounters and divine revelations.

Spiritual Clarity and Discernment through Fasting

One of the profound benefits of fasting is its role in seeking spiritual clarity and discernment. By quieting the noise of the world and the distractions of the flesh, fasting helps individuals to hear God's voice more clearly (Isaiah 58:6-11). It opens the heart and mind to receive divine guidance and wisdom, providing clarity in decision-making and discernment of God's purposes (Acts 13:2-3).

Biblical Instances

Numerous biblical figures practiced fasting to seek God's guidance and discernment. Moses fasted for forty days and nights on Mount Sinai, receiving the Ten Commandments and divine instructions for the Israelites (Exodus 34:28). Esther called for a fast among the Jews before approaching King Xerxes to save her people from destruction, demonstrating fasting's power in moments of crisis and decision-making (Esther 4:16). Jesus Himself fasted for forty days in the wilderness, preparing for His ministry and overcoming temptation (Matthew 4:1-2).

Forms of Fasting

Fasting can take various forms, including abstaining from food entirely, restricting certain types of food, or fasting from activities or luxuries that consume time and attention. The duration of fasting can range from a single day to extended periods, depending on individual spiritual goals and convictions (Daniel 10:2-3).

Spiritual Benefits

Beyond clarity and discernment, fasting can lead to spiritual renewal and breakthroughs. It strengthens faith, increases sensitivity to the Holy Spirit, and fosters a deeper dependence on God's grace (Isaiah 58:8). Fasting also enhances spiritual discipline, aligns priorities with God's kingdom, and prepares the heart for revival and transformation (Joel 2:12-13).

Supplications Prayers for Financial Blessings

Seeking Divine Direction

Gracious Lord, as I seek spiritual clarity through fasting, I also seek Your divine direction for my financial journey. Guide me in paths of righteousness and prosperity, according to Your perfect will (Isaiah 30:21). Help me discern opportunities that align with Your plans for my life and grant me the courage to step into them with faith. I surrender my financial goals to Your sovereign care, trusting that You will establish the work of my hands for Your glory. In Jesus' name, Amen.

Scripture Reference: Isaiah 30:21
"Your ears shall hear a word behind you, saying, 'This is the way, walk in it,' whenever you turn to the right hand or whenever you turn to the left."

Stewardship and Generosity

Lord God, I acknowledge that all good things come from You, and I am grateful for Your provision in my life. Teach me to be a faithful steward of the resources You have entrusted to me (1 Corinthians 4:2). Help me to manage my finances with wisdom and integrity, so that I may honor You in all that I do. Grant me a spirit of generosity, knowing that as I give, it will be given back to me—pressed down, shaken together, and running over (Luke 6:38). Use me as a vessel of Your blessings to bless others and advance Your kingdom on earth. In Jesus' name, Amen.

Scripture Reference: 1 Corinthians 4:2
"Moreover it is required in stewards that one be found faithful."

Protection from Financial Struggles

Heavenly Father, I pray for Your divine protection over my finances as I fast and seek Your wisdom. Guard me against financial struggles and challenges that may come my way. Your Word promises that the righteous will not be forsaken nor their children begging for bread (Psalm 37:25). I claim Your promise of provision and protection over my life and declare Your peace that surpasses all understanding to guard my heart and mind in Christ Jesus (Philippians 4:7). Grant me discernment to make sound financial decisions that honor You and align with Your will. In Jesus' name, Amen.

Scripture Reference: Psalm 37:25
"I have been young, and now am old; yet I have not seen the righteous forsaken, nor his descendants begging bread."

Generational Blessings and Financial Legacy

Heavenly Father, I pray for Your blessings over my finances and my family's financial legacy. Your Word promises that the wealth of the sinner is stored up for the righteous (Proverbs 13:22), and You desire to bless generations to come (Psalm 103:17). May Your blessings flow through me and into future generations, establishing a financial legacy of faithfulness and stewardship. Help me to sow seeds of generosity and wisdom that will bear fruit in due season. Guide my steps and grant me discernment to make decisions that honor You and bless my family for generations to come. In Jesus' name, Amen.

Scripture Reference: Proverbs 13:22
"A good man leaves an inheritance to his children's children, but the wealth of the sinner is stored up for the righteous."

Godly Navigation in Investment Opportunities

Heavenly Father, I seek Your divine guidance as I navigate financial investments and opportunities. Your Word instructs me to seek counsel and wisdom (Proverbs 15:22), and I ask for Your discernment in every financial decision I make. Grant me insight to recognize opportunities that align with Your will and to steward resources wisely for Your glory. Protect me from the lure of quick gains and guide me to investments that will bring long-term prosperity. May my financial endeavors honor You and reflect Your kingdom principles. In Jesus' name, Amen.

Scripture Reference: Proverbs 15:22
"Without counsel, plans go awry, but in the multitude of counselors they are established."

Wisdom in Career and Business Endeavors

Heavenly Father, I lift up my career and business endeavors to You. Your Word teaches that diligent hands will rule, but laziness ends in forced labor (Proverbs 12:24). Grant me wisdom and diligence in my work, that I may excel and prosper according to Your will. Open doors of opportunity that align with Your purpose for my life and bless the work of my hands. May my career and business endeavors bring glory to Your name and serve as a testimony of Your faithfulness and provision. In Jesus' name, Amen.

Scripture Reference: Proverbs 12:24
"Diligent hands will rule, but laziness ends in forced labor."

Breaking Financial Curses and Strongholds

Heavenly Father, I come against any financial curses or strongholds that may be hindering Your blessings in my life. Your Word declares that Christ redeemed us from the curse of the law by becoming a curse for us (Galatians 3:13). I claim the power of Christ's blood over every generational curse or financial bondage that seeks to hold me back. Break every chain of poverty, lack, and debt in my life, and release Your abundant blessings of financial prosperity and freedom. May Your kingdom come and Your will be done in my financial life as it is in heaven. In Jesus' name, Amen.

Scripture Reference: Galatians 3:13
"Christ redeemed us from the curse of the law by becoming a curse for us."

Provision for Family and Loved Ones

Lord God, I lift up my family and loved ones before You, trusting in Your provision and care. Your Word promises that those who honor You will lack no good thing (Psalm 34:9-10). Provide for the financial needs of my family according to Your riches in glory. Grant me wisdom to lead and provide for them and bless the work of their hands. May Your favor rest upon my household, bringing peace, prosperity, and unity. Use me as a channel of Your blessings to bless my family abundantly. In Jesus' name, Amen.

Scripture Reference: Psalm 34:9-10
"Oh, fear the Lord, you His saints! There is no want to those who fear Him. The young lions lack and suffer hunger; but those who seek the Lord shall not lack any good thing."

Thankfulness for Financial Blessings

Dear Lord, I thank You for Your abundant blessings and provision in my life. Your Word teaches us to give thanks in all circumstances, for this is Your will for us in Christ Jesus (1 Thessalonians 5:18). I praise You for the financial blessings You have bestowed upon me, both big and small. Help me to cultivate a heart of gratitude and generosity, knowing that every good gift comes from You. May my life be a testament to Your goodness and provision, and may I continually acknowledge Your faithfulness in all areas of my life. In Jesus' name, Amen.

Scripture Reference: 1 Thessalonians 5:18
"In everything give thanks; for this is the will of God in Christ Jesus for you."

Trusting in God's Provision

Heavenly Father, I come before You with a heart filled with gratitude for Your faithfulness and provision in my life. Your Word assures me that You are Yahweh Jireh, my provider (Genesis 22:14). I choose to trust in Your provision completely while fasting, as I passionately seek Your face. Help me to rely on Your promises and to walk by faith, knowing that You will supply all my needs according to Your riches in glory (Philippians 4:19). Strengthen my trust in You, even in times of financial uncertainty, and grant me peace that surpasses all understanding. In Jesus' name, Amen.

Scripture Reference: Genesis 22:14
"And Abraham called the name of the place, The-Lord-Will-Provide; as it is said to this day, 'In the Mount of the Lord it shall be provided.'"

Financial Blessings for Generosity

Heavenly Father, I thank You for the blessings You have entrusted to me. Your Word teaches us that it is more blessed to give than to receive (Acts 20:35), and I desire to be a cheerful giver. Grant me a generous heart and opportunities to bless others financially. Use me as Your instrument of provision and compassion in the lives of those in need. May my giving reflect Your love and grace, and may it bring glory to Your name. Bless me abundantly so that I may continue to sow into Your kingdom and impact lives for Your glory. In Jesus' name, Amen.

Scripture Reference: Acts 20:35
"I have shown you in every way, by laboring like this, that you must support the weak. And remember the words of the Lord Jesus, that He said, 'It is more blessed to give than to receive.'"

Release from Financial Burdens

Heavenly Father, I come before You burdened by financial challenges and debt. Your Word teaches us that the borrower is servant to the lender (Proverbs 22:7), but You have promised to set the captives free (Luke 4:18). I ask for Your mercy and grace to release me from the bondage of debt and financial strain. Provide for all my needs according to Your riches in glory (Philippians 4:19) and grant me wisdom to steward my resources wisely. May Your supernatural provision bring freedom and peace to my financial situation. In Jesus' name, Amen.

Scripture Reference: Proverbs 22:7
"The rich rules over the poor, and the borrower is servant to the lender."

Discernment in Financial Partnerships

Dear Lord, I seek Your discernment and wisdom in financial partnerships and collaborations. Your Word instructs us to walk with the wise and become wise, but the companion of fools suffers harm (Proverbs 13:20). Guide me in choosing trustworthy and God-fearing partners who will honor You in our financial endeavors. Protect me from partnerships that may lead to harm or financial loss. Grant me clarity of mind and heart as I fast and seek Your guidance. May my partnerships be fruitful and bring glory to Your name. In Jesus' name, Amen.

Scripture Reference: Proverbs 13:20
"He who walks with wise men will be wise, but the companion of fools will be destroyed."

Abundance and Overflowing Blessings

Dear Lord, I lift up to You my desire for abundance and overflowing blessings in my finances. Your Word promises that You are able to bless me abundantly, so that in all things, at all times, having all that I need, I will abound in every good work (2 Corinthians 9:8). I claim Your promise of abundance and prosperity.

Financial Peace and Contentment

Dear Lord, I seek Your peace and contentment in my financial life. Your Word teaches us that godliness with contentment is great gain (1 Timothy 6:6), and I desire to be content with what You provide. Grant me peace that surpasses all understanding as I abstain and ardently seek Your countenance. Help me to trust in Your timing and provision, knowing that You hold my future in Your hands. Remove any anxieties or worries about finances and fill my heart with Your peace that transcends circumstances. In Jesus' name, Amen.

Scripture Reference: 1 Timothy 6:6
"Now godliness with contentment is great gain."

Wisdom in Inheritance and Legacy

Dear Lord, I pray for wisdom and discernment in matters of inheritance and legacy. Your Word teaches us to leave an inheritance for our children's children (Proverbs 13:22), and I seek Your guidance in stewarding resources for future generations. Grant me wisdom to make decisions that honor You and bless my descendants. Protect my inheritance from loss or misuse and guide me in creating a lasting legacy that reflects Your kingdom values. May my actions today impact future generations for Your glory. In Jesus' name, Amen.

Empowering Affirmations for Economic Achievement

I Am Blessed to Be a Blessing

I affirm that I am blessed to be a blessing (Genesis 12:2). As I seek spiritual discernment through fasting, I embrace the opportunity to bless others with my financial resources, knowing that God multiplies what I sow.

Scripture Reference: Genesis 12:2
"I will make you a great nation; I will bless you and make your name great; and you shall be a blessing."

I Am a Good Steward of God's Blessings

I affirm that I am a good steward of God's blessings. I manage my finances with integrity and diligence, honoring God in all my financial dealings (Luke 16:10-11).

Scripture Reference: Luke 16:10-11
"He who is faithful in what is least is faithful also in much; and he who is unjust in what is least is unjust also in much. Therefore, if you have not been faithful in the unrighteous mammon, who will commit to your trust the true riches?"

My Financial Steps Are Ordered by God

I affirm that God orders my financial steps according to His perfect plan for my life (Psalm 37:23). I trust in His guidance and direction as I fast and seek His will.

Scripture Reference: Psalm 37:23
"The steps of a good man are ordered by the Lord, and He delights in his way."

I Choose Faith Over Fear in Financial Matters

I affirm that I choose faith over fear in all financial matters. God has not given me a spirit of fear but of power, love, and a sound mind (2 Timothy 1:7). I confidently trust in His provision and care for me.

Scripture Reference: 2 Timothy 1:7
"For God has not given us a spirit of fear, but of power and of love and of a sound mind."

I Am Debt-Free and Financially Secure

I affirm that I am debt-free and financially secure. God's Word declares that the borrower is servant to the lender (Proverbs 22:7), and I am empowered by God to live a life of financial freedom.

I Receive Divine Ideas for Financial Increase

I affirm that I receive divine ideas and strategies for financial increase and prosperity. God grants me wisdom and creativity to generate wealth and bless others (Deuteronomy 8:18).

I Release Generously and Reap Abundantly

I affirm that I release generously and reap abundantly. God's Word assures me that whoever sows sparingly will also reap sparingly, and whoever sows generously will also reap generously (2 Corinthians 9:6).

I Am Empowered to Create Wealth

I affirm that I am empowered by God to create wealth and to prosper for His kingdom purposes (Deuteronomy 8:18). I accept my role as a steward of His resources and a conduit of His blessings.

I Trust God's Timing for Financial Breakthroughs

I affirm that I trust God's timing for financial breakthroughs in my life. His Word assures me that He makes everything beautiful in its time (Ecclesiastes 3:11). I patiently wait on Him and His perfect timing.

I Am a Channel of God's Generosity and Compassion

I affirm that I am a channel of God's generosity and compassion. His love flows through me, prompting acts of kindness and financial blessings toward others (2 Corinthians 9:8).

I Receive Divine Guidance for Financial Decisions

I affirm that I receive divine guidance for all my financial decisions. God directs my steps and gives me wisdom to make choices that align with His will and purposes (Proverbs 3:5-6).

I Choose Contentment and Gratitude in Every Financial Season

I affirm that I choose contentment and gratitude in every financial season. I am content with what God provides, knowing that godliness with contentment is great gain (1 Timothy 6:6).

I Declare Financial Breakthroughs and Victories

I affirm that I declare financial breakthroughs and victories in Jesus' name. Through His love, I am empowered to conquer every challenge (Romans 8:37), and I claim His promises of prosperity and success.

Scripture Reference: Romans 8:37
"Yet in all these things we are more than conquerors through Him who loved us."

I Am a Channel of God's Abundant Blessings

I affirm that I am a channel of God's abundant blessings. His Word promises that the generous soul will be made rich, and he who waters will also be watered himself (Proverbs 11:25). As I fast and seek spiritual clarity, I accept a lifestyle of generosity and expect God's abundant provision in return.

Scripture Reference: Proverbs 11:25
"The generous soul will be made rich, and he who waters will also be watered himself."

I Declare God's Provision and Prosperity Over My Finances

I affirm that I declare God's provision and prosperity over my finances. His Word declares that the Lord will command the blessing on my storehouses and in all to which I set my hand (Deuteronomy 28:8). As I fast and seek His face, I walk in confidence that His blessings are upon me.

Scripture Reference: Deuteronomy 28:8
"The Lord will command the blessing on you in your storehouses and in all to which you set your hand, and He will bless you in the land which the Lord your God is giving you."

I Am Empowered to Achieve Wealth for Kingdom Purposes

I declare that God has empowered me to generate abundance and thrive in His divine mission to achieve wealth and prosperity for His kingdom purposes. His Word affirms that He gives me power to get wealth, that He may establish His covenant with me (Deuteronomy 8:18). I accept my role as a faithful steward of His resources.

I Walk in Financial Freedom and Generosity

I affirm that I walk in financial freedom and generosity. God's Word encourages me to be generous and ready to share, storing up for myself a good foundation for the future

(1 Timothy 6:18-19). As I fast and seek His guidance, I accept a lifestyle of generosity and abundance.

Scripture Reference: 1 Timothy 6:18-19
"Let them do good, that they be rich in good works, ready to give, willing to share, storing up for themselves a good foundation for the time to come, that they may lay hold on eternal life."

I Release Fear and Anxiety About Finances

I affirm that I release fear and anxiety about my finances. I am fortified by God with a spirit of courage, affection, and a disciplined mind (2 Timothy 1:7). I trust in His provision and sovereignty over every financial concern.

I Walk in God's Abundance and Overflow

I affirm that I walk in God's abundance and overflow in every area of my life, including my finances. His Word promises that He will open the windows of heaven and pour out blessings that cannot be contained (Malachi 3:10). I receive His abundant blessings as I seek Him through fasting and prayer.

I Release Past Financial Mistakes and Embrace God's Restoration

I affirm that I release past financial mistakes and embrace God's restoration and redemption in my finances. His Word promises that He will restore to me the years that the locust has eaten (Joel 2:25), and I trust in His faithfulness to bring healing and renewal.

I Am Empowered by God's Spirit to Achieve Financial Goals

I acknowledge that God has entrusted me with the capacity to produce wealth and thrive in His purpose to achieve my financial goals. His Word assures me that with God, all things are possible (Matthew 19:26), and I confidently pursue His purposes for my life.

Scripture Reference: Matthew 19:26
"But Jesus looked at them and said to them, 'With men this is impossible, but with God all things are possible.'"

Fasting to heighten spiritual awareness is a sacred practice that invites believers into deeper communion with God. With prayer, affirmation, and dependence on God's Word, individuals can experience spiritual renewal, discern His will, and grow in intimacy with Him. May these prayers and affirmations strengthen your faith journey as you seek God's guidance and clarity through fasting.

Chapter 7:
Fasting for Emotional Healing and Renewal

Fasting is not only a means of spiritual discipline but also a powerful tool for emotional healing and renewal. This chapter explores how fasting facilitates inner healing, emotional restoration, and freedom from past hurts and wounds. By surrendering your emotions to Yahweh through fasting, you open channels for His healing touch to mend brokenness, restore joy, and renew your mind. Accept fasting as a transformative journey toward emotional wholeness, allowing Yahweh to heal your heart and empower you to walk in emotional freedom and abundance.

Yahweh desires to heal and restore every aspect of your being, including your emotional well-being. As you start on this journey of fasting for emotional healing, trust in Yahweh's promise to bind up your wounds and restore your soul. Release any burdens or pain into His loving care, knowing that He is faithful to bring healing and renewal to your heart. Welcome the emotional healing process with courage and faith, knowing that Yahweh's grace and compassion surround you, guiding you toward emotional wholeness and abundance in Him.

Fasting has been practiced across cultures and religions for centuries, not only as a physical discipline but also as a spiritual and emotional tool for healing and renewal. When focusing on emotional healing through fasting, it involves abstaining from food or certain activities to draw closer to a higher spiritual power, often God. This practice is rooted in the belief that fasting enhances spiritual clarity, strengthens faith, and facilitates emotional healing by addressing deep-seated wounds and restoring inner peace.

Healing from Within

Discuss how fasting contributes to emotional healing by addressing deep-seated hurts, trauma, and emotional wounds. Explore the psychological benefits of fasting in promoting emotional resilience, inner peace, and healing.

Understanding Emotional Healing and Renewal through Fasting

1. **Emotional Healing**: Fasting provides a pathway for emotional healing by creating space for introspection and prayer. It allows individuals to confront emotional pain, trauma, and negative patterns in a focused manner, seeking divine intervention for healing.
2. **Renewal of Mind and Spirit**: By abstaining from physical nourishment, fasting redirects attention from worldly concerns to spiritual matters. This shift fosters a renewed perspective on life's challenges, fostering resilience and hope.
3. **Spiritual Connection**: Fasting deepens spiritual connection by quieting external distractions, enabling individuals to hear from God more clearly. This communion can bring comfort, guidance, and a sense of purpose amid emotional turmoil.
4. **Beating Spiritual Barriers**: Fasting is recognized as a powerful method for breaking down spiritual barriers and disrupting negative cycles that obstruct emotional well-being. It signifies reliance on God's power to conquer internal battles.
5. **Holistic Healing**: Combining fasting with prayer, meditation, and Scripture reading promotes holistic healing, addressing emotional wounds from a spiritual perspective. It encourages forgiveness, reconciliation, and the release of burdens.

Perceiving the Distinctive Strength and Virtue of Fasting

Fasting involves more than just not eating; it is a spiritual discipline that opens doors to profound encounters with God. It is a time of surrendering your physical needs to focus on spiritual nourishment, inviting God's transformative presence into every aspect of your life, especially your emotional health. In the depths of fasting, you discover a divine reset—a chance to release the pain and embrace God's healing touch.

God has uniquely crafted you with a purpose and destiny. Despite the challenges and setbacks, you may face, He has planted seeds of greatness within you. Through fasting, you unlock the potential to walk in the fullness of His plan for your life, including emotional healing and renewed strength. Your journey through fasting is not just about personal healing but also about stepping into the greatness that God has ordained for you.

Scriptural Foundation: God's Promises of Healing and Restoration

Throughout the Bible, we see God's promises of healing and restoration for His people. From the Psalms that declare His faithfulness to the New Testament passages that speak of His healing power through Jesus Christ, Scripture is filled with assurances of God's love and care for your emotional well-being. As you begin on this journey of fasting for emotional healing and renewal, let these promises anchor your faith and inspire your heart:

Psalm 34:17-18
"The righteous cry out, and the Lord hears them; he delivers them from all their troubles. The Lord is close to the brokenhearted and saves those who are crushed in spirit."

Isaiah 40:31
"But those who hope in the Lord will renew their strength. They will soar on wings like eagles; they will run and not grow weary, they will walk and not be faint."

James 5:16
"Therefore confess your sins to each other and pray for each other so that you may be healed. The prayer of a righteous person is powerful and effective."

How Fasting Leads to Emotional Healing

Fasting creates a space for God to work deeply within your heart and mind. As you deny yourself physically, you become more attuned to the spiritual realm. Here's how fasting facilitates emotional healing:

- **Surrender and Dependence on God**: Fasting breaks the hold of physical appetites and fosters dependence on God alone. In this state of surrender, God's presence brings comfort and healing to emotional wounds.

- **Clarity and Renewed Perspective**: Removing distractions allows for clarity of mind and a renewed perspective on past hurts or anxieties. God's truth shines through, offering peace and understanding.

- **Healing from Trauma and Pain**: Fasting can uncover deep-seated emotions and trauma. Through prayer and seeking God, healing flows into areas once wounded, bringing freedom and restoration.

Empowerment and Emotional Strength: As you fast, God strengthens you emotionally. His presence empowers you to overcome fear, anxiety, and doubt, equipping you with emotional resilience.

Prayers for Emotional Healing and Renewal

Surrendering to God's Healing Touch

Heavenly Father, I come before You in humility and surrender, acknowledging my need for Your healing touch in my emotions. You are the God who heals the brokenhearted and binds up their wounds (Psalm 147:3). I release all pain, hurt, and anxiety into Your loving hands. Pour out Your peace that surpasses all understanding upon me, and mend the broken pieces of my heart. May Your healing flow through every part of my emotional being, restoring me to wholeness in Your presence. In Jesus' name, Amen.

Scripture Reference: Psalm 147:3
"He heals the brokenhearted and binds up their wounds."

Finding Comfort in God's Presence

Lord, Your Word assures me that You are close to the brokenhearted and save those who are crushed in spirit (Psalm 34:18). In the midst of my emotional turmoil, I seek Your comforting presence. Wrap Your arms of love around me, O Lord, and fill me with Your peace. Let Your presence bring healing to every wound and bring restoration to my soul. I trust in Your faithfulness to heal and renew me. Amen.

Releasing Past Hurts and Forgiving Others

Heavenly Father, I bring before You all the hurts and wounds from my past. Help me, Lord, to forgive those who have caused me pain, just as You have forgiven me (Ephesians 4:32). Release me from bitterness and resentment, and fill my heart with Your love and compassion. Grant me the strength to let go of the past and walk in freedom and emotional healing. Thank You, Lord, for Your grace that empowers me to forgive and move forward. Amen.

Scripture Reference: Ephesians 4:32
"Be kind to one another, tenderhearted, forgiving one another, as God in Christ forgave you."

Seeking God's Guidance and Direction

Heavenly Father, as I fast for emotional healing and renewal, I seek Your guidance and direction in every area of my life. Your Word enlightens my path and guides my course (Psalm 119:105). Lead me by Your Spirit, Lord, and show me the steps to take for emotional wholeness. Give me wisdom and discernment to navigate through challenges and to embrace Your healing work in my life. I trust in Your perfect plan and timing. Amen.

Scripture Reference: Psalm 119:105
"Your word is a lamp to my feet and a light to my path."

Trusting in God's Timing for Healing

Heavenly Father, Your Word assures me that there is a time for everything, including healing and renewal (Ecclesiastes 3:1-3). Grant me patience and faith to trust in Your timing as I seek emotional healing through fasting. Strengthen my heart and mind with Your peace, knowing that You make everything beautiful in its time. I surrender my emotions into Your loving care and await Your healing touch with hope and expectation. Amen.

Scripture Reference: Ecclesiastes 3:1-3
"To everything there is a season, a time for every purpose under heaven: a time to be born, and a time to die; a time to plant, and a time to pluck what is planted; a time to kill, and a time to heal; a time to break down, and a time to build up."

Declaring God's Peace and Stability

Lord Jesus, You are the Prince of Peace who brings stability to my emotions (Isaiah 26:3). I declare Your peace over my mind and heart, during my fast to restore and rejuvenate emotions. Guard me against anxiety and turmoil and fill me with Your presence that calms every storm. Thank You for Your promise to keep me in perfect peace as I trust in You. I receive Your peace that surpasses all understanding. Amen.

Scripture Reference: Isaiah 26:3
"You will keep him in perfect peace, whose mind is stayed on You, because he trusts in You."

Embracing God's Love and Acceptance

Heavenly Father, Your love for me is unconditional and everlasting (Jeremiah 31:3). In times of emotional struggle, remind me of Your deep affection and acceptance. Heal the wounds of rejection and loneliness with Your overwhelming love. Help me to see myself through Your eyes, cherished and valued. Fill me with Your love that casts out all fear and brings emotional wholeness. I receive Your love and acceptance today. Amen.

Scripture Reference: Jeremiah 31:3
"The Lord has appeared of old to me, saying: 'Yes, I have loved you with an everlasting love; therefore with lovingkindness I have drawn you.'"

These prayers are crafted to help you seek emotional healing and renewal through the power of fasting and prayer. Each prayer is accompanied by a scripture reference to ground your faith in God's promises. If you'd like to continue with affirmations, psalms for protection, or psalms for financial breakthrough, please let me know!

Psalms for Protection Part 2

Psalm 91: Prayer of Protection

"He who dwells in the secret place of the Most High shall abide under the shadow of the Almighty. I will say of the Lord, 'He is my refuge and my fortress; My God, in Him I will trust.' Surely, He shall deliver you from the snare of the fowler and from the perilous pestilence. He shall cover you with His feathers, and under His wings you shall take refuge; His truth shall be your shield and buckler..."

Scripture Reference: Psalm 91:1-4

Psalm 121: Assurance of God's Protection

"I will lift up my eyes to the hills—From whence comes my help? My help comes from the Lord, who made heaven and earth. He will not allow your foot to be moved; He who keeps you will not slumber. Behold, He who keeps Israel shall neither slumber nor sleep..."

Scripture Reference: Psalm 121:1-4

Psalm 34: Deliverance from Fear

"I sought the Lord, and He heard me, and delivered me from all my fears. They looked to Him and were radiant, and their faces were not ashamed. This poor man cried out, and the Lord heard him, and saved him out of all his troubles..."

Scripture Reference: Psalm 34:4-6

Psalms for Financial Breakthrough Part 2

Psalm 112: Prosperity of the Righteous

"Praise the Lord! Blessed is the man who fears the Lord, who delights greatly in His commandments. His descendants will be mighty on earth; The generation of the upright will be blessed. Wealth and riches will be in his house, and his righteousness endures forever..."

Scripture Reference: Psalm 112:1-3

Psalm 128: Prosperity of Those Who Fear the Lord

"Blessed is everyone who fears the Lord, who walks in His ways. When you eat the labor of your hands, you shall be happy, and it shall be well with you. Your wife shall be like a fruitful vine in the very heart of your house, your children like olive plants all around your table..."

Scripture Reference: Psalm 128:1-3

Psalm 1: Prosperity of the Righteous

"Blessed is the man who walks not in the counsel of the ungodly, nor stands in the path of sinners, nor sits in the seat of the scornful; but his delight is in the law of the Lord, and in His law, he meditates day and night. He shall be like a tree planted by the rivers of water, that brings forth its fruit in its season, whose leaf also shall not wither; and whatever he does shall prosper..."

Scripture Reference: Psalm 1:1-3

Psalm 65: Abundance Through God's Provision

"You visit the earth and water it, You greatly enrich it; the river of God is full of water; You provide their grain, for so You have prepared it. You water its ridges abundantly, You settle its furrows; You make it soft with showers, You bless its growth..."

Scripture Reference: Psalm 65:9-10

Psalm 67: God's Blessing and Prosperity

"God be merciful to us and bless us, and cause His face to shine upon us, that Your way may be known on earth, Your salvation among all nations. Let the peoples praise You, O God; Let all the peoples praise You. Oh, let the nations be glad and sing for joy! For You shall judge the people righteously, and govern the nations on earth..."

Scripture Reference: Psalm 67:1-4

Psalm 46: God, Our Refuge and Strength

"Therefore, we will not fear, even though the earth be removed, and though the mountains be carried into the midst of the sea; though its waters roar and be troubled, though the mountains shake with its swelling..."

Scripture Reference: Psalm 46:2-3

Psalm 138: God's Faithfulness and Protection

"Though I walk in the midst of trouble, You will revive me; You will stretch out Your hand against the wrath of my enemies, and Your right hand will save me. The Lord will perfect that which concerns me; Your mercy, O Lord, endures forever..."

Scripture Reference: Psalm 138:7-8

Psalm 23: Assurance of God's Provision

"You prepare a table before me in the presence of my enemies; You anoint my head with oil; My cup runs over. Surely goodness and mercy shall follow me all the days of my life; and I will dwell in the house of the Lord forever."

Scripture Reference: Psalm 23:5-6

Affirmations for Emotional Healing and Renewal

I Am Secure in God's Love and Acceptance

I affirm that I am secure in God's unconditional love and acceptance. His love casts out all fear and brings healing to every part of my being. I embrace His love as the foundation of my emotional wholeness.

Scripture Reference: 1 John 4:18
"There is no fear in love; but perfect love casts out fear, because fear involves torment. But he who fears has not been made perfect in love."

I Release Past Hurts and Embrace Forgiveness

I affirm that I release past hurts and choose to forgive as Christ forgave me. Forgiveness sets me free from bitterness and restores peace to my heart. I walk in the freedom that comes from extending grace to others.

Scripture Reference: Colossians 3:13
"Bearing with one another, and forgiving one another, if anyone has a complaint against another; even as Christ forgave you, so you also must do."

I Embrace God's Healing Touch on My Emotions

I affirm that I embrace God's healing touch on my emotions. His presence brings comfort, healing, and restoration to every broken area of my heart.

I Walk in Emotional Resilience and Strength

I affirm that I walk in emotional resilience and strength through Christ who strengthens me. His power enables me to overcome challenges and to stand firm in His promises.

Scripture Reference: Philippians 4:13
"I can do all things through Christ who strengthens me."

I Choose Faith Over Fear in Every Circumstance

I affirm that I choose faith over fear in every circumstance. With God on my side, I have nothing to fear. I trust in His protection and provision for my life.

Scripture Reference: Psalm 56:3-4
"Whenever I am afraid, I will trust in You. In God (I will praise His word), In God I have put my trust; I will not fear. What can flesh do to me?"

I Experience Joy and Peace Overflowing

I affirm that I experience joy and peace overflowing in my life. God's joy is my strength, and His peace fills my heart, guiding me through every storm.

Scripture Reference: Romans 15:13
"Now may the God of hope fill you with all joy and peace in believing, that you may abound in hope by the power of the Holy Spirit."

I Am Renewed Daily by God's Word and Spirit

I affirm that I am renewed daily by God's Word and His Spirit. His truth refreshes my soul, bringing clarity and understanding to my emotions.

Scripture Reference: 2 Corinthians 4:16
"Therefore we do not lose heart. Even though our outward man is perishing, yet the inward man is being renewed day by day."

I Walk in Victory Over Emotional Turmoil

I affirm that I walk in victory over emotional turmoil. Christ has overcome the world, and His victory is mine. I stand firm in His promises of peace and restoration.

I Am Empowered by God's Spirit to Overcome Challenges

I assert that God has enabled me to create prosperity and prosper in alignment with His kingdom's goals to overcome every challenge. His strength is made perfect in my weakness, and I rely on His power to navigate through difficulties.

Scripture Reference: 2 Corinthians 12:9
"And He said to me, 'My grace is sufficient for you, for My strength is made perfect in weakness.' Therefore most gladly I will rather boast in my infirmities, that the power of Christ may rest upon me."

I Walk in Forgiveness and Freedom

I affirm that I walk in forgiveness and freedom. Christ has set me free from bondage and condemnation. I choose to forgive myself and others, releasing the weight of unforgiveness.

Scripture Reference: Romans 8:1
"There is therefore now no condemnation to those who are in Christ Jesus, who do not walk according to the flesh, but according to the Spirit."

I Am Renewed Daily in God's Presence

I affirm that I am renewed daily in God's presence. His mercies are new every morning, and I receive His grace to face each day with hope and joy.

Scripture Reference: Lamentations 3:22-23
"Through the Lord's mercies we are not consumed, because His compassions fail not. They are new every morning; great is Your faithfulness."

I Walk in Harmony and Peace

I affirm that I walk in harmony and peace with others. God's love fills my heart, enabling me to extend grace and kindness to those around me.

Scripture Reference: Romans 12:18
"If it is possible, as much as depends on you, live peaceably with all men."

I Am a Vessel of God's Love and Compassion

I affirm that I am a vessel of God's love and compassion to those in need. His love flows through me, bringing healing and restoration to others as I serve with humility.

Scripture Reference: 1 John 4:12
"No one has seen God at any time. If we love one another, God abides in us, and His love has been perfected in us."

I Rejoice in God's Promises for My Life

I affirm that I rejoice in God's promises for my life. His word is my foundation, and His promises are yes and amen in Christ Jesus. I stand firm in His truth and walk by faith.

Scripture Reference: 2 Corinthians 1:20
"For all the promises of God in Him are Yes, and in Him Amen, to the glory of God through us."

I Surrender My Worries and Anxieties to God

I affirm that I surrender my worries and anxieties to God. He cares for me deeply, and His peace guards my heart and mind. I cast all my cares upon Him because He cares for me.

Scripture Reference: 1 Peter 5:7
"Casting all your care upon Him, for He cares for you."

I Am Strengthened by God's Word and Presence

I affirm that I am strengthened by God's Word and His presence in my life. His Word is a lamp to my feet and a light to my path, guiding me through every season of life.

I Walk in Freedom from Past Hurts and Pains

I affirm that I walk in freedom from past hurts and pains. Christ has redeemed me from the bondage of my past, and I embrace His healing and restoration in my life.

I Choose Joy and Gratitude Daily

I affirm that I choose joy and gratitude daily. God's joy is my strength, and His blessings overflow in my life. I rejoice in His goodness and faithfulness.

Scripture Reference: Psalm 118:24
"This is the day the Lord has made; We will rejoice and be glad in it."

I Walk in Obedience to God's Word

I affirm that I walk in obedience to God's Word. His commands are for my good, and I delight in following His ways. I receive His blessings as I obey His instructions.

Scripture Reference: Psalm 119:1-2
"Blessed are the undefiled in the way, who walk in the law of the Lord! Blessed are those who keep His testimonies, who seek Him with the whole heart!"

I Am a Vessel of God's Love and Grace

I affirm that I am a vessel of God's love and grace to those around me. His love compels me to show kindness and compassion, reflecting His character in all I do.

Scripture Reference: Ephesians 2:10
"For we are His workmanship, created in Christ Jesus for good works, which God prepared beforehand that we should walk in them."

I Rejoice in God's Salvation and Deliverance

I affirm that I rejoice in God's salvation and deliverance. He has rescued me from darkness and brought me into His marvelous light. I celebrate His victory in my life.

Scripture Reference: Psalm 18:2
"The Lord is my rock and my fortress and my deliverer; my God, my strength, in whom I will trust; my shield and the horn of my salvation, my stronghold."

I Walk in Unity and Harmony with Others

I affirm that I walk in unity and harmony with others. God's love binds us together in perfect harmony, and I seek to build up and encourage those around me.

Scripture Reference: Colossians 3:14
"But above all these things put on love, which is the bond of perfection."

In closing, fasting for emotional healing and renewal is a powerful spiritual discipline that invites God's transformative work into our lives. Through prayers of petition and affirmation, we declare our faith in God's healing power and open ourselves to His divine restoration. May this time of fasting bring forth emotional healing, renewed strength, and a deeper understanding of God's unfailing love and grace.

Chapter 8:
Fasting as a Catalyst for Social Justice and Compassion

Fasting transcends personal spiritual growth to become a catalyst for social justice, compassion, and advocacy for the marginalized and oppressed. This chapter explores how fasting awakens your heart to social injustices, empowers you to advocate for change, and aligns your actions with Yahweh's heart for justice. By fasting with a heart of compassion and solidarity, you stand in solidarity with the marginalized, seek justice for the oppressed, and demonstrate Yahweh's love in tangible ways. Embrace fasting as a transformative tool for societal transformation and a testament to Yahweh's call to pursue justice and compassion in the world.

Yahweh calls you to be His hands and feet in bringing justice and compassion to a broken world. As you fast with a heart aligned with His, He empowers you to advocate for the voiceless, uplift the oppressed, and bring healing to communities in need. Let your fasting be a testament to Yahweh's love and justice, igniting a passion for social change and transformation. Trust in Yahweh's guidance and provision as you stand for justice and compassion, knowing that He blesses those who seek His kingdom and righteousness with abundance and favor.

Historical and Cultural Context: Throughout history, fasting has been intertwined with movements for social justice and compassion. In various religious traditions, prophets, leaders, and followers have employed fasting to advocate for justice, challenge oppression, and express solidarity with the disadvantaged. Examples include Gandhi's use of fasting as a nonviolent resistance tool during India's independence movement and fasting as a means of protest systemic injustices.

Spiritual and Psychological Impact: Fasting is not merely a physical discipline but also a spiritual and psychological one. It fosters empathy by sensitizing individuals to the suffering of others and cultivates humility by challenging material dependencies. This heightened awareness often leads to a deeper commitment to social justice causes and a renewed sense of compassion for marginalized communities.

Within you lies a potential waiting to be awakened—a power bestowed upon you by the divine. You are crafted with purpose, intricately designed to bring about change and goodness in the world. Fasting, often overlooked in its profound spiritual and transformative capacities, is a gift from God—an avenue through which you can tap into spiritual strength, clarity of purpose, and profound compassion for others.

The Sacred Gift of Fasting

Fasting, in its essence, is not merely abstaining from food and drink. It is a spiritual discipline that transcends the physical realm, reaching into the depths of your soul. It is a sacred act of devotion, a deliberate choice to humble oneself before the Almighty, seeking His guidance and grace. Through fasting, you open a channel for divine intervention, inviting God to work miracles in your life and in the lives of those around you.

Unveiling the Power Within

As you embark on this journey of fasting, understand that you are engaging in a profound spiritual battle—one that shapes not only your inner being but also the world you inhabit. Through fasting, you harness the power to dismantle injustice, to speak for the voiceless, and to advocate for those oppressed. It is a tool of empowerment, equipping you with clarity of mind and purity of heart to pursue justice with unwavering conviction.

Fasting and Compassion

Compassion, born out of fasting, is a force that bridges divides, heals wounds, and restores dignity. When you deny yourself the comforts of the world, you awaken to the struggles of others. Your heart softens, your empathy deepens, and you become a beacon of hope and kindness in a world often marred by indifference. Fasting cultivates a spirit of compassion that compels you not only to see the plight of others but also to take action to alleviate their suffering.

Scriptural Foundations

Throughout history, fasting has been a practice embraced by prophets, saints, and spiritual leaders. In the Bible, we see how fasting brought about profound change—turning the hearts of kings, healing nations, and securing divine favor. Jesus Himself fasted for forty days in the wilderness, demonstrating the rejuvenating effects of fasting in preparing for His ministry.

Motivation to Act

God has created you with a purpose—to be a light in the darkness, a voice for the marginalized, and a catalyst for justice. Your journey of fasting is not merely a personal endeavor but a spiritual commitment to bring about positive change in your community and beyond. Embrace this sacred discipline with faith and perseverance, knowing that God honors your sacrifice and uses it to accomplish His will on earth.

Entreaties for Economic Flourishing Through Fasting

Surrendering Financial Concerns to God

Heavenly Father,

As I board this journey of fasting, I surrender all my financial concerns into Your capable hands. You are the provider of all things, and I trust in Your divine provision for my life. Grant me wisdom and discernment in managing my finances, that I may glorify You in all that I do. Open doors of opportunity and bless the work of my hands, that I may prosper and be a blessing to others. May my financial success be a testimony to Your faithfulness and grace.

Seeking Divine Guidance in Financial Decisions

Dear Lord,

In the midst of uncertainty, I seek Your divine guidance and wisdom in all financial decisions. Grant me clarity of mind and discernment to make wise investments and steward my resources faithfully. May my choices reflect Your will and align with Your purpose for my life. Thank You for Your promise to guide me along the right path, leading to prosperity and abundance in You.

Scripture Reference: **Proverbs 3:5-6** - "Trust in the Lord with all your heart, and do not lean on your own understanding. In all your ways acknowledge him, and he will make straight your paths."

Breaking Financial Barriers Through Faith

Gracious Father,

I come before You with faith, believing in Your power to break every financial barrier in my life. Through fasting, I declare freedom from debt, lack, and financial struggle. Strengthen my faith, Lord, that I may see Your mighty hand at work, providing abundantly beyond all I can ask or imagine. Let my testimony of financial breakthroughs bring glory to Your name and inspire others to trust in Your unfailing promises.

Scripture Reference: **Matthew 17:20** - "He said to them, 'Because of your little faith. For truly, I say to you, if you have faith like a grain of mustard seed, you will say to this mountain, 'Move from here to there,' and it will move, and nothing will be impossible for you.'"

Blessing Others Through Financial Abundance

O Lord of Blessings,

As You bless me with financial abundance through fasting and prayer, I pray that I may be a channel of Your blessings to others. Use me to support those in need, to contribute to worthy causes, and to advance Your kingdom on earth. May my generosity reflect Your heart of compassion and justice, bringing hope and transformation to lives around me. Thank You, Lord, for entrusting me with resources to make a difference in this world.

Scripture Reference: **2 Corinthians 9:11** - "You will be enriched in every way to be generous in every way, which through us will produce thanksgiving to God."

Embracing Contentment and Gratitude

Heavenly Father,

In the midst of striving for financial success, I pray for a heart of happiness and appreciation. Help me to appreciate Your blessings and to find joy in every circumstance. Teach me the value of spiritual riches that surpass material wealth, that I may seek Your kingdom first above all else. Thank You for Your faithfulness and provision, which sustain me through fasting and prayer.

Scripture Reference: **Hebrews 13:5** - "Keep your life free from love of money, and be content with what you have, for he has said, 'I will never leave you nor forsake you.'"

Seeking God's Guidance in Career and Business Endeavors

Heavenly Father,

During my fasting period, as I diligently seek Your presence, I lift up my career and business endeavors before You. Guide me in choosing paths that align with Your will and purpose for my life. Grant me favor and wisdom in my workplace or business dealings. May I be a light of integrity and compassion, reflecting Your values in all I do. Thank You for equipping me with skills and opportunities to excel and contribute positively to society.

Scripture Reference: **Psalm 32:8** - "I will instruct you and teach you in the way you should go; I will counsel you with my eye upon you."

Receiving Divine Favor in Financial Negotiations and Opportunities

Gracious Father,

As I fast and pray, I ask for Your divine favor to accompany me in every financial negotiation and opportunity. Open doors that no one can shut and grant me favor in the eyes of those I interact with. May Your presence go before me, guiding me to fruitful outcomes and prosperous partnerships. Thank You for Your promise to bless the work of my hands and make me a lender and not a borrower.

Scripture Reference: **Deuteronomy 28:12** - "The Lord will open to you his good treasury, the heavens, to give the rain to your land in its season and to bless all the work of your hands. And you shall lend to many nations, but you shall not borrow."

Healing and Restoration of Financial Health

Merciful God,

I come to You with a heart burdened by financial challenges and setbacks. Through fasting, I seek Your healing touch and restoration in my financial health. Heal every area of lack and debt and restore what has been lost or broken. Grant me the discipline and wisdom to steward my finances wisely, honoring You with my resources. Thank You for Your promise of restoration and abundant blessings poured out upon those who seek You.

Scripture Reference: **Joel 2:25** - "I will restore to you the years that the swarming locust has eaten, the hopper, the destroyer, and the cutter, my great army, which I sent among you."

Strengthening Faith Amidst Financial Challenges

Dear Lord,

In the midst of financial challenges and uncertainties, I come before You with faith and trust. Strengthen my faith, O God, that I may not waver in my belief in Your provision and promises. Through fasting, deepen my reliance on You and renew my hope in Your unfailing love. May my faith grow stronger, even in the face of adversity, knowing that you are my caregiver and my source.

Wisdom in Financial Planning and Investments

Wise God,

I humbly seek Your wisdom and guidance as I plan for my financial future and make investments. Grant me insight into opportunities that align with Your will and purposes. May I steward my resources wisely, honoring You with every financial decision. Thank You for Your promise that when we seek Your wisdom, You generously give it without reproach.

Patience and Perseverance During Financial Challenges

Heavenly Father,

In times of financial hardship and waiting, grant me patience and perseverance. Help me to trust in Your perfect timing and to remain steadfast in faith. Through fasting, cultivate in me a spirit of endurance and hope, understanding that You are orchestrating all things for my betterment. Strengthen my resolve to keep pressing forward with confidence in Your promises.

Scripture Reference: **Romans 12:12** - "Rejoice in hope, be patient in tribulation, be constant in prayer."

Humility and Gratitude in Financial Success

Loving Father,

As You bless me with financial success through fasting, keep me humble and grateful before You. Guard my heart from pride and selfish ambition and fill me with a spirit of gratitude for Your abundant blessings. Help me to use my resources wisely and generously, honoring You in all that I do.

Scripture Reference: **James 4:10** - "Humble yourselves before the Lord, and he will exalt you."

Boldness in Using Financial Resources for Kingdom Impact

Heavenly Father,

Grant me boldness and courage to use the financial resources You provide through fasting for kingdom impact. Help me to invest in missions, support ministries, and care for the marginalized and oppressed. May my generosity and compassion shine as a beacon of Your love and justice in a world in need. Use me as Your instrument to bring about transformation and healing in communities and nations.

Faithfulness in Tithing and Offering

Faithful Provider,

As You bless me abundantly through fasting, instill in me a heart of faithfulness in tithing and offering. Help me to honor You with the first fruits of all my increase, trusting in Your promise to pour out blessings that I cannot contain. May my obedience in financial stewardship be a testimony of Your faithfulness and provision to others, drawing them closer to You.

Scripture Reference: **Malachi 3:10** - "Bring the full tithe into the storehouse, that there may be food in my house. And thereby put me to the test, says the Lord of hosts, if I will not open the windows of heaven for you and pour down for you a blessing until there is no more need."

Wisdom in Handling Financial Windfalls and Blessings

Heavenly Father,

As I fast and seek Your wisdom, grant me discernment and wisdom in handling financial windfalls and blessings. Help me to steward these resources with integrity and generosity, honoring You in all my decisions. May I use these blessings to bless others, to advance Your kingdom, and to bring glory to Your name. Thank You for Your promise that You will bless those who are faithful with little and entrust them with more.

Scripture Reference: **Luke 16:10** - "One who is faithful in a very little is also faithful in much, and one who is dishonest in a very little is also dishonest in much."

Protection from Greed and Materialism

Gracious God,

Guard my heart from the allure of greed and materialism as I experience financial success through fasting. Help me to prioritize eternal treasures over temporary riches, seeking first Your kingdom and righteousness. Keep me humble and content in Your provision, knowing that true wealth is found in knowing and serving You. Thank You for Your promise to satisfy the desires of those who fear You.

Scripture Reference: **Matthew 6:19-21** - "Do not lay up for yourselves treasures on earth, where moth and rust destroy and where thieves break in and steal, but lay up for yourselves treasures in heaven, where neither moth nor rust destroys and where thieves do not break in and steal. For where your treasure is, there your heart will be also."

Patience and Trust During Financial Waiting Periods

Faithful Provider,

In seasons of financial waiting and uncertainty, grant me patience and unwavering trust in Your timing and provision. Help me to wait upon You with hope and expectancy, knowing that You are working behind the scenes for my good. Strengthen my faith through fasting, Lord, that I may rest in Your promises and persevere in prayer. Thank You for Your assurance that those who wait upon You will renew their strength.

Financial Freedom and Liberation from Debt

Merciful Savior,

I come to You with a heart burdened by debt and financial bondage. Through fasting, I seek Your supernatural intervention and liberation from all forms of financial oppression. Break every chain of debt and lack in my life, and release me into the freedom and abundance You have promised. Thank You for Your covenant to satisfy all my needs from Your infinite resources.

Seeking Financial Wisdom and Discernment

Wise and Sovereign God,

As I fast and seek Your wisdom, grant me discernment and understanding in financial matters. Help me to make wise decisions that honor You and align with Your purposes.

May I seek Your counsel in every financial transaction and endeavor, trusting in Your guidance and provision. Thank You for Your promise that if anyone lacks wisdom, they should ask You, who gives generously to all without finding fault.

Divine Alignment of Financial Goals with Your Will

Heavenly Father,

Align my financial goals and ambitions with Your perfect will and purposes. Help me to seek first Your kingdom and righteousness, trusting that all other things will be added unto me. May my desires align with Your desires for my life, that I may steward my resources faithfully and generously. Thank You for Your promise to guide me along paths of righteousness for Your name's sake.

Scripture Reference: **Psalm 23:3** - "He leads me in paths of righteousness for his name's sake."

Financial Abundance to Bless Others

Heavenly Father,

As You bless me with financial abundance through fasting, give me a heart to bless others generously. Help me to be a channel of Your love, compassion, and provision to those in need. Guide me to use my resources wisely and strategically to alleviate poverty, support missions, and bring healing to broken communities. May my generosity reflect Your character and bring glory to Your name.

Financial Abundance Affirmations

Affirmation of Generosity and Compassion

"I affirm a spirit of generosity and compassion in my financial success. Through fasting, I align my heart with God's heart for the marginalized and needy. As **2 Corinthians 9:7** encourages, 'Each one must give as he has decided in his heart, not reluctantly or under compulsion, for God loves a cheerful giver.' I embrace a lifestyle of generous giving, reflecting God's love and compassion."

Affirmation of Debt Freedom and Financial Liberation

"I affirm freedom from debt and financial bondage through fasting. Scripture assures me in **Psalm 37:21**, 'The wicked borrows but does not pay back, but the righteous is generous and gives.' I declare freedom from all forms of financial oppression and commit to stewarding my finances in alignment with God's principles of abundance and blessing."

Affirmation of Strategic Financial Planning and Success

"I affirm success in my financial endeavors through fasting and prayer. As **Proverbs 16:3** states, 'Commit your work to the Lord, and your plans will be established.' I align my financial goals with God's purposes, seeking His guidance and favor in every endeavor. I declare success, prosperity, and divine favor in all my financial undertakings."

Affirmation of Trusting God in Financial Uncertainty

"I affirm unwavering trust in God's provision during financial uncertainty. Through fasting, I anchor my faith in God's promises. As **Psalm 56:3** assures me, 'When I am afraid, I put my trust in you.' I trust in God's unfailing provision and guidance, knowing that He is faithful to sustain me in every season of financial challenge."

Affirmation of Financial Excellence and Fruitfulness

"I affirm financial excellence and fruitfulness in my endeavors through fasting. As **Deuteronomy 28:8** promises, 'The Lord will command the blessing on you in your barns and in all that you undertake. And he will bless you in the land that the Lord your God is giving you.' I declare God's favor and blessing upon my work, investments, and financial decisions."

Affirmation of Thankfulness for God's Faithfulness in Financial Matters

"I affirm thankfulness for God's faithfulness in all financial matters through fasting. As **Psalm 9:1** proclaims, 'I will give thanks to the Lord with my whole heart; I will recount all of your wonderful deeds.' I praise God for His faithfulness, provision, and blessings in my finances. I declare gratitude and praise for His continued faithfulness in every aspect of my financial journey."

Affirmation of God's Promises of Provision

"I affirm God's promises of provision in my life through fasting. As **Psalm 34:10** declares, 'The young lions suffer want and hunger; but those who seek the Lord lack no good thing.' I trust in God's abundant provision for all my needs, both now and in the future. I declare that I lack no good thing because God is my faithful provider."

Assertion of Monetary Liberty and Liberation

"I affirm my journey towards financial freedom and liberation through fasting. Scripture assures me in **Proverbs 22:7**, 'The rich rules over the poor, and the borrower is the slave of the lender.' Through fasting, I declare freedom from debt and financial bondage, and I commit to stewarding my finances in alignment with God's principles of freedom and abundance."

Affirmation of Favor and Blessings in Financial Endeavors

"I affirm God's favor and blessings upon my financial endeavors through fasting. Scripture promises in **Psalm 5:12**, 'For you bless the righteous, O Lord; you cover him with favor as with a shield.' I declare God's favor to surround me like a shield in all my financial dealings, opening doors of opportunity and prosperity according to His abundant grace."

Affirmation of Diligence and Hard Work in Financial Success

"I affirm diligence and hard work as pathways to financial success through fasting. As **Proverbs 10:4** teaches, 'A slack hand causes poverty, but the hand of the diligent makes rich.' Through fasting, I commit to working diligently and faithfully in my endeavors, trusting God to bless the work of my hands and to multiply my efforts for His glory."

Affirmation of Honoring God with Financial Resources

"I affirm my commitment to honoring God with my financial resources through fasting. As **Proverbs 3:9-10** instructs, 'Honor the Lord with your wealth and with the first fruits of all your produce; then your barns will be filled with plenty, and your vats will be bursting with wine.' I declare my intention to steward my finances in ways that glorify God and advance His kingdom."

Affirmation of Faith in God's Ability to Provide Abundantly

"I affirm my faith in God's ability to provide abundantly for all my needs through fasting. As **Ephesians 3:20** assures me, 'Now to him who is able to do far more abundantly than all that we ask or think, according to the power at work within us.' I declare that God is able to exceed my expectations and provide for me beyond measure."

Affirmation of Patience and Trust in God's Timing for Financial Breakthroughs

"I affirm patience and trust in God's timing for financial breakthroughs through fasting. As **Psalm 27:14** encourages, 'Wait for the Lord; be strong, and let your heart take courage; wait for the Lord!' I declare my trust in God's perfect timing for financial blessings and breakthroughs, knowing that He works all things together for my good."

Affirmation of Financial Wisdom to Manage and Grow Resources

"I affirm financial wisdom to manage and grow resources through fasting. Scripture assures me in **Proverbs 24:3-4**, 'By wisdom a house is built, and by understanding it is established; by knowledge the rooms are filled with all precious and pleasant riches.' I declare my desire to steward my financial resources wisely, seeking God's wisdom to build a solid foundation for prosperity."

Affirmation of Joy and Contentment in Every Financial Season

"I affirm joy and contentment in every financial season through fasting. As **Philippians 4:11-12** states, 'Not that I am speaking of being in need, for I have learned in whatever situation I am to be content. I know how to be brought low, and I know how to abound. In any and every circumstance, I have learned the secret of facing plenty and hunger, abundance and need.' I declare my contentment and joy in God's provision, regardless of the financial circumstances."

Affirmation of Using Wealth to Serve God's Purposes and Advance His Kingdom

"I affirm my commitment to use wealth to serve God's purposes and advance His kingdom through fasting. Scripture instructs me in **1 Timothy 6:17-19**, 'As for the rich in this present age, charge them not to be haughty, nor to set their hopes on the uncertainty of riches, but on God, who richly provides us with everything to enjoy. They are to do good, to be rich in good works, to be generous and ready to share, thus storing up treasure for themselves as a good foundation for the future, so that they may take hold of that which is truly life.' I declare my intention to use my resources to bless others, support missions, and bring glory to God."

In inference, fasting as a catalyst for social justice and compassion is a profound spiritual discipline that calls believers to action. It empowers individuals and communities to confront systemic injustices, extend compassion to the marginalized, and advocate for a more just and equitable society. Grounded in scriptural principles and motivated by God's love, fasting for social justice embodies the revolutionary impact of faith in action.

Chapter 9:
Fasting for Physical Health and Wellness

Fasting is not only a spiritual discipline but also a powerful practice for enhancing physical health and wellness. This chapter delves into how fasting promotes detoxification, boosts metabolism, and supports overall well-being. By abstaining from food and focusing on Yahweh's nourishment, you give your body time to heal, regenerate, and achieve optimal health. Embrace fasting as a holistic approach to wellness, aligning your physical health with your spiritual journey toward wholeness and vitality.

Your body is a temple entrusted to you by Yahweh, and fasting offers a transformative opportunity to honor Him through stewardship of your health. As you fast for physical wellness, invite Yahweh's presence into your journey, trusting in His provision and guidance to nourish and strengthen your body. Embrace this season of fasting as a pathway to renewed energy, vitality, and well-being, knowing that Yahweh desires your health and flourishing in every aspect of your life.

Fasting, practiced for centuries across various cultures and religions, has gained attention in modern times for its potential health benefits beyond spiritual reasons. When done correctly and under guidance, fasting can contribute significantly to physical health and overall well-being. This section explores different fasting methods, their benefits, considerations, and the spiritual connection that enhances the experience.

In the depths of your soul, there lies a divine spark, a flicker of light that connects you to the vastness of eternity. From the dawn of creation, God formed you with purpose and intention, breathing His life into your very being. You are not merely a collection of atoms but a vessel crafted by the hands of the Almighty, destined for greatness and imbued with the capacity to experience His power in extraordinary ways.

Fasting, a practice as ancient as humanity itself, is not just a ritual of abstaining from food; it is a profound spiritual discipline that unlocks doors to both physical health and spiritual enlightenment. God, in His infinite wisdom, ordained fasting not only as a means to seek His face but also as a transformative journey toward holistic well-being. Through fasting, you embark on a sacred pilgrimage, traversing the realms of the physical and the spiritual, cultivating compassion for yourself and others, and nurturing a deeper communion with the Divine.

The Special Power and Gift of Fasting

Fasting is a gift bestowed upon you by a loving Father who desires your wholeness in every aspect of life. It is a spiritual tool that sharpens your focus, strengthens your resolve, and purifies your intentions. Beyond its physical benefits, fasting holds the key to unlocking supernatural breakthroughs in your spiritual journey. It is a pathway to encounter Yahweh's power in profound ways, aligning your heart with His will and opening floodgates of blessings that transcend earthly limitations.

Imagine standing at the precipice of transformation, poised to break free from the chains that bind you—whether they be physical ailments, emotional wounds, or spiritual barriers. Fasting empowers you to reclaim your health, renew your spirit, and realign your priorities with the eternal purposes of God. It is a sacred invitation to partner with Yahweh in co-creating a life marked by vitality, compassion, and divine favor.

Fasting to Boost Physical Vitality

Fasting, in its essence, is a voluntary abstinence from food for spiritual purposes, often accompanied by prayer and meditation. Scientifically, fasting has been recognized for its profound effects on the body, including detoxification, cellular repair, and metabolic enhancement. Spiritually, fasting serves as a catalyst for deeper intimacy with God, fostering clarity of mind, and amplifying spiritual sensitivity.

When approached with reverence and intentionality, fasting becomes a transformative journey toward physical health and wellness. It allows your body to rest and rejuvenate, purging toxins and restoring balance. Moreover, fasting cultivates discipline and self-control, virtues that spill over into every area of your life, enabling you to make healthier lifestyle choices and honor your body as a temple of the Holy Spirit.

Holistic Wellbeing

Explore the physical benefits of fasting, including improved metabolism, detoxification, and overall health. Discuss scientific research and medical perspectives on intermittent fasting and its positive impacts on longevity and disease prevention.

Balancing Spiritual and Physical Health

Offer practical advice on maintaining balance between spiritual fasting practices and physical health. Address concerns such as hydration, nutrition, and potential health risks associated with prolonged fasting.

Health Benefits of Fasting:

Research suggests several health benefits of fasting:

- **Fasting and Metabolic Benefits:** Fasting may aid in reducing body fat, enhancing insulin sensitivity, and balancing blood sugar levels.
- **Cellular Repair and Longevity:** Autophagy, the cellular cleaning process activated during fasting, may promote longevity and protect against diseases like Alzheimer's and Parkinson's.
- **Heart Health:** Fasting may lower blood pressure, improve cholesterol levels, and reduce inflammation, benefiting cardiovascular health.
- **Cognitive Benefits of Fasting:** Fasting has the potential to improve brain health, enhance cognitive function, and provide protection against neurodegenerative diseases.

Requests for Monetary Blessings Through Fasting for Enhanced Physical Fitness:

Prayer for Financial Provision and Blessing

Heavenly Father, as I start this journey of fasting to promote physical health, I lift up to You my financial needs and aspirations. You are the Provider of all things, and I trust in Your abundant provision for my life. Grant me wisdom and discernment to manage my finances wisely, honoring You with every decision I make.

Prayer for God's Favor and Opportunities

Lord, I seek Your favor and divine opportunities in my financial endeavors. Open doors of blessing and prosperity that align with Your will for my life. Guide me in paths of righteousness, where financial success and spiritual fulfillment intersect. May Your grace abound in my financial affairs as I honor You through fasting.

Scripture Reference: Psalm 90:17 - "Let the favor of the Lord our God be upon us, and establish the work of our hands upon us; yes, establish the work of our hands!"

Prayer for Breakthrough in Financial Challenges

Heavenly Father, I bring before You every financial challenge and obstacle I face. Through fasting, I surrender these burdens into Your capable hands. Grant me breakthrough and victory over financial struggles, providing solutions and resources beyond my expectations. Strengthen my faith as I trust in Your promises of provision.

Scripture Reference: Isaiah 41:10 - "Fear not, for I am with you; be not dismayed, for I am your God; I will strengthen you, I will help you, I will uphold you with my righteous right hand."

Prayer for Wisdom in Financial Stewardship

Lord, bless me with divine wisdom and discernment in financial stewardship. Teach me to be faithful in managing the resources You entrust to me, so that I may honor You in every financial decision. May my fasting be a catalyst for clarity of mind and spiritual insight regarding financial matters.

Prayer for Supernatural Increase and Multiplication

Lord, I pray for supernatural increase and multiplication in my finances as I honor You through fasting. Pour out Your abundance upon me, exceeding my expectations and meeting every financial need. Let Your blessings overflow in my life, enabling me to be a blessing to others and glorifying Your name.

Scripture Reference: Deuteronomy 1:11 - "May the Lord, the God of your fathers, make you a thousand times as many as you are and bless you, as he has promised you!"

Prayer for Courage to Step into Financial Opportunities

Heavenly Father, grant me courage and boldness to step into new financial opportunities and ventures that You place before me. Remove any fear or doubt that hinders me from walking in obedience to Your leading. May my fasting empower me with confidence, knowing that You go before me and make a way where there seems to be no way.

Scripture Reference: Joshua 1:9 - "Have I not commanded you? Be strong and courageous. Do not be frightened, and do not be dismayed, for the Lord your God is with you wherever you go."

Prayer for Alignment with God's Will in Financial Goals

Lord, align my financial goals and aspirations with Your perfect will for my life. May my desires be shaped by Your wisdom and guided by Your Spirit. Grant me patience and perseverance as I pursue financial success through fasting, trusting in Your divine timing and purpose for my life.

Scripture Reference: Proverbs 16:3 - "Commit your work to the Lord, and your plans will be established."

Prayer for Divine Guidance in Financial Decisions

Heavenly Father, I seek Your divine guidance and wisdom in every financial decision I make. Grant me clarity of mind and discernment to recognize Your leading and to distinguish between opportunities that align with Your will and those that do not. During my fast to promote physical health and well-being, illuminate the path of financial prosperity You have prepared for me.

Scripture Reference: Psalm 25:4-5 - "Make me to know your ways, O Lord; teach me your paths. Lead me in your truth and teach me, for you are the God of my salvation; for you I wait all day long."

Supplication for Financial Independence and Debt Release

Lord, I lift up to You my financial burdens and debts. As I fast, release me from the chains of financial bondage and grant me supernatural provision to settle every debt. Provide opportunities for financial freedom and increase the chance that I may live a life of generosity and stewardship according to Your kingdom principles.

Scripture Reference: Psalm 37:21 - "The wicked borrows but does not pay back, but the righteous is generous and gives."

Prayer for Divine Strategy and Insight in Financial Planning

Lord, grant me divine strategy and insight as I plan for my financial future. Guide me in making wise investments and financial decisions that align with Your kingdom purposes. Throughout my fasting journey for physical vitality and wellness, sharpen my mind and illuminate opportunities that will bring glory to Your name and benefit Your kingdom.

Prayer for Business and Career Success

Heavenly Father, bless the work of my hands and prosper the endeavors of my business or career. As I fast, grant me favor and success in all my professional pursuits. Open doors of opportunity and promotion that I may excel and be a light for Your kingdom in the marketplace. May my financial success glorify Your name.

Scripture Reference: Deuteronomy 8:18 - "You shall remember the Lord your God, for it is he who gives you power to get wealth, that he may confirm his covenant that he swore to your fathers, as it is this day."

Prayer for Generational Blessings and Legacy

Lord, I pray for generational blessings and a lasting legacy of financial stewardship in my family. As I fast, break every generational curse of poverty and lack, and establish a heritage of abundance and generosity. May my children and descendants walk in Your favor and experience Your provision throughout their lives.

Scripture Reference: Psalm 112:2 - "His offspring will be mighty in the land; the generation of the upright will be blessed."

Prayer for Patience and Trust in God's Timing

Heavenly Father, teach me patience and trust in Your perfect timing regarding my financial goals and aspirations. As I fast, cultivate in me a spirit of patience and perseverance, knowing that Your plans for me are good and Your timing is flawless. Strengthen my faith to wait upon You and to walk in obedience to Your leading.

Scripture Reference: Habakkuk 2:3 - "For still the vision awaits its appointed time; it hastens to the end—it will not lie. If it seems slow, wait for it; it will surely come; it will not delay."

Prayer for Supernatural Debt Cancellation

Heavenly Father, I come before You with faith, believing in Your power to cancel debts supernaturally. As I abstain to enhance my physical health and overall well-being, I ask for Your intervention in my financial situation. Release me from the burden of debt and financial obligations that weigh heavy on my heart. Provide a way where there seems to be no way, and let Your grace abound in my finances.

Scripture Reference: Psalm 37:5 - "Commit your way to the Lord; trust in him, and he will act."

Prayer for Increased Financial Income and Opportunities

Heavenly Father, I pray for increased income and divine opportunities for financial growth. While fasting to improve my physical health and wellness, open doors of abundance and prosperity in my career, business, investments, and endeavors. Bless the work of my hands and multiply my resources according to Your riches in glory.

Prayer for Favor in Financial Negotiations and Transactions

Lord, grant me favor and grace in all financial negotiations and transactions. As I fast, let Your favor surround me like a shield, influencing decisions and outcomes in my favor. May I walk in integrity and wisdom, reflecting Your character in every financial interaction I have.

Scripture Reference: Proverbs 3:4 - "So you will find favor and good success in the sight of God and man."

Prayer for Financial Protection and Security

Heavenly Father, I pray for Your divine protection and security over my finances. Guard me against financial loss, theft, and unforeseen expenses. During my fasting period for the sake of physical well-being, place a hedge of protection around my finances and possessions. Let Your angels encamp around me and keep me safe from harm.

Prayer for Generosity and Heart for Giving

Lord, cultivate within me a generous heart and a spirit of cheerful giving. As I fast, teach me the joy of sharing my financial blessings with others in need. Show me opportunities to bless others abundantly and to sow into Your kingdom purposes. May my generosity reflect Your love and compassion to those around me.

Prayer for Supernatural Increase in Savings and Investments

Heavenly Father, I pray for a supernatural increase in my savings and investments. As I refrain to support my physical health and holistic wellness, multiply my financial resources and bless my efforts to save and invest wisely. Grant me discernment in identifying opportunities that yield fruitful returns, aligning with Your will for my financial stewardship.

Scripture Reference: Ecclesiastes 11:1 - "Cast your bread upon the waters, for you will find it after many days."

Prayer for Wisdom in Budgeting and Financial Planning

Lord, grant me wisdom and discipline in budgeting and financial planning. As I fast, help me to prioritize spending and to allocate resources according to Your wisdom. Guide me in creating a financial plan that honors You and prepares me for future needs and opportunities.

Scripture Reference: Luke 14:28 - "For which of you, desiring to build a tower, does not first sit down and count the cost, whether he has enough to complete it?"

Prayer for Patience and Endurance During Financial Challenges

Heavenly Father, grant me patience and endurance during times of financial challenges and trials. Throughout my fast to support physical health and holistic well-being, strengthen my faith to persevere with hope and trust in Your provision. Teach me to rely on Your timing and to wait upon You with confident expectation.

Scripture Reference: Romans 5:3-4 - "Not only that, but we rejoice in our sufferings, knowing that suffering produces endurance, and endurance produces character, and character produces hope."

Scripture Reference: Hebrews 11:1 - "Now faith is the assurance of things hoped for, the conviction of things not seen."

These prayers are fashioned to align your financial aspirations with God's promises of provision and blessing, while incorporating the transformative practice of fasting for better physical conditioning. May they inspire faith, foster trust in God's faithfulness, and empower you to pursue financial success in harmony with His divine will.

Fasting to strengthen physical resilience integrates ancient wisdom with modern scientific understanding. It offers a holistic approach to improving metabolic health, supporting weight management, and fostering spiritual growth. When practiced mindfully and with proper guidance, fasting can be a powerful tool for enhancing overall well-being.

Affirmative Statements for Monetary Growth for Comprehensive Physical Fitness

Affirmation of God's Favor and Open Doors

God's favor rests upon me, opening doors of opportunity and prosperity in my career, business, and investments. During my fasting period to promote physical well-being and holistic health, I step into new levels of financial blessing and breakthrough.

Affirmation of Supernatural Increase and Multiplication

I experience supernatural increase and multiplication in my finances through fasting. God's blessings overflow in my life, exceeding my expectations and enabling me to walk in His abundance.

Affirmation of Financial Wisdom and Success

I operate in financial wisdom and success as I seek God's guidance through fasting. My financial endeavors prosper, and I am empowered to achieve my financial goals with excellence.

Affirmation of Faith in God's Promises for Financial Breakthrough

I declare faith in God's promises for financial breakthrough and prosperity. As I fast for physical health and wellness, I receive His blessings and provision abundantly, walking in His divine favor and grace.

Affirmation of Patience and Trust in God's Timing for Financial Miracles

I patiently trust in God's perfect timing for financial miracles and breakthroughs. As I fast, I wait upon the Lord with expectancy, knowing that He will fulfill His promises and exceed my expectations.

Affirmation of Abundant Harvest and Financial Increase

I sow seeds of faith and obedience, expecting an abundant harvest and financial increase. Through fasting, God multiplies my efforts and blesses me beyond measure, fulfilling His plans for my prosperity.

Scripture Reference: Galatians 6:9 - "And let us not grow weary of doing good, for in due season we will reap, if we do not give up."

Affirmation of Supernatural Provision in Financial Challenges

I receive supernatural provision and divine solutions in every financial challenge I face. Through fasting, God turns obstacles into opportunities, demonstrating His faithfulness and power in my financial circumstances.

Affirmation of Confidence and Boldness in Financial Pursuits

I walk in confidence and boldness in all my financial pursuits. Through fasting, God equips me with courage and faith to pursue His plans for financial success and kingdom impact.

Affirmation of Strategic Financial Planning and Management

I engage in strategic financial planning and management guided by God's wisdom. As I fast, He directs my steps and empowers me to steward His resources with excellence and integrity.

Affirmation of Stability and Security in God's Provision

I am anchored in God's provision, experiencing stability and security in all financial matters. Through fasting, He establishes my finances on His promises, ensuring that I lack no good thing.

Scripture Reference: Psalm 16:5-6 - "The Lord is my chosen portion and my cup; you hold my lot. The lines have fallen for me in pleasant places; indeed, I have a beautiful inheritance."

Affirmation of Obedience and Blessings in Financial Matters

I obey God's principles of financial stewardship, knowing that obedience brings blessings. Through fasting, I align my finances with His kingdom purposes, and He blesses me abundantly beyond measure.

Affirmation of Confidence in God's Financial Plan

I trust in God's perfect financial plan for my life. As I fast, I surrender my financial concerns to Him, believing that His plan is good, pleasing, and perfect.

Scripture Reference: Romans 13:8 - "Owe no one anything, except to love each other, for the one who loves another has fulfilled the law."

Affirmation of Generational Blessings and Wealth Transfer

I affirm generational blessings and wealth transfer in my family line. Through fasting, I position myself to receive and steward God's blessings for future generations.

Scripture Reference: Proverbs 13:22 - "A good man leaves an inheritance to his children's children, but the sinner's wealth is laid up for the righteous."

Affirmation of Strategic Financial Investments

I make strategic financial investments that align with God's wisdom and principles. As I fast, I discern opportunities that yield fruitful returns and honor God's kingdom purposes.

Scripture Reference: Proverbs 21:5 - "The plans of the diligent lead surely to abundance, but everyone who is hasty comes only to poverty."

Affirmation of Favor in Business Ventures and Career Advancement

I walk in God's favor in my business ventures and career advancement. Through fasting, doors of opportunity open for me, and I excel in all my professional pursuits.

Affirmation of Faith in God's Provision for Future Plans

I have faith in God's provision for my plans and aspirations. Through fasting, I trust Him to guide me in achieving financial goals that align with His purpose and glory.

These affirmations are designed to align your thoughts and declarations with God's promises of financial success and abundance, while integrating the transformative practice of fasting for physical harmony and health. May they inspire faith, cultivate gratitude, and empower you to walk confidently in God's provision and blessings.

Chapter 10:
How to Begin Your Fast and Awakening Your Potential

Entering on a fast is more than abstaining from food; it is a deliberate spiritual practice that requires preparation, intentionality, and alignment with Yahweh's purpose. This chapter explores practical steps and strategies for beginning your fast, including setting intentions, choosing fasting methods, and preparing spiritually and physically. By cultivating a heart of expectancy and readiness, you position yourself to experience Yahweh's transformative power and awaken your potential for spiritual and financial breakthrough.

Yahweh has uniquely designed you with limitless potential and purpose. As you embark on your fasting journey, accept the opportunity to align your heart and mind with His divine plan for your life. Invite Yahweh to awaken dormant gifts, talents, and dreams within you, trusting in His guidance and provision to empower you for spiritual and financial success. Accept each moment of preparation as a sacred opportunity to draw closer to Yahweh and step into the fullness of your calling and destiny.

The purpose of fasting is to draw closer to God, a spiritual discipline rooted in Biblical teachings. Fasting involves setting aside distractions to reset our inner selves, allowing God to renew us deeply. It's a time to celebrate God's mercy and prepare our hearts to receive His blessings. Your personal fast should challenge you appropriately while considering your health and seeking divine guidance through prayer.

In the vast expanse of time and eternity, there lies a profound truth: God has destined you for greatness. From the moment of your creation, His hand has guided your steps, weaving a tapestry of purpose and promise. As you start on the journey of fasting, you are not merely abstaining from food; you are awakening to the divine potential within you.

Fasting is a sacred practice, a spiritual discipline that transcends the physical realm and connects you intimately with the Creator. It is a pathway to spiritual clarity, a channel through which you can hear the whispers of God's voice amidst the noise of life. By denying your flesh, you open your spirit to receive revelations, guidance, and empowerment that transcend human understanding.

Imagine standing at the threshold of your destiny, with Yahweh Himself beckoning you forward. He has placed dreams in your heart and purpose in your spirit. Through fasting, you align your will with His, forging a partnership that unlocks doors and dismantles barriers. It is a testament to your faith, a declaration that you trust in His provision and guidance.

Fasting is not about deprivation but about dedication. It is a deliberate choice to seek Yahweh's face, to lay down distractions and worldly comforts in pursuit of something greater. As you begin this journey, remember that you are not alone. The same power that raised Christ from the dead resides within you, ready to breathe life into your prayers and aspirations.

To fast effectively is to understand its significance beyond physical act. It is a spiritual weapon against the forces of darkness, a means of fortifying your soul against temptation and doubt. In fasting, you declare your dependence on God, surrendering your weaknesses and insecurities at His feet. It is a journey of purification, where your heart is cleansed and your spirit renewed.

There are different types of fasts:

1. **Complete Fast:** Drinking only liquids, typically water with optional light juices.
2. **Selective Fast:** Removing specific elements from your diet, like the Daniel Fast which excludes meat, sweets, and bread.
3. **Partial Fast:** Abstaining from food during specific times of the day or sunup to sundown.
4. **Soul Fast:** Focusing on abstaining from non-food activities like social media or TV to rebalance life priorities.

How to Begin Your Fast: Starting your fast with clear objectives enhances its spiritual impact. Seek the Holy Spirit's guidance for renewal, healing, or resolving challenges (2 Chronicles 7:14). Commit to your fast duration, type, prayer focus, and spiritual activities beforehand to stay committed amid temptations.

Steps to Fasting:

1. **Set Your Objective:** Clarify why you're fasting and what spiritual goals you aim to achieve.
2. **Make Your Commitment:** Decide on the type and duration of your fast, aligning it with prayer and Scripture (Matthew 6:16-18).
3. **Prepare Yourself Spiritually:** Repentance and seeking forgiveness are foundational. Prepare your heart by confessing sins and surrendering fully to God (1 John 1:9; Ephesians 5:18).
4. **Prepare Yourself Physically:** Consult a physician if needed and gradually adjust your diet before fasting to ease the transition.

During Your Fast: Allocate ample time for prayer and reflection, listening to God's guidance through Scripture and worship (Philippians 2:13). Manage physical aspects like hydration and moderate exercise, anticipating temporary discomforts.

Breaking Your Fast: Gradually reintroduce solid foods to avoid digestive issues, starting with light, easily digestible options like fruits and vegetables. Ending your fast properly supports both physical and spiritual well-being.

Expect Results: Approach fasting with expectation, believing in heightened spiritual awareness and answered prayers (John 14:21). Each fast is a step toward deeper spiritual growth, building your faith and resilience over time.

Fasting isn't a quick fix but a journey of spiritual strengthening. If challenges arise, persevere and continue fasting with faith. Let's commit to fasting and prayer for personal renewal and revival in our communities and beyond.

A Dietary Routine for Fasting: Maintaining a consistent dietary routine during fasting is crucial. You must have a structured schedule:

- **Early Morning (4 a.m. - 6 a.m.):** Freshly squeezed fruit juices diluted with distilled water, such as apple, pear, or grapefruit juices.
- **Late Morning (10:00 a.m. - noon):** Fresh vegetable juice blend of lettuce, celery, and carrots.
- **Afternoon (1:30 p.m. – 3:30 p.m.):** Herbal tea with a touch of honey, avoiding caffeinated teas.
- **Evening (6 p.m. - 8:00 p.m.):** Broth made from potatoes, celery, and carrots, consumed after boiling.

Advice for Juice Fasting:

- Fruit juices can alleviate hunger pangs and provide natural sugar energy, motivating and strengthening you to continue.
- opt for juices made from fresh fruits and vegetables like watermelon, lemons, apples, and leafy greens.
- Adjust your intake to weather conditions and personal preference, mixing acidic juices like orange or tomato with water to avoid stomach discomfort.
- Steer clear of caffeinated beverages and gum, which can stimulate digestive activity.

Breaking Your Fast Gradually: When concluding your fast, it's crucial to reintroduce solid foods gradually to prevent adverse physical and spiritual effects:

- Start with light options like watermelon when ending an extended water fast.
- Continue with fruit and vegetable juices, gradually adding a raw salad, baked or boiled potatoes without butter or seasoning, and steamed vegetables over the following days.
- Eventually transition back to your regular diet, beginning with small, frequent meals to maintain the benefits of your fast.

Expecting Results: Approach your fasting journey with faith and expectation, trusting in God's promise to strengthen and renew you spiritually, mentally, and physically (John 14:21). While a single fast isn't a cure-all, regular fasting can foster ongoing spiritual growth and deepened intimacy with God.

As you get on this journey of fasting and prayer, remember that each step is a part of your spiritual development. Accept the challenges and blessings that come with fasting, knowing that your commitment and faithfulness will be honored by God. Together, let's pursue revival in our lives, our communities, and beyond through the transformative potential of fasting and prayer.

Challenges and Growth in Fasting: Fasting presents challenges that test and strengthen our spiritual resolve. It's a discipline that not only detoxifies our bodies but also purifies our hearts and minds before God. As you navigate through the physical and spiritual challenges of fasting, remember that these difficulties are opportunities for growth and deeper connection with God.

Support and Community in Fasting: Engaging in fasting with others can provide support and encouragement. Whether participating in communal prayer sessions or sharing insights with fellow believers, community involvement can enhance the spiritual impact of fasting. Together, we can uplift and inspire one another to persevere in faith during our fasting journeys.

Scriptural Foundation of Fasting: Throughout the Bible, fasting is portrayed as a powerful tool for spiritual breakthrough and intimacy with God. Scriptures such as Isaiah 58:6-7 emphasize the importance of fasting with a heart aligned with God's will, leading to acts of justice and compassion towards others. Jesus Himself fasted for forty days and nights, demonstrating the spiritual discipline we are called to follow (Matthew 4:2).

Continuing in Prayer and Reflection: As you continue in your fasting journey, prioritize prayer and reflection. Dedicate time daily to seek God's presence, listen to His voice, and align your heart with His purposes. Allow the Holy Spirit to guide your prayers and illuminate His Word, leading you deeper into spiritual understanding and revelation.

Long-Term Benefits of Fasting: While the immediate benefits of fasting include spiritual renewal and clarity, the long-term effects extend to every aspect of our lives. Fasting can strengthen our faith, deepen our relationship with God, and empower us to overcome spiritual obstacles and strongholds. By consistently engaging in fasting as a spiritual discipline, we position ourselves to experience ongoing growth and transformation in Christ.

In inference, fasting is not merely a ritual or religious practice but a powerful means of drawing nearer to God and experiencing His transformative presence in our lives. Accept the journey with faith, knowing that God honors the sincere efforts of His children to seek Him with all their hearts. May your fasting be a catalyst for revival, both personally and corporately, as we seek to glorify God and fulfill His purposes on earth.

Maintaining Spiritual Discipline: Consistency in fasting fosters spiritual discipline and resilience. Just as physical exercise strengthens muscles, regular fasting builds spiritual endurance and fortitude. Stay committed to your fasting practice, knowing that each period of sacrifice and seeking God's presence contributes to your spiritual growth and maturity.

Wisdom in Fasting Practices: Seeking wisdom in how and when to fast is essential. Consultation with spiritual mentors or trusted leaders can provide guidance tailored to your spiritual journey. Whether undertaking a short fast for clarity or an extended fast for breakthrough, approach each fast with prayerful consideration and dependence on God's leading.

Integration of Fasting into Daily Life: Integrate the principles of fasting beyond designated periods into your daily life. Cultivate habits of prayer, meditation on Scripture, and spiritual reflection that sustain spiritual vitality and sensitivity to God's voice. Let fasting become a lifestyle of consecration and devotion rather than a sporadic practice.

Transformation Through Fasting: Fasting not only detoxifies the body but also purifies the soul and spirit. It opens avenues for God to heal, restore, and renew us holistically—mentally, emotionally, and spiritually. Accept the transformative journey of fasting to align your life with God's will and experience His abundant grace and power.

Encouragement and Support: During challenging moments in your fasting journey, draw strength from the promises of God's Word and the encouragement of fellow believers. Share testimonies of God's faithfulness and breakthroughs experienced through fasting, inspiring others to persevere in their own spiritual disciplines.

Continual Growth and Reflection: As you continue to grow in fasting and prayer, reflect on the lessons learned and the spiritual milestones achieved. Celebrate the victories and learn from the challenges, trusting that God uses every season of fasting to shape you into His likeness and empower you for His purposes.

Blessings Prayers for Financial Fulfillment: How to Begin Your Fast and Realizing Your Potential

Opening Prayer

Heavenly Father, as I begin this sacred journey of fasting, I surrender my financial concerns and aspirations into Your loving hands. You are the God of abundance and provision, and I trust in Your perfect timing and provision during this time of consecration. Open my eyes to see Your blessings and opportunities and grant me wisdom to steward them faithfully. In Jesus' name, Amen. (Philippians 4:19)

Prayer for Divine Guidance

Lord God, I seek Your guidance as I fast and pray for financial breakthrough. Lead me on the path of righteousness and prosperity, according to Your will. Illuminate my mind with Your wisdom and insight, that I may make sound financial decisions that honor You. Protect me from schemes and distractions that seek to hinder Your blessings in my life. May Your favor surround me as a shield, and may Your peace guard my heart and mind in Christ Jesus. Amen. (Proverbs 3:5-6)

Prayer for Breaking Financial Barriers

Almighty God, I declare Your authority over every financial barrier and stronghold in my life. By the power of Your Holy Spirit, I break every chain of debt, lack, and poverty that has held me captive. Your Word says that You came to give us life abundantly; therefore, I claim Your promises of prosperity and abundance in my finances. Let Your light shine upon my financial situation, bringing clarity, provision, and supernatural breakthroughs. In Jesus' name, Amen. (John 10:10)

Prayer for Provision and Blessings

Gracious Father, You are the source of all blessings and the giver of every good gift. I thank You for the financial blessings You have bestowed upon me and for those yet to come. During this time of fasting, I ask for Your continued provision and favor in my career, business endeavors, and investments. Bless the work of my hands and multiply my resources, that I may be a channel of Your generosity to others. Let Your blessings overflow in my life, bringing glory and honor to Your name. Amen. (James 1:17)

Prayer for Courage and Faith

Dear Lord, as I step out in faith to fast and pray for financial breakthrough, strengthen my courage and increase my faith. Help me to trust in Your promises and to remain steadfast in prayer, even in times of uncertainty. Fill me with Your peace that surpasses all understanding and with the confidence that You are working all things together for my good. Let Your will be done in my life, and may Your name be glorified through the testimony of Your provision and faithfulness. Amen. (Mark 11:24)

Closing Prayer of Thanksgiving

Gracious God, I thank You for the privilege of fasting and seeking Your face for spiritual and financial breakthroughs. Thank You for hearing my prayers and for Your promises that are yes and amen in Christ Jesus. As I continue this journey, I trust in Your faithfulness and provision. May Your name be exalted and glorified through the testimonies of Your goodness in my life. In Jesus' name, Amen. (Psalm 34:1)

Prayer for Financial Healing and Restoration

Heavenly Father, I lift up to You any areas of financial loss, setback, or hardship in my life. You are the God who restores and heals, and I ask for Your healing touch in my finances. Restore what the enemy has stolen from me and bring forth restoration and abundance according to Your promises. Let Your peace reign in my heart as I trust in Your provision and plan for my financial well-being. In Jesus' name, Amen. (Joel 2:25-26)

Prayer for Family Financial Blessing

Lord Jesus, I pray for my family's financial situation and well-being. Provide for all our needs according to Your riches in glory. Bless our home with financial stability, peace, and unity. Protect us from financial strain and hardship and let Your love and grace overflow in our family finances. May we be a testimony of Your faithfulness and provision to those around us. In Jesus' name, Amen. (Philippians 4:19)

Prayer for Generational Wealth and Legacy

Gracious God, I lift up to You the desire to leave a godly legacy of wealth and blessing for future generations. Help me to be a faithful steward of the resources You entrust to me, that I may leave an inheritance of righteousness and provision to my children and grandchildren. Guide me in making wise investments and financial decisions that will impact future generations for Your glory. May Your kingdom purposes be advanced through the wealth You entrust to me. In Jesus' name, Amen. (Proverbs 13:22)

Prayer for Financial Favor and Opportunities

Lord God, I pray for Your divine favor and supernatural opportunities in my financial endeavors. You are the God who opens doors that no one can shut, and I ask for Your favor to be upon me as I seek to advance in my career, business, and financial investments. Let Your wisdom and discernment guide me in seizing every opportunity You place before me. May Your favor set me apart and lead to success and prosperity for Your glory. In Jesus' name, Amen. (Psalm 5:12)

Prayer for Thankfulness and Praise

Heavenly Father, I thank You for the honor of fasting and pursuing Your face for financial breakthrough. Thank You for Your promises that are yes and amen in Christ Jesus. I praise You for Your faithfulness and provision in my life. As I continue this journey, I trust in Your unfailing love and provision. May Your name be lifted and praised through the testimonies of Your goodness and financial miracles in my life. In Jesus' name, Amen. (Psalm 103:1-5)

Prayer for Financial Stability

Heavenly Father, I lift up to You my desire for financial stability and security. Your Word assures me that You are my rock and my fortress, my deliverer and my refuge. I trust in Your promises of protection and provision. Grant me wisdom and discernment to manage my resources wisely. Strengthen me with Your peace and assurance, knowing that You are my provider in every season of life. In Jesus' name, Amen. (Psalm 62:5-8)

Prayer for Divine Strategies and Ideas

Lord God, I seek Your divine strategies and creative ideas for financial success. Your Word declares that You give wisdom generously to all who ask in faith. I ask for Your wisdom to innovate and excel in my profession, enterprise, and monetary investments. Open my mind to new opportunities and possibilities that align with Your will. Let Your Spirit guide me in implementing these strategies for Your glory and the advancement of Your kingdom. In Jesus' name, Amen. (James 1:5)

Prayer for Financial Abundance

Father God, I pray for the gift of financial freedom and independence. Your Word promises that where the Spirit of the Lord is, there is freedom. I declare freedom from debt, lack, and financial bondage in my life. By Your power, break every chain that hinders my financial breakthrough. Grant me wisdom to steward my resources faithfully and generously. May my life reflect Your abundance and generosity to others. In Jesus' name, Amen. (2 Corinthians 3:17)

Prayer for God's Provision in Times of Need

Gracious Father, I come to You with my financial needs and concerns. Your Word assures me that You will supply all my needs according to Your riches in glory by Christ Jesus. I trust in Your provision, even in times of uncertainty and economic challenges. Provide for me and my family abundantly, that we may testify to Your faithfulness and goodness. Thank You for Your promises and for Your unfailing love toward us. In Jesus' name, Amen. (Philippians 4:19)

Prayer for Supernatural Increase in Income

Lord Jesus, I pray for supernatural increase in my income and financial resources. Your Word teaches us that You can do exceedingly abundantly above all that we ask or think. I ask for Your divine multiplication upon my finances, that I may have more than enough to meet every need and to bless others. Open doors of opportunity for promotion, bonuses, and unexpected financial blessings. May Your name be glorified through the overflow of Your provision in my life. In Jesus' name, Amen. (Ephesians 3:20)

Prayer for Generosity and Open-hearted Giving

Lord God, You are the ultimate Giver of every good gift. Teach me the joy of open-hearted giving and cheerful generosity. Your Word encourages us to give freely, knowing that it will be given back to us in good measure, pressed down, shaken together, and running over. Help me to sow seeds of kindness, generosity, and financial support into the lives of others. Bless my giving abundantly, that Your kingdom purposes may be advanced, and Your name glorified. In Jesus' name, Amen. (Luke 6:38)

Prayer for Favor in Business and Career

Gracious Father, I pray for Your favor and blessings upon my business endeavors and career pursuits. Your Word declares that You delight in the prosperity of Your servants. I ask for Your favor to open doors of opportunity, promotion, and success in my professional life. Let Your favor distinguishes me and set me apart for greatness in my field. May my work be a testimony of Your grace and provision, bringing glory to Your name. In Jesus' name, Amen. (Psalm 90:17)

Prayer for Perseverance and Faith

Lord Jesus, strengthen my faith and perseverance as I continue to seek Your face for financial breakthrough. Your Word assures us that those who wait upon the Lord shall renew their strength. Help me to remain steadfast in prayer and unwavering in faith, knowing that You are faithful to fulfill Your promises. May my perseverance in fasting and prayer bring forth a harvest of financial blessings and spiritual growth. In Jesus' name, Amen. (Isaiah 40:31)

Declarations for Financial Prosperity: How to Begin Your Fast and Activating Your Potential

I am a steward of God's abundance, and His blessings overflow in my life.

Scripture Reference: "The Lord will open to you His good treasure, the heavens, to give the rain to your land in its season, and to bless all the work of your hand. You shall lend to many nations, but you shall not borrow." - Deuteronomy 28:12

I am empowered to create wealth and prosper in all my endeavors.

Scripture Reference: "But you shall remember the Lord your God, for it is He who gives you power to get wealth, that He may establish His covenant which He swore to your fathers, as it is this day." - Deuteronomy 8:18

Every setback is a setup for a greater financial comeback in God's perfect timing.

Scripture Reference: "And we know that all things work together for good to those who love God, to those who are the called according to His purpose." - Romans 8:28

I am a channel of God's generosity, blessing others with the abundance He has given me.

Scripture Reference: "He who has a generous eye will be blessed, for he gives of his bread to the poor." - Proverbs 22:9

I am surrounded by divine favor, attracting success, prosperity, and divine connections.

Scripture Reference: "The Lord will make you the head and not the tail; you shall be above only, and not be beneath, if you heed the commandments of the Lord your God." - Deuteronomy 28:13

My mind is renewed with God's promises of financial abundance and prosperity.

Scripture Reference: "And do not be conformed to this world, but be transformed by the renewing of your mind, that you may prove what is that good and acceptable and perfect will of God." - Romans 12:2

I sow seeds of faith and generosity, knowing that God multiplies my harvest abundantly.

I am empowered by God's Spirit to overcome financial challenges and achieve success.

Scripture Reference: "But you shall receive power when the Holy Spirit has come upon you; and you shall be witnesses to Me in Jerusalem, and in all Judea and Samaria, and to the end of the earth." - Acts 1:8

I declare breakthroughs in my finances, as God's promises manifest in my life.

Scripture Reference: "For with God nothing will be impossible." - Luke 1:37

I am anointed for financial success and divine prosperity in every area of my life.

Scripture Reference: "But you have an anointing from the Holy One, and you know all things." - 1 John 2:20

God's favor goes before me, making a way where there seems to be no way in my financial journey.

Scripture Reference: "The Lord will fight for you, and you shall hold your peace." - Exodus 14:14

I am blessed to be a blessing, and God's goodness follows me all the days of my life.

I trust in God's faithfulness to fulfill His promises of prosperity and abundance in my life.

Scripture Reference: "For I am the Lord your God who takes hold of your right hand and says to you, Do not fear; I will help you." - Isaiah 41:13

I am aligned with God's timing and His perfect will for my financial breakthrough.

Scripture Reference: "But let patience have its perfect work, that you may be perfect and complete, lacking nothing." - James 1:4

I am a child of God, and His blessings of prosperity and success are upon me.

Scripture Reference: "Blessed is the man who trusts in the Lord, and whose hope is the Lord. For he shall be like a tree planted by the waters, which spreads out its roots by the river, and will not fear when heat comes; but its leaf will be green, and will not be anxious in the year of drought, nor will cease from yielding fruit." - Jeremiah 17:7-8

My faith in God's provision unlocks doors of opportunity and financial favor.

Scripture Reference: "Now faith is the substance of things hoped for, the evidence of things not seen." - Hebrews 11:1

I am diligent in my work, and God rewards my efforts with prosperity and success.

Scripture Reference: "The soul of a lazy man desires, and has nothing; but the soul of the diligent shall be made rich." - Proverbs 13:4

I declare breakthroughs in my finances, believing in God's promises of abundance and provision.

Scripture Reference: "For assuredly, I say to you, whoever says to this mountain, 'Be removed and be cast into the sea,' and does not doubt in his heart, but believes that those things he says will be done, he will have whatever he says." - Mark 11:23

I am a wise steward of God's resources, and He multiplies my efforts for His glory.

Scripture Reference: "Well done, good and faithful servant; you were faithful over a few things, I will make you ruler over many things. Enter into the joy of your lord." - Matthew 25:21

I release any fear of lack or scarcity and embrace God's abundance and provision in my life.

Scripture Reference: "Fear not, for I am with you; be not dismayed, for I am your God. I will strengthen you, yes, I will help you, I will uphold you with My righteous right hand." - Isaiah 41:10

My thoughts are aligned with God's promises of prosperity and abundance, manifesting in my life.

In closing, fasting is a sacred discipline that aligns our hearts with God's purposes and prepares us to receive His blessings and guidance. Approach fasting with reverence and expectation, believing in the paradigm-shifting energy of God to work mightily in and through your life. May your fasting journey be marked by deep intimacy with God, spiritual breakthroughs, and a renewed passion to live in obedience and holiness before Him.

Chapter 11:

Important Strategies for Fasting: 40, 21, 14, 7, or 3 Days

Fasting spans a spectrum of durations, from short-term to extended periods, each offering unique spiritual and physical benefits. This chapter explores the significance and strategies of various fasting durations—40, 21, 14, 7, or 3 days —guiding you through the spiritual and practical considerations of each. Whether you choose a brief fast for immediate breakthrough or a prolonged fast for deeper spiritual alignment, Yahweh meets you in your commitment, guiding you toward spiritual clarity, renewal, and empowerment.

The duration of your fast is a personal journey of faith and surrender to Yahweh's timing and purpose. Whether you embark on a short-term or extended fast, trust in Yahweh's provision and presence to sustain you through every moment. Accept the discipline and sacrifice of fasting as a testament to your commitment to Yahweh and His promises. Allow Yahweh to deepen your faith, refine your character, and lead you into a season of profound spiritual and financial breakthroughs as you align your heart with His perfect will.

Fasting, whether for 40, 21, 14, 7, or 3 days, is a spiritual discipline practiced across various cultures and religions. It involves abstaining from food for a specific period, often seeking spiritual clarity, renewal, and deeper connection with the divine. Here are some essential strategies for fasting:

1. **Prepare Spiritually and Physically:** Before fasting, prepare your heart and mind through prayer, meditation, and seeking guidance from spiritual mentors or leaders. Physically, gradually reduce caffeine, sugar, and processed foods to ease fasting.
2. **Set Clear Intentions:** Define your purpose for fasting—whether it's seeking spiritual breakthroughs, healing, guidance, or clarity. Write down your intentions and keep them in mind throughout your fasting period.

3. **Choose the Right Type of Fast:** Decide on the type of fast based on your health, spiritual goals, and experience. Options include water fasts, juice fasts, Daniel fasts (eating only fruits and vegetables), or partial fasts (such as abstaining from specific foods or meals).
4. **Establish a Routine of Prayer and Meditation:** Use the extra time gained from not eating to deepen your prayer life and meditation. Reflect on scripture, journal your thoughts, and listen attentively to God's voice.
5. **Stay Hydrated and Rest:** During extended fasts, drink plenty of water and herbal teas to stay hydrated. Ensure adequate rest to support your body and mind through the fasting process.
6. **Break the Fast Mindfully:** When concluding your fast, reintroduce food gradually and mindfully. Start with light, easily digestible foods to avoid overwhelming your system.
7. **Seek Community and Support:** Engage with a supportive community of fellow believers or fasting partners. Share your experiences, struggles, and victories to encourage and uplift one another.
8. **Evaluate and Reflect:** After fasting, reflect on your experiences and insights gained. Evaluate how your spiritual life has been enriched and set goals for ongoing spiritual growth.

Fasting stands as the pinnacle of Christian disciplines, offering a profound avenue for spiritual transformation through prayer. When approached with a sincere heart and a desire to seek God's face rather than His hand, fasting becomes a powerful catalyst for personal and communal healing. This conviction, rooted in Scripture, personal testimony, and careful observation, assures us that God responds to the repentant cries of His people by healing lives, churches, communities, and nations.

Moreover, the impact of fasting extends beyond individual lives; it can precipitate revival on a national and global scale, redirecting the course of nations and advancing the Great Commission. This extraordinary spiritual power can flow through anyone who fasts under the guidance of the Holy Spirit.

Fasting has unfortunately been overlooked in many spiritual practices for so long that practical guidance on its nuances can be scarce. When I embarked on my initial extended fast, I struggled to find resources on the biblical nature of fasting, preparation, physical and spiritual expectations, and proper conclusion of a fast.

This series aims to address your practical concerns about fasting and alleviate any apprehensions you may have. Throughout this resource, you will discover:

- The significance of fasting

- Safe fasting practices
- Choosing the appropriate duration and type of fast
- Spiritual and physical preparation tips
- Managing daily routines while fasting
- Handling responses from family and friends
- Maximizing your spiritual journey
- Maintaining health and nutritional balance with specific juice and broth recipes
- Anticipated physical benefits
- Gradual transition from fasting to normal eating patterns

Why You Should Fast

If you are unfamiliar with the profound impact and importance of fasting, consider these compelling reasons:

- Fasting was an established practice in both the Old and New Testaments. Moses and Jesus Himself set powerful examples through their forty-day fasts.
- Fasting and prayer can restore a fervent love for Christ and deepen your intimacy with Him.
- Fasting humbles you before God, aligning your heart with His purposes (Psalm 35:13; Ezra 8:21).
- It allows the Holy Spirit to reveal your spiritual state, leading to repentance and transformation.
- Scripture becomes alive and meaningful, deepening your understanding of God's truth.
- Your prayer life can be revitalized and personalized through fasting.
- Personal revival can ignite your spiritual journey and impact others.
- Fasting and prayer fulfill the conditions of 2 Chronicles 7:14, promising spiritual healing and renewal.

Through fasting, you will experience humbling moments and discover increased time for prayer and seeking God's presence. As you confess and repent of sin, expect God's special blessings and guidance.

How to Fast Safely

Beginning a fast often raises concerns from loved ones about your health. It's crucial to assure them that fasting, when approached correctly, not only enhances spiritual growth but also benefits physical well-being. Consulting with your doctor before starting a fast is prudent, though their familiarity with fasting practices may be limited. A physical examination ensures you're fit for fasting and highlights any health concerns that may require caution or adjustment in your fasting plans.

Despite the safety and rewards of fasting, certain individuals should not fast without professional oversight, including those with eating disorders, chronic illnesses, or specific medical conditions.

Choosing the Right Type and Duration of Fast

For newcomers to fasting, gradual progression is key. Start with small steps—such as fasting a single meal or a day per week—to build spiritual endurance. There's no singular "correct" way to fast; the focus should be on the condition of your heart and God's leading. As you mature spiritually, longer fasts, even up to forty days, can become spiritually enriching experiences.

Scriptural Types of Fasts

The Bible highlights two main types of fasting:

- Partial fasts, as exemplified by Daniel's abstention from delicacies (Daniel 10:3).
- Absolute or supernatural absolute fasts, involving complete abstention from food and water, as seen in instances like Paul's three-day fast (Acts 9:9) and Moses' and Elijah's forty-day fasts (Deuteronomy 9:9; 1 Kings 19:8).

How to Prepare Spiritually and Physically

Spiritual Preparation: Before fasting, examine your heart for unconfessed sin. Confession precedes God's response to prayers (Psalm 66:16-20). Address both obvious and subtle sins, such as spiritual apathy or neglect of God's Word and prayer.

Physical Preparation: While fasting primarily impacts the spirit, starting with physical readiness is essential. Gradually reduce meal sizes and eliminate caffeine and sugar to ease into the fast. Adjusting your workload and incorporating times of prayer and Scripture reading enhances the fasting experience.

Managing Your Schedule During Fasting

Adapt your daily routine to accommodate fasting. Depending on your occupation, adjust workloads or opt for partial fasting if physically demanding tasks are involved. Avoid fasting during major holidays to minimize disruptions and temptations.

Balancing physical limitations and spiritual aspirations during fasting ensures a holistic approach to the discipline. Prioritize intimate communion with God through extended times of prayer and Scripture meditation.

Dealing with Responses from Friends and Loved Ones

Many individuals hesitate to disclose their fasting practice to avoid the sin of the Pharisees—fasting solely for public recognition. This mindset often stems from a misunderstanding of Christ's teachings and is a tactic of the enemy, discouraging both the act of fasting and the sharing of its benefits with loved ones, neighbors, and friends.

By isolating ourselves from fellow believers, we become vulnerable to doubts and negative influences, both human and spiritual. It's crucial to have the prayer support of Christian friends and family, as they can uplift us during moments of loneliness or when tempted by the enemy, like how Jesus was tested in the wilderness (Matthew 4:1-11).

While people may eventually notice your abstaining from food, daily acquaintances often overlook skipped meals. If asked, a brief response suffices for non-believers, while Christians understand and support your fasting intentions.

If loved one's express health concerns, reassure them of your vigilance. Let them know you will cease fasting if it jeopardizes your health, or upon divine guidance, and involve your doctor if any health doubts arise.

It's generally unnecessary to inform strangers or casual acquaintances of your fasting, as it may lead to unwanted inquiries. Use discernment and God's guidance in deciding whom to inform about your fast.

How to Make Your Spiritual Experience the Best It Can Be

Achieving God's profound blessings through fasting demands unwavering commitment. Dedicate specific daily intervals to commune with God, especially during periods of weakness, vulnerability, or irritability.

- Engage in prayer and scripture reading during usual mealtimes.
- Meditate on God even in moments of wakefulness during the night.
- Offer praises to Him freely and frequently.
- Center every action on worshiping the Heavenly Father.

By persistently seeking God's presence, you align with His command to "pray without ceasing" (1 Thessalonians 5:17). Recognize that Satan will attempt to distract you from prayer and Bible study. Combat these assaults by immediately turning to God in prayer for strength and resilience against trials and temptations.

Satan perceives fasting as a potent Christian discipline and endeavors to thwart your spiritual growth. Remain steadfast in prayer, shielding yourself against his tactics. Fasting for personal revival, national awakening, and fulfilling the Great Commission underscores its broader significance. Intercede humbly for personal needs, loved ones, church, community, nation, and the world, amplifying your impact through fasting (Matthew 6:16-18).

However, avoid becoming so absorbed in personal and intercessory prayer that you neglect revering and praising God. Authentic spiritual fasting centers on God Himself. Surrender to Him all aspects of your being—thoughts, actions, motives, desires, and speech. Confess sins as the Holy Spirit convicts, focusing solely on God for potent and effective prayers (James 5:16).

While fasting often yields a renewed closeness with God and heightened spiritual sensitivity, don't be disheartened if it doesn't result in an immediate "mountaintop experience." Some report feeling God's presence profoundly, while others encounter no outward manifestation. Nevertheless, persevere with faithfulness, knowing that God honors genuine seeking hearts (Jeremiah 29:13).

Maintaining Nutritional Balance and Health from Beginning to End

Facing extended periods without food may concern some individuals, but maintaining nutritional adequacy and health during fasting is achievable through prudent practices.

For prolonged fasting, consider hydrating with water and nutrient-rich fruit and vegetable juices. These juices, especially when freshly prepared, provide essential energy and motivational flavor. Opt for natural fruit juices without added sugars or other additives.

During a juice fast, prioritize juices like carrot, grape, celery, apple, cabbage, or beet for their cleansing and restorative benefits. "Green drinks" from leafy vegetables detoxify effectively and support electrolyte balance crucial for heart function.

To sustain health during fasting, consider a liquid formula like:

- One-gallon distilled water
- 1-1/2 cups lemon juice
- 3/4 cup pure maple syrup

- 1/4 teaspoon cayenne pepper

Lemon juice offers flavor and vitamin C, maple syrup provides energy, while cayenne pepper aids in detoxifying the body. If allergic to cayenne, exercise caution, as it can provoke severe reactions in sensitive individuals.

Prefer juices like pure white grape and peach, avoiding caffeinated drinks, which undermine fasting benefits. Moderate physical activity supports well-being during juice fasting, though avoid strenuous exercise without specialist oversight during water fasting.

What Physical Effects to Expect

While fasting brings profound spiritual benefits, it may also provoke physical and mental discomforts. Be prepared for these challenges as part of your disciplined journey.

- **Hunger Pangs:** Typically, intense during the initial days as your body transitions from digesting food to consuming stored fats.
    - **Relief:** Psyllium bulk helps curb hunger and aids in cleansing. Silymarin tablets protect and enhance liver detoxification.
- **Physical Discomforts:** Include coldness, bad breath, heightened body odor, changes in elimination, light-headedness, altered sleep patterns, and body aches.
    - **Relief:** Symptoms often diminish after the first weeks of extended fasting. Persistent discomfort may indicate fat tissue elimination, which is beneficial but seek medical advice for prolonged pain.
- **Withdrawal Symptoms:** Headaches or stomachaches from salt, sugar, or caffeine withdrawal.
    - **Relief:** Gradually eliminating these items from your diet before fasting reduces discomfort.
- **Dehydration Signs:** Lower back pain suggests dehydration.
    - **Relief:** Increase fluid intake to alleviate symptoms.
- **Dizziness:** Occurs with sudden position changes.
    - **Relief:** Move slowly and pause briefly to regain balance. Seek medical evaluation if symptoms persist.
- **Minor Discomforts:** Address with psyllium seed powder for toxin elimination and alfalfa tablets for breath freshness and system cleansing.

Ways to Finish Your Fast in a Healthy Way

Breaking fast is a critical phase that demands cautious handling to avoid digestive distress and potential health risks. After fasting, when your body rests and digestive functions slow, reintroduce solid foods gradually over several days.

Begin with light, nourishing foods like fresh fruits and steamed vegetables. Avoid meats, fats, dairy, starches, and processed foods initially to prevent shock and discomfort. Opt for plant-based foods, slowly reintroducing other food groups.

The Daniel Fast, inspired by Daniel's scriptural fasting experience, involves abstaining from specific foods as an act of consecration to God. It fosters spiritual intimacy and dependence on God, promoting a closer relationship with Him.

As you undertake the Daniel Fast, focus less on food restrictions and more on drawing near to God through prayer and spiritual growth. Accept the opportunity to deepen your faith and seek His presence earnestly.

The conclusion of a fast is just as crucial as its beginning and duration. Properly ending a fast is essential for maintaining the benefits of spiritual discipline while safeguarding physical health. During a fast, your body adjusts to reduced food intake, and your digestive system may become less active. Therefore, reintroducing solid foods gradually is paramount to avoid digestive distress or complications.

After a prolonged fast, such as a 40-day period, it's recommended to transition back to regular eating habits over several days. This gradual approach allows your body to readjust slowly and reap the full benefits of fast. Rushing into consuming solid foods can lead to physical discomforts like diarrhea, nausea, or even serious conditions due to the shock of sudden food intake.

Breaking a Fourteen-Day Fast:

- **Evening of the 14th Day:** Begin with peeled and chopped tomatoes boiled lightly until soft. Allow them to cool to a comfortable eating temperature before consuming as many as desired.
- **Morning of the 15th Day:**
    - **Breakfast:** A salad of grated carrots and cabbage, with the juice of half an orange squeezed over it.
    - **Mid-Morning:** Steamed greens and peeled tomatoes (such as spinach, Swiss chard, or mustard greens). Boil the greens briefly and then allow them to cool.
    - **Snack:** Two slices of 100% whole-wheat toast, toasted until completely dry ("Melba toast").

- **Throughout the Day:**
  - Drink as much distilled water as desired.
- **Dinner of the 15th Day:**
  - Another salad of grated carrots chopped celery, and cabbage, dressed with orange juice.
  - Two servings of cooked vegetables: one leafy green like spinach or kale, and one variety like string beans or steamed celery.
  - Two pieces of whole grain "Melba toast."
  - Avoid any oils in your meals during this transition phase.

Morning of the 16th Day:

- **Breakfast:** Fresh fruit of your choice, such as banana, pineapple, orange slices, grapefruit, or apple slices. Sprinkle with two tablespoons of raw wheat germ and sweeten with no more than one tablespoon of honey.
- **Midday:**
  - Another salad of grated carrots, cabbage, and celery.
  - One cooked vegetable and one slice of "Melba toast."
- **Dinner of the 16th Day:**
  - Salad with lettuce, watercress, parsley, and tomatoes.
  - Two servings of cooked vegetables.

It's crucial to avoid adding oils to your meals during this reintroduction phase. Begin with lighter foods, focusing on vegetables, fruits, and minimal grains. Stop eating before you feel full, as your stomach capacity may have decreased during the fast.

General Recommendations for Breaking a Fast:

- **Start Slowly:** Introduce foods gradually over several days to allow your digestive system to adjust.
- **Avoid Heavy Foods:** Steer clear of meats, dairy products, fats, and heavy starches like potatoes or bread for at least a week.
- **Stay Hydrated:** Continue to drink plenty of water to support your body's hydration and cleansing processes.
- **Monitor Physical Reactions:** Pay attention to how your body responds to different foods reintroduced during this phase.
- **Consultation:** If you have specific health concerns or conditions, consider consulting with a healthcare professional before and after fasting to ensure it's done safely.

By observing these principles, you can conclude your fast in a way that maximizes both spiritual benefits and physical well-being. Remember, the disciplined approach to ending a fast honor the journey and enhances the lasting impact of your spiritual devotion.

MAINTAIN SPIRITUAL AND PHYSICAL BALANCE AFTER FASTING

After completing a fast, maintaining the spiritual and physical benefits involves establishing healthy routines and mindsets. Here's a guide to help you maintain balance and continue reaping the rewards of your fasting experience:

1. Spiritual Nourishment:

- **Prayer and Meditation:** Continue dedicating time for prayer and meditation daily. Use this time to reflect on your spiritual journey during the fast and to seek guidance for the future.
- **Scripture Reading:** Engage in regular reading of sacred texts or inspirational literature to deepen your spiritual understanding and connection.
- **Gratitude Practice:** Cultivate an attitude of gratitude by reflecting on the blessings in your life. Write down or verbalize your gratitude daily to maintain a positive mindset.

2. Healthy Eating Habits:

- **Balanced Diet:** Transition back to a balanced diet that includes a variety of fruits, vegetables, whole grains, lean proteins, and healthy fats. Avoid processed foods, excessive sugars, and fats to support your overall well-being.
- **Hydration:** Continue drinking plenty of water throughout the day to stay hydrated and aid in detoxification.
- **Meal Planning:** Plan your meals ahead of time to ensure they are nutritious and balanced. Incorporate fresh ingredients and home-cooked meals whenever possible.

3. Physical Activity:

- **Exercise Routine:** Establish a regular exercise routine that includes cardiovascular activities, strength training, and flexibility exercises. Aim for at least 30 minutes of moderate intensity exercise most days of the week.
- **Outdoor Time:** Spend time outdoors to enjoy nature and fresh air, which can enhance your overall sense of well-being.

4. Emotional and Mental Well-being:

- **Stress Management:** Practice stress-relieving techniques such as deep breathing, yoga, or mindfulness meditation to manage stress effectively.
- **Social Connections:** Maintain healthy relationships with family and friends who support your spiritual and personal growth. Stay connected and share your experiences with others.

5. Continued Growth and Reflection:

- **Journaling:** Keep a journal to document your post-fast experiences, insights, and reflections. Use this journal as a tool for self-discovery and personal growth.
- **Learning and Development:** Pursue opportunities for learning and personal development that align with your spiritual and life goals. Attend workshops, seminars, or classes that inspire and challenge you.

6. Professional Guidance:

- **Healthcare Provider:** If you have any concerns about your health or nutrition post-fast, consult with a healthcare professional or registered dietitian for personalized advice and guidance.

By integrating these practices into your daily life, you can maintain the spiritual and physical balance achieved through fasting. Remember that consistency and mindful living are key to sustaining your well-being and spiritual growth over time.

If there are any specific aspects you'd like to focus on further or if you have more content in mind, feel free to let me know!

7. Renewing Spiritual Practices:

- **Continued Fasting:** Consider periodic fasting as a spiritual discipline to maintain spiritual clarity and renewal. This could involve regular fasting days or seasons of fasting throughout the year, as guided by your spiritual beliefs and practices.
- **Community and Fellowship:** Engage in spiritual communities or fellowships that support your journey. Participate in group prayers, worship services, or study groups to foster spiritual connection and accountability.

8. Service and Giving:

- **Acts of Service:** Extend your spiritual experience by engaging in acts of service and charity. Volunteer in your community, support charitable organizations, or help those in need to express gratitude and compassion.
- **Generosity:** Practice generosity by sharing your resources, time, and talents with others. This can include financial contributions, mentoring relationships, or simply offering a listening ear to someone in distress.

9. Reflection and Adjustment:

- **Self-Assessment:** Regularly assess your spiritual growth and personal development. Reflect on areas where you have grown and identify areas that may require further attention or improvement.
- **Adjustment and Adaptation:** Be open to adjusting your spiritual practices and routines based on your evolving spiritual journey and life circumstances. Remain flexible while staying true to your core beliefs and values.

10. Spiritual Guidance:

- **Mentorship:** Seek guidance from spiritual mentors, leaders, or advisors who can provide wisdom and insight into your spiritual path. Their experience and perspective can offer valuable guidance and encouragement.
- **Retreats and Pilgrimages:** Consider participating in spiritual retreats, pilgrimages, or sacred journeys to deepen your spiritual connection and experience profound spiritual renewal.

11. Celebration and Gratitude:

- **Celebrate Milestones:** Acknowledge and celebrate milestones in your spiritual journey, such as breakthroughs, insights, or moments of clarity. Share these experiences with others to inspire and encourage them on their own paths.
- **Gratitude Practices:** Cultivate a daily practice of gratitude to acknowledge the blessings and lessons gained from your fasting experience. Express gratitude to the divine, yourself, and those who have supported you along the way.

12. Integration and Application:

- **Integrate Learnings:** Apply the insights and lessons learned from your fasting experience into your daily life. Incorporate spiritual principles, virtues, and values into your decisions, actions, and interactions with others.

- **Purposeful Living:** Live with purpose and intentionality, guided by your spiritual beliefs and aspirations. Align your goals and priorities with your spiritual journey to experience fulfillment and inner peace.

These practices aim to support you in maintaining a balanced and fulfilling spiritual life after fasting. Accept these principles with sincerity and dedication, knowing that each step contributes to your ongoing growth and spiritual well-being.

Prayers of Invocations for Economic Success: Important Strategies for Fasting (40, 21, 14, 7, or 3 Days)

Prayer for Clear Vision and Divine Guidance

Heavenly Father, as I begin on this fasting journey to seek Your face and receive divine guidance, I humbly come before You. Grant me clarity of vision regarding my financial goals and aspirations. Guide my steps according to Your perfect will, that I may make decisions aligned with Your Word and purposes. Let Your Holy Spirit lead me into paths of prosperity and success as I fast and pray. May Your wisdom illuminate my mind and heart, bringing forth breakthroughs in my financial endeavors. In Jesus' name, Amen.

Prayer for Debt Freedom and Financial Liberation

Heavenly Father, I lift up my financial burdens and debts before You. Your Word teaches us to owe no one anything except to love one another. Grant me the wisdom and diligence to manage my finances wisely during this time of fasting. Break every chain of debt and financial bondage in my life. Provide divine strategies and opportunities to settle all debts and walk in financial freedom. Let Your peace reign in my financial affairs, knowing that You are my provider and deliverer. In Jesus' name, Amen.

Scripture Reference: "Owe no one anything except to love one another, for he who loves another has fulfilled the law." - Romans 13:8

Prayer for Divine Strategies in Business and Career

Heavenly Father, I commit my business/career aspirations to Your hands. You have promised to give wisdom generously to all who ask in faith. During this time of fasting, I seek Your divine strategies and guidance for success in my business/career endeavors. Open doors of opportunity that align with Your perfect will. Grant me favor and influence in the marketplace. May my work bring glory to Your name and be a testimony of Your provision and faithfulness. In Jesus' name, Amen.

Prayer for Supernatural Favor and Open Doors

Gracious Father, as I start this fasting journey, I pray for Your supernatural favor and open doors of opportunity in my finances. You are the God who uncovers avenues that remain accessible. I declare Your favor over my job interviews, business deals, and financial investments. Let Your hand of blessing be upon me, O Lord, as I trust in Your divine provision and guidance. In Jesus' name, Amen.

Scripture Reference: "I know your works. See, I have set before you an open door, and no one can shut it; for you have a little strength, have kept My word, and have not denied My name." - Revelation 3:8

Prayer for Courage and Boldness in Financial Decisions

Heavenly Father, Your Word encourages us to be strong and courageous, for You are with us wherever we go. While I fast and diligently seek Your divine presence for financial breakthroughs, I pray for courage and boldness in making wise decisions. Help me to step out in faith and obedience, knowing that You go before me. Remove any fear or doubt that hinders me from walking in Your perfect will for my finances. May Your peace and confidence fill my heart as I trust in You completely. In Jesus' name, Amen.

Scripture Reference: "Have I not commanded you? Be strong and of good courage; do not be afraid, nor be dismayed, for the Lord your God is with you wherever you go." - Joshua 1:9

Prayer for Peace and Contentment in Financial Journey

Heavenly Father, I thank You for Your faithfulness and provision in my life. Throughout my fasting journey, as I strive to find Your presence for financial breakthroughs, I pray for Your peace and contentment to fill my heart. Help me to find satisfaction in You alone, regardless of my financial circumstances. Teach me to trust in Your timing and to rest in Your promises of abundance and prosperity. May Your joy be my strength as I navigate through the ups and downs of my financial journey. In Jesus' name, Amen.

Prayer for Supernatural Business Expansion

Lord God, You are the God of growth and expansion. Your Word declares that the righteous shall flourish like a palm tree and grow like a cedar in Lebanon. As I commit to fasting and seeking Your face, I pray for supernatural expansion in my business endeavors. Open doors of opportunity in the marketplace. Multiply my client base and increase my influence. May my business be a beacon of Your light and provision. I declare Your favor and prosperity over every aspect of my business. In Jesus' name, Amen.

Scripture Reference: "The righteous shall flourish like a palm tree, he shall grow like a cedar in Lebanon. Those who are planted in the house of the Lord shall flourish in the courts of our God." - Psalm 92:12-13

Prayer for Wisdom and Discernment in Financial Planning

Heavenly Father, Your Word instructs us to plan diligently and seek Your wisdom in all our ways. As I fast and intensely seek Your divine presence, I pray for wisdom and discernment in financial planning. Help me to set goals that honor You and to make decisions that align with Your will. Guide me in budgeting, saving, and investing for the future. Grant me peace and confidence in Your provision and timing. May my financial decisions bring glory to Your name. In Jesus' name, Amen.

Scripture Reference: "The plans of the diligent lead surely to plenty, but those of everyone who is hasty, surely to poverty." - Proverbs 21:5

Prayer for Supernatural Favor in Negotiations and Contracts

Gracious God, You are the God who grants us the capability to foster prosperity and affirms His covenant with His people. As I commit to fasting and seeking Your face, I pray for Your supernatural favor in negotiations and contracts. Go before me, O Lord, and prepare the way. Grant me wisdom and tact in communication. May Your favor rest upon me, opening doors of opportunity and securing favorable outcomes. I trust in Your provision and leading in every business endeavor. In Jesus' name, Amen.

Prayer for Divine Connections and Strategic Partnerships

Lord God, You are the God who connects us with divine appointments and strategic partnerships. Throughout my fasting period, as I humbly seek Your face for financial breakthroughs, I pray for Your divine connections in my life. Bring into my path those who will uplift and support me in my financial journey. Grant me wisdom to recognize divine opportunities and partnerships that align with Your kingdom purposes. May Your name be glorified through these connections, and may they bear fruit in abundance. In Jesus' name, Amen.

Scripture Reference: "Two are better than one, because they have a good reward for their labor." - Ecclesiastes 4:9

Prayer for Strength and Perseverance in Financial Challenges

Heavenly Father, Your Word assures us that in this world we will face trials, but You have overcome the world. As I commit to fasting and seeking Your face, I pray for strength and perseverance in financial challenges. Help me to stand firm on Your promises of provision and protection. Fill me with Your peace that surpasses understanding. Strengthen my faith to endure and overcome every obstacle. I trust in Your unfailing love and grace to sustain me through all trials. In Jesus' name, Amen.

Scripture Reference: "These things I have spoken to you, that in Me you may have peace. In the world you will have tribulation; but be of good cheer, I have overcome the world." - John 16:33

Prayer for Divine Favor in Business Negotiations

Lord God, You are the God who gives us the ability to produce wealth and establish Your covenant. As I commit to fasting and seeking Your face, I pray for Your divine favor in all my business negotiations. Go before me, O Lord, and prepare the hearts of those I will engage with. Please grant me favor and influence in my professional endeavors. May Your wisdom guide my words and actions, securing favorable outcomes and fruitful partnerships. I put my confidence in Your provision and guidance for every business pursuit. In Jesus' name, Amen.

Prayer for Supernatural Increase in Business Profitability

Heavenly Father, You are the God who blesses the work of our hands and causes us to prosper. As I abstain and wholeheartedly seek Your divine presence, I pray for supernatural increase in the profitability of my business. Multiply my earnings and expand my client base. Grant me divine strategies to streamline operations and enhance productivity. May my business be a testimony of Your faithfulness and provision. I declare Your favor and blessings over every aspect of my business. In Jesus' name, Amen.

Prayer for Supernatural Increase in Generosity

Gracious Father, You are the God who blesses us to be a blessing to others. As I commit to fasting and seeking Your face, I pray for Your supernatural increase in generosity. Open my heart to give freely and cheerfully, knowing that You will multiply my seed sown. Use me to bless others abundantly, both financially and spiritually. May Your love and compassion flow through me, touching lives and transforming hearts for Your kingdom. In Jesus' name, Amen.

Scripture Reference: "But this I say: He who sows sparingly will also reap sparingly, and he who sows bountifully will also reap bountifully." - 2 Corinthians 9:6

Wealth Manifestation Affirmations: Important Strategies for Fasting (40, 21, 14, 7, or 3 Days)

Affirmation of Financial Freedom

I affirm that through fasting and seeking God's wisdom, I am breaking free from financial bondage and debt. As Deuteronomy 15:6 declares, "For the Lord your God will bless you just as He promised you; you shall lend to many nations, but you shall not borrow; you shall reign over many nations, but they shall not reign over you."

Affirmation of Supernatural Increase in Income

I affirm that God is opening doors for supernatural increase in my income and financial resources. Isaiah 48:17 reminds me, "Thus says the Lord, your Redeemer, the Holy One of Israel: 'I am the Lord your God, who teaches you to profit, who leads you by the way you should go.'" Therefore, I receive His divine strategies for financial prosperity.

Affirmation of Wisdom in Stewardship

I affirm that I am a wise steward of God's blessings, managing resources with integrity and diligence. Luke 16:10 encourages me, one who is trustworthy in small matters will also be trustworthy in larger responsibilities; and he who is unjust in what is least is unjust also in much. Therefore, I honor God through wise financial stewardship and accountability.

Affirmation of Supernatural Favor in Career Advancement

I affirm that God's favor promotes me and opens doors of opportunity in my career. Psalm 75:6-7 affirms, "For exaltation comes neither from the east nor from the west nor from the south. But God is the Judge: He puts down one and exalts another." Therefore, I walk in divine favor, advancing in my career and achieving success beyond measure.

Confirmation of Prosperous Harvest

I affirm that I sow seeds of faith and generosity, expecting an abundant harvest in due season. Galatians 6:9 encourages me, "And let us not grow weary while doing good, for in due season we shall reap if we do not lose heart." Therefore, I sow generously and expect God's multiplication and provision in every area of my life.

Affirmation of Financial Security in God's Hands

I affirm that my financial security rests securely in God's hands. Psalm 62:5-8 affirms, "My soul, wait silently for God alone, for my expectation is from Him. He only is my rock and my salvation; He is my defense; I shall not be moved." Therefore, I trust in God's unfailing protection and provision, knowing He sustains me through every season of life.

Affirmation of Prosperity in All I Do

I affirm that everything I set my hand to prospers and succeeds through God's grace. Joshua 1:8 promises, "This Book of the Law shall not depart from your mouth, but you shall meditate in it day and night, that you may observe according to all that is written in it. For then you will make your way prosperous, and then you will have good success." Therefore, I align with God's Word and prosper in every endeavor.

Affirmation of Fiscal Autonomy and Debt Release

I affirm that through fasting and prayer, I am released from financial burdens and debt. Psalm 37:21 declares, "The wicked borrows and does not repay, but the righteous shows mercy and gives." Therefore, I trust in God's provision to clear debts and bring financial freedom into my life.

Affirmation of Generosity and Seed Sowing

I affirm that I am favored to share blessings with those around me to others through my generosity. Luke 6:38 encourages me, "Give, and it will be given to you: good measure, pressed down, shaken together, and running over will be put into your bosom. For with the same measure that you use, it will be measured back to you." Therefore, I sow seeds of generosity, knowing that God multiplies them for His kingdom.

Affirmation of Wisdom in Financial Investments

I affirm that God grants me wisdom in financial investments and stewardship. Proverbs 19:20 advises me, "Listen to counsel and receive instruction, that you may be wise in your latter days." Therefore, I seek God's guidance and wisdom in every financial decision and investment I make.

Affirmation of Abundance in Every Area of Life

I affirm that God's abundance flows into every area of my life, including my finances. John 10:10 declares, "The thief does not come except to steal, and to kill, and to destroy.

I have come that they may have life, and that they may have it more abundantly." Therefore, I receive God's abundant life and blessings in every aspect of my life.

Affirmation of Steadfast Trust in God's Financial Guidance

I affirm steadfast trust in God's guidance and direction for my financial decisions. Psalm 37:5 advises me, "Commit your way to the Lord, trust also in Him, and He shall bring it to pass." Therefore, I commit my finances to God's care and trust Him to lead me into financial prosperity and success.

Affirmation of Wisdom and Discernment in Financial Planning

I affirm wisdom and discernment in my financial planning and stewardship. Proverbs 24:3-4 encourages me, "Through wisdom a house is built, and by understanding it is established; by knowledge the rooms are filled with all precious and pleasant riches." Therefore, I seek God's wisdom and understanding to build a secure financial future.

Affirmation of Financial Increase through God's Grace

I affirm financial increase through God's grace and provision. 2 Corinthians 9:8 assures me, "And God is able to make all grace abound toward you, that you, always having all sufficiency in all things, may have an abundance for every good work." Therefore, I receive God's abundant grace for financial abundance and prosperity.

Affirmation of Contentment and Satisfaction in God's Blessings

I affirm contentment and satisfaction in God's blessings and provision. Philippians 4:11-13 inspires me, "Not that I speak in regard to need, for I have learned in whatever state I am, to be content: I know how to be abased, and I know how to abound. Everywhere and in all things, I have learned both to be full and to be hungry, both to abound and to suffer need. Through Christ's empowerment, I am equipped to achieve all tasks." Therefore, I find true contentment in God's abundant blessings and provision.

Important strategies for fasting involve careful preparation, spiritual focus, community support, and mindful reflection. When approached with reverence and intentionality, fasting becomes a transformative journey of spiritual growth, healing, and alignment with God's purposes. May these practices enrich your spiritual life and deepen your relationship with the Divine.

Chapter 12:

In-Depth Overview of Different Fasting Approaches and Their Health Benefits

Fasting encompasses a variety of types, each offering distinct spiritual and physical benefits. This chapter explores different types of fasting—such as water fasts, juice fasts, intermittent fasting, and partial fasts—and their respective impacts on spiritual growth and physical health. By understanding the nuances of each fasting type and its benefits, you can tailor your fasting practice to align with your goals for spiritual enrichment, physical wellness, and overall transformation.

Yahweh invites you to explore the diversity of fasting practices to draw closer to Him and experience His transformative power. Adopt the opportunity to discover which fasting type resonates with your spiritual and physical needs, trusting in Yahweh's guidance to lead you toward greater spiritual clarity, vitality, and breakthrough. As you embark on this journey of exploring different fasting methods, remain open to Yahweh's revelation and blessing, knowing that He meets you in your pursuit of intimacy and wholeness in Him.

Understanding the Types of Fasting

Fasting manifests in various forms, each carrying its own significance and benefits. Whether it's a water fast, a partial fast, or a Daniel fast, each type serves a specific purpose in drawing you closer to God and opening doors to His blessings. By choosing the right type of fast based on your spiritual goals, you position yourself to receive supernatural guidance and breakthroughs.

The Spiritual Power of Fasting

Fasting isn't just about physical discipline; it's a spiritual weapon that demolishes strongholds and paves the way for divine intervention. Through fasting, you declare your dependence on God and invite His presence to work mightily in your life. As you dedicate time to seek Him in fasting, He promises to reveal His plans and provide abundantly beyond your expectations.

The Gift of Spiritual Discernment

One of the profound gifts of fasting is heightened spiritual discernment. By denying your physical appetites, you sharpen your spiritual senses to recognize God's voice more clearly. This discernment empowers you to make wise decisions, discern opportunities, and discern spiritual attacks, ensuring that you walk in alignment with God's will for your life.

Unlocking Financial Breakthroughs

Beyond spiritual benefits, fasting also holds the key to financial breakthroughs. As you commit to fasting with faith, you activate God's promises of provision and prosperity. The Bible is replete with examples of individuals who experienced miraculous financial turnarounds through fasting and prayer. Your financial breakthrough awaits as you align your fasting with God's promises of abundance.

You are uniquely designed by God with a purpose and destiny that only you can fulfill. Through fasting, you step into your identity as a chosen vessel of God's power and favor. He has called you to greatness, equipped you with spiritual tools such as fasting, and empowered you to overcome every obstacle standing in the way of your divine destiny.

Scripture Reference

- **Isaiah 58:6-7**: "Is not this the fast that I choose: to loose the bonds of wickedness, to undo the straps of the yoke, to let the oppressed go free, and to break every yoke? Is it not to share your bread with the hungry and bring the homeless poor into your house; when you see the naked, to cover him, and not to hide yourself from your own flesh?"
- **Matthew 6:16-18**: "And when you fast, do not look gloomy like the hypocrites, for they disfigure their faces that their fasting may be seen by others. Truly, I say to you, they have received their reward. But when you fast, anoint your head and wash your face, that your fasting may not be seen by others but by your Father who is in secret. And your Father who sees in secret will reward you."

Fasting is a practice that has been embraced across cultures and religions for centuries, celebrated not only for its spiritual significance but also for its profound impact on health and well-being. Different types of fasting offer unique pathways to physical vitality, mental clarity, emotional balance, and spiritual enrichment. Let's explore the various types of fasting and their benefits in detail:

1. Intermittent Fasting

Intermittent fasting involves cycling between periods of eating and fasting. Popular methods include the 16/8 method (16 hours of fasting with an 8-hour eating window) or the 5:2 diet (five days of regular eating and two non-consecutive days of very low-calorie intake). Intermittent fasting (IF) has gained popularity for its diverse health benefits, promoting both physical wellness and cognitive clarity through structured periods of eating and fasting. This approach to eating doesn't focus on what you eat but rather when you eat, cycling between eating windows and fasting periods. Here's a thorough brief of the benefits of intermittent fasting:

Physical Benefits

1. **Weight Management**: Intermittent fasting is effective for weight loss and body fat reduction. By restricting the eating window, it naturally reduces overall calorie intake and promotes fat burning through metabolic processes like ketosis.
2. **Metabolic Health**: IF improves insulin sensitivity and regulates blood sugar levels, reducing the risk of type 2 diabetes. It also lowers cholesterol and triglyceride levels, contributing to better heart health.
3. **Cellular Repair and Longevity**: During fasting periods, cellular repair processes like autophagy are activated. This helps cells remove dysfunctional components and promotes longevity.
4. **Inflammation Reduction**: IF lowers markers of inflammation in the body, potentially reducing the risk of chronic inflammatory diseases such as arthritis and cardiovascular diseases.

Cognitive Enhancements

1. **Improved Cognitive Function**: Intermittent fasting boosts the production of brain-derived neurotrophic factor (BDNF), a protein crucial for neuronal health, enhancing cognitive function and stabilizing mood.
2. **Mental Clarity and Focus**: Fasting periods promote mental clarity and sharpness. Many individuals report improved concentration, focus, and productivity during fasting hours.

3. **Neurological Protection**: IF may protect against neurodegenerative diseases like Alzheimer's and Parkinson's by reducing oxidative stress and inflammation in the brain.

Psychological and Emotional Advantages

1. **Stress Reduction**: IF reduces cortisol levels, the body's primary stress hormone, promoting better stress management and emotional resilience.
2. **Mood Regulation**: Stable blood sugar levels and improved neurotransmitter function during fasting periods contribute to enhanced mood stability and emotional well-being.

Holistic Wellness

1. **Digestive Health**: Intermittent fasting gives the digestive system a break, improving gut health, digestion, and nutrient absorption.
2. **Immune System Support**: IF boosts immune function by reducing inflammation and promoting cellular repair, enhancing the body's ability to fight infections and diseases.
3. **Longevity**: Studies suggest that intermittent fasting can extend lifespan and improve overall health span by reducing the risk of age-related diseases and promoting cellular health.

Lifestyle and Practical Benefits

1. **Simplicity and Convenience**: IF is flexible and adaptable to various lifestyles, making it easier to maintain long-term compared to traditional calorie-restricted diets.
2. **Cultural and Social Adaptability**: IF can be practiced in diverse cultural settings and social environments, allowing individuals to enjoy meals with family and friends while still reaping its health benefits.

Presumption

Intermittent fasting offers a holistic approach to health and wellness, encompassing physical benefits such as weight management, metabolic health, and inflammation reduction, along with cognitive enhancements and emotional well-being. Incorporating intermittent fasting as part of a balanced lifestyle, combined with nutritious eating and regular physical activity, can optimize health outcomes and promote longevity.

However, it's important to approach intermittent fasting with awareness of individual health needs and consult with healthcare professionals, especially for those with underlying medical conditions or unique dietary requirements. With proper guidance and mindful practice, intermittent fasting can be a sustainable and effective strategy for achieving overall health, vitality, and well-being.

2. Water Fasting

Water fasting, a practice involving the consumption of only water for a specified period, typically ranging from 24 hours to several days, offers a range of compelling benefits that span physical health, mental clarity, and overall well-being. This method of fasting has been involved for centuries across cultures and religions, celebrated not only for its spiritual significance but also for its transformative effects on the body and mind.

Bodily Benefits

Water fasting promotes significant physiological changes that contribute to enhanced health and vitality:

1. **Detoxification**: By abstaining from solid food and relying solely on water intake, water fasting allows the body to detoxify and eliminate accumulated toxins and metabolic waste. This process supports liver function and promotes overall cellular health.
2. **Cellular Repair and Regeneration**: Fasting triggers autophagy, a process where cells break down and remove damaged components. This cellular "clean-up" not only rejuvenates cells but also enhances their resilience and longevity.
3. **Weight Loss and Metabolic Health**: Water fasting induces ketosis, a metabolic state where the body burns stored fat for energy. This promotes effective weight loss while preserving muscle mass. Moreover, fasting improves insulin sensitivity, regulates blood sugar levels, and may reduce the risk of type 2 diabetes.
4. **Inflammation Reduction**: Chronic inflammation is a precursor to many diseases. Water fasting helps lower inflammation markers in the body, potentially reducing the risk of inflammatory conditions such as arthritis and cardiovascular diseases.

Mental and Emotional Benefits

Water fasting isn't just beneficial for the body; it also enhances cognitive function and emotional well-being:

1. **Clarity and Focus**: Fasting promotes mental clarity, sharpens cognitive function, and enhances concentration. This is partly due to increased production of brain-derived neurotrophic factor (BDNF), a protein that supports brain health and synaptic plasticity.
2. **Stress Reduction**: The physiological changes induced by water fasting, such as reduced cortisol levels and improved hormonal balance, contribute to lower stress levels and improved resilience to psychological stressors.
3. **Emotional Balance**: Many individuals report an increased sense of emotional balance and stability during water fasting. This may be attributed to the mind-body connection facilitated by fasting practices, fostering introspection and emotional regulation.

Spiritual

Water fasting is also valued for its spiritual benefits:

1. **Spiritual Renewal**: Across various spiritual traditions, water fasting is practiced as a means of purification and spiritual renewal. It encourages introspection, mindfulness, and a deeper connection to spiritual principles or higher consciousness.

Considerations and Inference

While water fasting offers numerous benefits, it's essential to approach it with caution and under appropriate guidance, especially for extended periods. Consulting with a healthcare professional is advisable, particularly for individuals with underlying health conditions or those new to fasting practices.

In review, water fasting stands as a powerful tool for health optimization, offering detoxification, weight loss, mental clarity, emotional balance, and spiritual renewal. By embracing water fasting mindfully and responsibly, individuals can harness its transformative potential to achieve holistic wellness and vitality.

3. Juice Fasting

Juice fasting, a practice where individuals consume only freshly squeezed juices from fruits and vegetables for a designated period, offers a variety of health benefits that can inspire personal transformation and holistic well-being. Involving this approach can be a profound journey towards rejuvenation, inner cleansing, and spiritual renewal, aligning with the natural rhythms of your body and the abundant gifts of creation.

Physical Renewal and Detoxification

Go aboard on a juice fast allows your digestive system to rest and rejuvenate. By consuming nutrient-dense juices, you provide your body with essential vitamins, minerals, and antioxidants that support cellular repair and detoxification processes. This gentle detox can help eliminate accumulated toxins, promote liver health, and enhance overall vitality.

Nutrient Absorption and Digestive Health

Fresh juices are rich in enzymes that aid digestion and facilitate nutrient absorption. During a juice fast, your body can efficiently absorb these nutrients without the burden of digesting solid foods. This supports optimal gut health, improves bowel regularity, and may alleviate symptoms of digestive discomfort such as bloating or constipation.

Weight Loss and Metabolic Benefits

Juice fasting can jumpstart weight loss by reducing calorie intake while providing essential nutrients. The cleansing effect of juices helps flush out excess water weight and promotes fat metabolism. Moreover, juice fasting improves insulin sensitivity, regulates blood sugar levels, and supports metabolic efficiency, contributing to sustainable weight management and overall metabolic health.

Mental Clarity and Emotional Balance

As your body detoxifies and becomes nourished with essential nutrients, you may experience heightened mental clarity and improved focus. The vitamins and minerals in fresh juices support brain function, enhance cognitive performance, and stabilize mood. Many individuals report feeling more centered, emotionally balanced, and resilient during and after a juice fast.

Spiritual and Emotional Renewal

Juice fasting is not just a physical cleanse but also a spiritual and emotional journey. By abstaining from solid foods and focusing on pure, living juices, you can deepen your spiritual connection, foster mindfulness, and cultivate inner peace. This practice of self-discipline and purification aligns with spiritual traditions worldwide, allowing you to tap into your inner strength and spiritual resilience.

Skin Health and Radiance

The abundance of antioxidants and hydration in fresh juices can promote radiant skin and overall complexion. During a juice fast, your skin may become clearer, smoother, and more youthful looking as toxins are eliminated and nutrients nourish from within. This external manifestation of health can boost confidence and enhance your natural beauty.

Enhanced Immune Function and Longevity

Juice fasting supports immune system function by reducing inflammation, supporting cellular repair, and enhancing immune responses. The vitamins C, A, and E found in juices strengthen immune defenses against infections and diseases. Over time, regular juice fasting may contribute to increased longevity and improved overall quality of life.

Holistic Well-being and Lifestyle Transformation

Juice fasting encourages a holistic approach to health and well-being, inspiring you to make mindful choices about nutrition, hydration, and self-care. It promotes a shift towards plant-based eating, sustainability, and appreciation for the abundance of natural resources provided by God. By embracing juice fasting as a lifestyle practice, you nurture your body, mind, and spirit in harmony with divine creation.

Adopt the Journey of Juice Fasting

As you get on a juice fasting journey, envision the limitless potential for transformation and renewal that lies ahead. Adopt this opportunity to honor your body as a sacred vessel, capable of healing and rejuvenation. Allow the vibrant colors, flavors, and nutrients of fresh juices to nourish not only your physical body but also your soul.

Remember, each sip of juice is a gift from God, offering you the nutrients and vitality needed to fulfill your purpose and embrace all the great things He has created you to become. Through discipline, faith, and gratitude, juice fasting can be a transformative experience that brings you closer to optimal health, inner peace, and spiritual fulfillment.

Commitment to Health and Vitality

By committing to a juice fasting regimen, you venture on a path of self-discovery and empowerment. Embrace this opportunity to align your body, mind, and spirit with the divine purpose for which you were created. Through the discipline of juice fasting, you demonstrate reverence for your body as a temple of God's creation, deserving of nourishment that enhances vitality and longevity.

Cultivating Discipline and Resilience

Juice fasting requires discipline and dedication, qualities that strengthen your character and fortify your resolve. As you navigate the challenges and rewards of fasting, you cultivate resilience and perseverance in overcoming obstacles. This journey teaches valuable lessons in self-control and mindfulness, empowering you to make conscious choices that honor your health and well-being.

Deepening Spiritual Connection

Beyond physical benefits, juice fasting offers a profound opportunity for spiritual growth and connection. As you abstain from solid foods and consume pure, living juices, you create space for spiritual reflection, prayer, and meditation. This practice of fasting is rooted in many spiritual traditions as a means of purification and communion with the divine. Allow the clarity and serenity of fasting to deepen your spiritual awareness and strengthen your faith.

Embracing Abundance and Gratitude

In embracing juice fasting, you celebrate the abundance of natural resources provided by God for your nourishment and sustenance. Each sip of fresh juice is a testament to His provision and care for your well-being. Practice gratitude for the vibrant colors, flavors, and nutrients that enrich your body and soul during this transformative journey.

Integrating Wellness into Daily Life

As you integrate juice fasting into your lifestyle, consider how this practice aligns with your broader goals of holistic wellness. Embrace plant-based nutrition, hydration, and mindful eating habits that support long-term health and vitality. Use this opportunity to explore new recipes, flavors, and combinations that nourish your body and delight your senses.

Sharing the Gift of Health

Your commitment to juice fasting can inspire and encourage others on their own wellness journeys. Share your experiences, insights, and the profound change induced by fasting with compassion and empathy. Offer support to those seeking guidance on improving their health and well-being through mindful nutrition and self-care practices.

Inference: Embrace the Journey of Juice Fasting

As you continue your juice fasting journey, remember that each day brings new opportunities for growth, healing, and renewal. Trust in the wisdom of your body and the guidance of God as you nurture your health and embrace all the great things He has created you to become. With faith, perseverance, and gratitude, may juice fasting be a source of strength, vitality, and spiritual fulfillment in your life.

4. Fasting for Breakthrough

Fasting for breakthrough is a powerful spiritual practice that transcends physical benefits, aiming to achieve spiritual clarity, divine guidance, and personal transformation. This form of fasting involves abstaining from food and sometimes other indulgences, focusing instead on prayer, meditation, and seeking God's direction in your life. Here's a widespread framework of its benefits for individual on their journey towards breakthrough:

Spiritual Purification and Renewal

Fasting for breakthrough is rooted in the belief that abstaining from earthly pleasures allows for spiritual purification and renewal. By denying yourself physical sustenance, you create space for God to work deeply within your heart and soul. This practice is exemplified in biblical teachings where fasting is seen as a means to draw closer to God and seek His will.

During a fast for breakthrough, you intentionally set aside time to commune with God through prayer and meditation. This spiritual discipline helps clear your mind of distractions and opens your heart to receive divine guidance and revelation.

For instance, you may choose to fast for several days, dedicating each day to specific prayers and petitions. As you immerse yourself in prayer and fasting, you experience a heightened sense of spiritual awareness and sensitivity to God's presence.

Imagine facing a significant decision in your life, such as choosing a career path or resolving a challenging relationship. Through fasting for breakthrough, you seek clarity and direction from God, trusting that He will reveal His perfect plan for your life.

Discernment and Wisdom

Fasting for breakthrough enhances your ability to discern God's voice and receive His wisdom. By quieting the noise of daily life and humbling yourself before Him, you sharpen your spiritual senses to recognize His guidance and understand His purposes for your life.

As you fast, you become attuned to the promptings of the Holy Spirit, discerning between your own desires and God's will. This discernment empowers you to make decisions that align with His purposes and bring glory to His name.

Consider a situation where you are seeking guidance on a major life transition, such as moving to a new city or embarking on a mission trip. Through fasting and prayer, you seek divine wisdom and clarity, trusting God to lead you step by step.

Picture yourself facing a season of uncertainty or adversity, unsure of the next steps to take. Through fasting for breakthrough, you surrender your fears and anxieties to God, seeking His peace and assurance that He has plans to prosper you and not to harm you, plans to give you hope and a future (Jeremiah 29:11).

Spiritual Strength and Victory

Fasting for breakthroughs strengthens your spiritual muscles and prepares you for spiritual battles. It is a declaration of faith and dependence on God's strength to overcome challenges, break strongholds, and experience spiritual victory in every area of your life.

During a fast, you draw upon God's promises of strength and victory found in Scripture. You rely on His grace to empower you to resist temptation, conquer spiritual obstacles, and experience breakthroughs in areas of personal struggle.

Think of a persistent challenge or temptation you have been facing, such as overcoming addiction or breaking free from negative thought patterns. Through fasting and prayer, you invite God's transformative power into your life, believing that He can deliver you and set you free.

Envision a season of spiritual dryness or desolation, where you long to experience a deeper intimacy with God. Through fasting for breakthrough, you seek revival and renewal in your spiritual walk, trusting God to revive your soul and restore your passion for Him.

Personal Transformation and Purpose

Fasting for breakthrough catalyzes personal transformation and aligns you with God's divine purpose for your life. It is a journey of surrender, allowing God to mold you into the person He created you to be and equipping you to fulfill His calling on your life.

As you fast, you surrender your ambitions, fears, and dreams to God, inviting Him to align your heart with His desires. This transformative process leads to personal growth, spiritual maturity, and a deeper understanding of God's unconditional love for you.

Consider a desire to serve others through a specific ministry or mission. Through fasting and prayer, you seek God's guidance and empowerment, trusting that He will equip you with the gifts and resources needed to fulfill His purpose in your life.

Imagine feeling stagnant or complacent in your spiritual journey, longing for a renewed passion and zeal for God. Through fasting for breakthrough, you invite God to ignite a fire within your soul, empowering you to live boldly for His kingdom and impact the world around you.

Inference: Fasting for Breakthrough

Fasting for breakthrough is not merely a religious ritual but a transformative spiritual practice that invites God's presence, power, and purpose into your life. As you get on this journey of fasting and prayer, may you experience the abundant blessings and supernatural breakthroughs that God has prepared for you. Trust in His faithfulness, lean on His strength, and embrace all the great things He has created you to become through fasting for breakthrough.

5. Fasting for Financial Breakthrough

Fasting for financial breakthrough is a spiritual discipline aimed at seeking God's provision, wisdom, and guidance in matters of finances and prosperity. It involves abstaining from food or certain luxuries while dedicating time to prayer, meditation, and aligning with biblical principles of stewardship and abundance. For individuals who are on their journey towards financial breakthrough:

Aligning with God's Principles of Provision

Fasting for financial breakthrough involves aligning your financial decisions and aspirations with biblical principles of stewardship, generosity, and trust in God's provision. It is a spiritual practice that emphasizes seeking God's guidance and wisdom in managing resources and pursuing financial stability.

During a fast for financial breakthrough, you focus on surrendering your financial concerns and goals to God, trusting Him to provide according to His riches in glory (Philippians 4:19). This practice cultivates a mindset of gratitude and reliance on divine provision rather than solely on human efforts.

Imagine committing to a period of fasting and prayer to seek God's direction regarding a significant financial decision, such as investing in a business venture or navigating debt repayment. Through fasting, you demonstrate faith in God's ability to multiply resources and bless your financial endeavors.

Picture yourself facing financial challenges, such as job loss, debt accumulation, or unexpected expenses. Through fasting for financial breakthrough, you seek God's intervention and guidance, believing that He can turn your financial circumstances around and provide for your needs abundantly.

Wisdom and Discernment in Financial Management

Fasting for financial breakthrough enhances your ability to discern God's will and make wise financial decisions. By seeking His wisdom through prayer and fasting, you gain clarity on financial priorities, investments, and stewardship practices that align with His purposes for your life.

As you fast, you meditate on Scripture and seek God's guidance on budgeting, savings, investments, and charitable giving. This intentional focus allows you to make informed financial decisions that honor God and contribute to long-term financial stability.

Consider a season where you are contemplating a career change or pursuing higher education to enhance your earning potential. Through fasting and prayer, you seek God's direction on how to best utilize your talents and resources for His kingdom purposes.

Envision a scenario where you desire to break free from financial bondage or unhealthy spending habits. Through fasting for financial breakthrough, you surrender these concerns to God, trusting Him to provide strategies and resources for financial freedom and abundance.

Supernatural Provision and Debt Elimination

Fasting for financial breakthrough invites God's supernatural provision and favor into your financial affairs. It is a declaration of faith in God's ability to bless and multiply your finances, including debt elimination, unexpected income, and opportunities for financial increase beyond human understanding.

During a fast, you proclaim God's promises of provision and prosperity found in Scripture. You believe in His faithfulness to supply all your needs according to His glorious riches (Philippians 4:19) and to bless the work of your hands (Deuteronomy 28:12).

Reflect on instances in your life where unexpected financial blessings or opportunities emerged following a period of fasting and seeking God's face. These manifestations of His provision reinforce your faith in His ability to intervene miraculously in your financial circumstances.

Imagine facing overwhelming debt or financial hardship that seems insurmountable. Through fasting for financial breakthrough, you trust God to supernaturally cancel debts, open doors for new income streams, and provide wisdom for sound financial management.

Emotional and Spiritual Freedom from Financial Stress

Fasting for financial breakthroughs brings emotional and spiritual freedom from anxiety, stress, and worry about finances. By surrendering your concerns to God through fasting and prayer, you experience peace that surpasses understanding and a renewed sense of trust in His divine provision.

As you fast, you release financial burdens and anxieties to God, embracing His promise to give you peace that guards your heart and mind (Philippians 4:6-7). This practice fosters emotional resilience and spiritual growth amidst financial challenges.

Consider a time when financial setbacks or uncertainties caused stress and anxiety in your life. Through fasting and prayer, you seek God's peace and assurance, believing that He cares deeply about your financial well-being and has a plan to prosper you (Jeremiah 29:11).

Picture yourself desiring to cultivate a spirit of generosity and stewardship in your financial journey. Through fasting for financial breakthrough, you seek God's guidance on how to use your resources wisely, bless others generously, and honor Him with your finances.

Summary: Fasting for Financial Breakthrough

Fasting for financial breakthrough is a transformative spiritual discipline that invites God's provision, wisdom, and supernatural intervention into your financial journey. As you commit to fasting and prayer, may you experience divine breakthroughs, financial freedom, and a deeper intimacy with God. Trust in His faithfulness, lean on His promises, and embrace all the great things He has created you to become through fasting for financial breakthrough.

6. Fasting for Employment and Job Opportunities

Fasting for employment and job opportunities is a spiritual practice aimed at seeking God's guidance, provision, and favor in securing meaningful work and career advancement. This form of fasting involves abstaining from food or other indulgences while dedicating focused time to prayer, meditation, and aligning with God's will for your professional life.

Here's a summary of its benefits, for each individual on their journey towards career breakthrough:

Questing for God's Counsel and Guidance

Fasting for employment is a deliberate act of longing for God's direction and guidance in your career journey. It involves setting aside distractions and focusing your heart and mind on discerning His will for your professional path. Through prayer and fasting, you invite God to illuminate the right opportunities and choices that align with His purpose for your life.

During a fast for employment, you intentionally seek God's wisdom and clarity on career decisions, job searches, and professional aspirations. This spiritual discipline helps you discern the next steps in your career journey and align your ambitions with His divine plan.

Imagine dedicating a period of fasting and prayer to seek God's direction on a career transition, such as moving into a new industry or pursuing leadership roles. Through fasting, you demonstrate faith in God's ability to guide your steps and open doors of opportunity.

Picture yourself facing a season of unemployment or job dissatisfaction. Through fasting for employment, you surrender your concerns to God, trusting Him to lead you to the right job that utilizes your skills, passions, and talents effectively.

Depending on Divine Provision and Timing

Fasting for employment cultivates a deep trust in God's provision and perfect timing. It is an expression of faith that acknowledges God as the ultimate provider of opportunities and blessings in your professional life. By fasting, you demonstrate reliance on His sovereignty over career outcomes and trust in His faithfulness to meet your needs.

As you fast, you release anxieties about job security, financial stability, and career progression to God. This practice strengthens your confidence in His ability to provide for you and orchestrate divine connections that lead to career advancement.

Consider a period of uncertainty when you are seeking a job after graduation or facing layoffs in your current position. Through fasting and prayer, you seek God's provision and divine intervention in securing a job that aligns with His purpose and fulfills your professional aspirations.

Imagine navigating a competitive job market or experiencing repeated rejections in your job search. Through fasting for employment, you surrender setbacks and disappointments to God, believing that He is preparing a position that exceeds your expectations and utilizes your unique gifts.

Enhancing Spiritual Discernment and Confidence

Fasting for employment enhances your spiritual discernment and confidence in God's guidance. It sharpens your ability to recognize His voice amidst career decisions, job interviews, and networking opportunities. By aligning your thoughts and actions with His will, you position yourself to seize God-ordained opportunities and pursue career paths that honor Him.

During a fast, you engage in fervent prayer and meditation on Scripture, seeking God's perspective on career choices and professional growth. This spiritual discipline deepens your sensitivity to His leading and empowers you to make informed career decisions.

Reflect on instances when God provided clarity and direction during a job interview or negotiation process after a period of fasting. These moments reinforce your faith in His ability to guide your career path and align you with opportunities that showcase your talents.

Envision a pivotal career decision, such as accepting a promotion or transitioning to a new geographic location for work. Through fasting for employment, you seek God's confirmation and peace, knowing that His plans for your career are filled with hope and prosperity (Jeremiah 29:11).

Cultivating Perseverance and Resilience

Fasting for employment cultivates perseverance and resilience in the face of challenges and setbacks. It fosters a spirit of endurance as you persistently seek God's favor and breakthrough in your job search or career advancement efforts. By fasting, you demonstrate commitment to trusting God's timing and believing in His ability to turn obstacles into opportunities.

As you fast, you draw strength from God's promises of provision and favor in your professional endeavors. This practice builds resilience against discouragement and empowers you to persevere in pursuing career goals with unwavering faith.

Consider a prolonged job search or unexpected career transition that tests your resolve. Through fasting and prayer, you renew your trust in God's plan for your career and embrace challenges as opportunities for growth and refinement.

Picture yourself navigating a competitive industry or seeking advancement in a challenging economic climate. Through fasting for employment, you maintain steadfast faith in God's ability to elevate your career trajectory and open doors that lead to professional fulfillment.

Embracing God's Purpose and Calling

Fasting for employment aligns your career aspirations with God's purpose and calling for your life. It invites Him to direct your steps and use your professional talents and skills for His glory. By fasting, you surrender your career ambitions to His divine guidance and commit to serving Him faithfully through your work.

During a fast for employment, you seek alignment with God's purpose and calling in your career. This spiritual discipline involves surrendering personal ambitions and allowing God to shape your professional journey according to His perfect plan.

Reflect on moments when God orchestrated career opportunities that aligned with your passions and values after a period of fasting. These experiences affirm His faithfulness in guiding your career path and using your talents for His kingdom purposes.

Imagine pursuing a career change that aligns with a sense of calling to make a positive impact in your community or industry. Through fasting and prayer, you seek God's confirmation and empowerment, trusting that He will equip you for the responsibilities and challenges ahead.

Review: Fasting for Employment and Job Opportunities

Fasting for employment is a transformative spiritual practice that invites God's provision, guidance, and favor into your career journey. As you commit to fasting and prayer, may you experience divine breakthroughs, professional fulfillment, and a deeper intimacy with God. Have faith in His steadfastness, rest on His assurances, and welcome the extraordinary destiny He has shaped for you through fasting for employment and job opportunities.

7. Fasting for Breaking Spiritual Strongholds

Fasting for breaking spiritual strongholds is a powerful spiritual practice aimed at overcoming obstacles, defeating spiritual oppression, and experiencing freedom in Christ. This form of fasting involves abstaining from food or certain activities while dedicating focused time to prayer, worship, and seeking God's intervention in areas of personal or spiritual struggle.

Here's a summary of its benefits for everyone on their journey towards breaking spiritual breakthrough:

Understanding Spiritual Strongholds

Fasting for breaking spiritual strongholds involves identifying and addressing areas of spiritual bondage or oppression in your life. These strongholds can manifest as persistent sin patterns, destructive habits, negative thought patterns, or spiritual attacks that hinder your relationship with God and others. Through fasting and prayer, you seek God's power and intervention to dismantle these strongholds and experience spiritual freedom.

During a fast for breaking spiritual strongholds, you engage in intentional spiritual warfare through prayer, repentance, and declaring God's Word over your life. This practice focuses on surrendering to God's authority and seeking His deliverance from areas of bondage and oppression.

Imagine committing to a period of fasting and prayer to overcome a specific spiritual stronghold, such as addiction, fear, unforgiveness, or spiritual dryness. Through fasting, you demonstrate your dependence on God's strength and invite His transformative power into areas of your life that need healing and restoration.

Picture yourself facing recurring patterns of sin or spiritual attacks that seem insurmountable on your own. Through fasting for breaking spiritual strongholds, you surrender these challenges to God, trusting in His promise to set you free and equip you with spiritual armor to withstand the enemy's schemes (Ephesians 6:10-18).

Experiencing Spiritual Renewal and Revival

Fasting for breaking spiritual strongholds leads to spiritual renewal and revival in your relationship with God. It is a catalyst for personal transformation as you seek intimacy with God, repentance from sin, and a deeper understanding of His grace and mercy. Through fasting, you position yourself to receive God's forgiveness, healing, and restoration in areas where you have struggled or faltered.

As you fast, you humble yourself before God and seek His presence through worship, meditation on Scripture, and heartfelt repentance. This spiritual discipline opens your heart to receive His love and experience His transforming power in areas of brokenness and spiritual dryness.

Reflect on moments in your spiritual journey when fasting led to breakthroughs in overcoming spiritual strongholds, renewing your faith, and deepening your walk with God. These experiences testify to God's faithfulness in bringing healing and revival to areas of your life that were once bound by darkness.

Envision a season of spiritual stagnation or complacency, where you long to experience God's presence and power in a fresh way. Through fasting for breaking spiritual strongholds, you seek revival and renewal, believing that God will pour out His Spirit and revive your passion for Him and His purposes.

Strengthening Spiritual Discernment and Authority

Fasting for breaking spiritual strongholds strengthens your spiritual discernment and authority in Christ. It equips you to discern the enemy's tactics, stand firm in your identity as a child of God, and exercise authority through prayer and declarations of

God's Word. By fasting, you declare your allegiance to God's kingdom and resist the schemes of the enemy with confidence and faith.

During a fast, you engage in spiritual warfare by declaring Scripture, renouncing lies and strongholds, and affirming your identity and authority in Christ. This practice empowers you to resist temptation, overcome spiritual attacks, and walk in victory over the powers of darkness.

Consider times when fasting empowered you to confront spiritual opposition or overcome persistent challenges in your spiritual life. Through fasting and prayer, you accessed God's strength and authority to break free from spiritual strongholds and live victoriously in Christ.

Imagine facing spiritual battles, such as doubt, temptation, or spiritual oppression that threaten your peace and joy in Christ. Through fasting for breaking spiritual strongholds, you engage in spiritual warfare, trusting in God's promise to equip you with everything you need for spiritual victory (2 Corinthians 10:4-5).

Embracing Freedom and Transformation

Fasting for breaking spiritual strongholds leads to freedom and transformation in Christ. It is a journey of surrender and restoration as you yield every area of your life to God's healing touch and transformative power. Through fasting, you embrace God's invitation to experience abundant life and walk in the fullness of His purposes for your life.

As you fast, you surrender areas of bondage and brokenness to God, inviting His Holy Spirit to bring healing, restoration, and freedom. This spiritual discipline opens doors to new beginnings, renewed strength, and a deeper sense of purpose in serving God and others.

Reflecting on moments when fasting for breaking spiritual strongholds resulted in profound personal transformation, renewed faith, and restored relationships. These testimonies illustrate God's faithfulness in redeeming your past, empowering your present, and securing your future in Him.

Picture yourself overcoming longstanding spiritual battles or cycles of defeat through fasting and prayer. As you seek God's intervention, His grace enables you to break free from bondage, experience inner healing, and embrace a life of freedom and victory in Christ.

Inference: Fasting for Breaking Spiritual Strongholds

Fasting for breaking spiritual strongholds is a transformative spiritual discipline that invites God's power, healing, and freedom into every area of your life. As you commit to fasting and prayer, may you experience divine breakthroughs, spiritual renewal, and a deeper intimacy with God. Have confidence in His consistency, rely on His pledges, and embrace the extraordinary person He has destined you to be through fasting for breaking spiritual strongholds.

8.   Fasting for Open Doors to Abundance

Fasting for open doors to abundance is a spiritual discipline that focuses on seeking God's favor, provision, and blessings in all areas of life. It involves abstaining from food or other activities while dedicating concentrated time to prayer, meditation, and aligning with God's will for your prosperity.

Here's a detailed summary of its benefits for individuals who are on their journey towards experiencing God's abundance:

Embracing God's Promises of Provision

Fasting for open doors to abundance begins with embracing God's promises of provision and blessing found throughout Scripture. It is an act of faith that acknowledges God as the ultimate source of all blessings, including financial prosperity, spiritual growth, and personal fulfillment. Through fasting, you position yourself to receive God's abundant provision and open doors to opportunities beyond your imagination.

During a fast for open doors to abundance, you intentionally seek God's face and align your desires with His purposes for your life. This spiritual discipline involves surrendering your financial worries, career aspirations, and personal dreams to God, trusting in His ability to provide according to His riches in glory.

Imagine committing to a period of fasting and prayer to seek God's favor in a specific area of your life, such as career advancement, financial breakthrough, or personal relationships. Through fasting, you demonstrate your reliance on God's wisdom and sovereignty to open doors that lead to abundance and fulfillment.

Picture yourself facing challenges in your career or financial situation where you desire breakthrough and divine intervention. Through fasting for open doors to abundance, you invite God to intervene supernaturally, trusting that He will orchestrate circumstances and opportunities that exceed your expectations.

Experiencing Spiritual Growth and Transformation

Fasting for open doors to abundance fosters spiritual growth and transformation in your relationship with God. It is a journey of deepening intimacy as you seek His presence, wisdom, and guidance in every area of your life. Through fasting, you cultivate a heart that is receptive to God's leading and empowered to walk in His purposes for your prosperity and well-being.

As you fast, you engage in heartfelt prayer, meditation on Scripture, and worship, seeking to align your thoughts and desires with God's kingdom values. This spiritual discipline opens channels for spiritual growth, renewal of mind, and transformation of heart, preparing you to steward abundance with wisdom and gratitude.

Reflect on moments when fasting led to breakthroughs in spiritual understanding, personal healing, or renewed passion for serving God. These experiences illustrate God's faithfulness in transforming lives and preparing hearts to receive His abundant blessings.

Envision a season of spiritual dryness or uncertainty where you long to experience God's presence and direction more deeply. Through fasting for open doors to abundance, you seek spiritual renewal and revival, trusting that God will pour out His Spirit and equip you to walk in His abundant blessings.

Aligning with God's Timing and Purpose

Fasting for open doors to abundance aligns your desires and aspirations with God's perfect timing and purpose for your life. It is a practice of surrendering control and trusting in His divine timing to unfold opportunities and blessings according to His will. Through fasting, you cultivate patience, perseverance, and faith in God's sovereign plan for your prosperity and success.

During a fast, you surrender your timeline and expectations to God, acknowledging His sovereignty over your life's journey. This spiritual discipline involves waiting on God's timing with expectancy and faith, knowing that He orchestrates all things for your good and His glory.

Consider instances when God answered prayers and opened doors in unexpected ways after a period of fasting and seeking His face. These testimonies highlight God's faithfulness in fulfilling His promises and guiding your steps towards abundant living.

Imagine pursuing a career opportunity, financial breakthrough, or personal goal that seems out of reach or delayed. Through fasting for open doors to abundance, you release anxieties and uncertainties to God, trusting that His timing is perfect and His plans for your prosperity are filled with hope and promise.

Receiving Supernatural Provision and Favor

Fasting for open doors to abundance invites God's supernatural provision and favor into your life. It is an expression of faith that positions you to receive blessings, opportunities, and breakthroughs that surpass human understanding. By fasting, you declare your dependence on God's grace and goodness to manifest His abundance in every area of your life.

As you fast, you declare God's promises of provision, favor, and blessing over your finances, career, relationships, and dreams. This spiritual discipline activates faith to believe in God's ability to do exceedingly abundantly above all that you ask or think (Ephesians 3:20).

Reflect on moments when God provided for your needs, orchestrated divine connections, or opened doors of opportunity that exceeded your expectations. These experiences testify to God's faithfulness in rewarding those who seek Him diligently through fasting and prayer.

Picture yourself facing financial challenges, career transitions, or personal obstacles where you need God's intervention and breakthrough. Through fasting for open doors to abundance, you position yourself to receive supernatural provision, divine favor, and unexpected blessings that testify to God's goodness and provision.

Closing: Fasting for Open Doors to Abundance

Fasting for open doors to abundance is a transformative spiritual discipline that invites God's provision, favor, and blessings into every area of your life. As you commit to fasting and prayer, may you experience divine breakthroughs, spiritual growth, and a deeper intimacy with God. Trust in His trustworthiness, depend on His assurances, and welcome the magnificent purpose He has ordained for you through fasting for open doors to abundance.

9. Fasting for Breaking Generational Curses

Fasting for breaking generational curses is a profound spiritual practice that seeks freedom from negative patterns, behaviors, and influences passed down through family lines. It involves abstaining from food or other distractions while dedicating focused time to prayer, repentance, and seeking God's intervention to break the cycle of generational bondage. Fasting for Breaking Generational Curses for individuals who are on their journey towards spiritual freedom and the realization of God's promises:

Understanding Generational Curses

Fasting for breaking generational curses begins with understanding the concept of generational curses in a biblical context. These curses are spiritual and emotional patterns that pass from one generation to another, affecting families and individuals in various ways. They can manifest as recurring patterns of addiction, dysfunction, poverty, sickness, or relational strife. Through fasting and prayer, you seek God's power and authority to break these negative cycles and experience His freedom and restoration.

During a fast for breaking generational curses, you engage in intentional spiritual warfare by renouncing and repenting of generational sins and patterns. This spiritual discipline involves acknowledging the impact of family history while surrendering these influences to God, trusting in His power to redeem and restore.

Imagine committing to a period of fasting and prayer to break specific generational curses, such as patterns of addiction or financial hardship, that have plagued your family lineage. Through fasting, you demonstrate your faith in God's ability to bring healing and transformation to areas of your life that have been negatively impacted by generational influences.

Picture yourself grappling with inherited challenges, such as emotional wounds or destructive habits, that seem to recur across generations. Through fasting for breaking generational curses, you invite God's intervention and healing, trusting that His grace is sufficient to break every chain and restore wholeness to your family lineage (Galatians 5:1).

Experiencing Spiritual and Emotional Healing

Fasting for breaking generational curses leads to spiritual and emotional healing. It is a journey of inner healing and restoration as you seek God's forgiveness, deliverance, and renewal of mind and spirit. Through fasting, you create space for God to heal past wounds, mend broken relationships, and release you from the emotional burdens inherited from previous generations.

As you fast, you engage in heartfelt prayer, repentance, and seeking God's face for inner healing and restoration. This spiritual discipline involves confronting and renouncing generational sins, bitterness, and unforgiveness while embracing God's grace and mercy to heal deep-seated wounds.

Reflect on moments when fasting and prayer led to breakthroughs in emotional healing and restoration within your family or personal life. These experiences illustrate God's power to redeem the past and transform pain into a testimony of His faithfulness and love.

Envision a season where unresolved conflicts, resentment, or emotional trauma impact your relationships or personal well-being. Through fasting for breaking generational curses, you release these burdens to God, trusting in His ability to heal broken hearts, mend fractured relationships, and restore peace and joy (Isaiah 61:1-3).

Breaking Destructive Patterns and Behaviors

Fasting for breaking generational curses empowers you to break destructive patterns and behaviors that have plagued your family lineage. It is an act of spiritual warfare that involves renouncing and breaking free from cycles of sin, addiction, poverty, sickness, or dysfunction that have persisted across generations. Through fasting and prayer, you align your thoughts, actions, and decisions with God's truth and authority to live a life of victory and freedom.

During a fast, you confront and renounce generational strongholds by declaring God's Word and promises over your life and family. This spiritual discipline involves replacing negative thought patterns and behaviors with God's truth and principles for abundant living.

Consider moments when fasting enabled you to break free from inherited patterns of addiction, financial struggles, or relational dysfunction. These testimonies demonstrate God's power to break every chain and empower you to walk in His freedom and victory.

Imagine facing recurring challenges or temptations that mirror patterns of behavior in your family history. Through fasting for breaking generational curses, you seek God's strength and deliverance, trusting in His ability to break destructive cycles and establish new patterns of righteousness and wholeness (2 Corinthians 5:17).

Receiving God's Promises of Blessing and Prosperity

Fasting for breaking generational curses positions you to receive God's promises of blessing, prosperity, and generational legacy. It is an opportunity to align your life with God's purposes and plans, releasing His abundant blessings to future generations. Through fasting, you declare your faith in God's ability to restore and establish His kingdom principles in your family lineage.

As you fast, you declare God's promises of blessing and generational legacy over your life and descendants. This spiritual discipline involves sowing seeds of faith, obedience, and generosity while trusting in God's faithfulness to fulfill His promises for your family's future.

Reflect on moments when God's faithfulness and provision were evident in your family's journey after a season of fasting and seeking His face. These testimonies illustrate God's desire to bless and prosper His children and their descendants, demonstrating His covenantal faithfulness across generations.

Picture yourself desiring to break the cycle of poverty, illness, or spiritual oppression that has affected your family for generations. Through fasting for breaking generational curses, you sow seeds of faith and obedience, trusting in God to establish a legacy of blessing, health, and spiritual abundance for future generations (Deuteronomy 30:19-20).

Renewing Mindsets and Aligning with God's Truth

Fasting for breaking generational curses involves renewing your mind and aligning your beliefs with God's truth and promises. It is a process of breaking free from negative mindsets, lies, and misconceptions that have been passed down through generations. Through fasting and prayer, you invite God to transform your thinking and empower you to walk in His truth and freedom.

During a fast, you engage in spiritual warfare by uprooting lies and negative beliefs that have hindered your spiritual growth and fulfillment. This spiritual discipline involves meditating on Scripture, declaring God's promises, and replacing worldly perspectives with God's kingdom principles.

Imagine confronting deeply ingrained beliefs of unworthiness, failure, or fear that have affected your family's legacy. Through fasting for breaking generational curses, you declare your identity in Christ, embracing God's truth that you are chosen, loved, and empowered to live a life of purpose and abundance.

Consider moments when generational beliefs or behaviors hindered your ability to pursue God's calling or experience His blessings fully. Through fasting, you seek God's wisdom and guidance to dismantle these strongholds, allowing His truth to renew your mind and empower you to walk in His divine purpose (Romans 12:2).

Healing Family Relationships and Restoring Unity

Fasting for breaking generational curses fosters healing and restoration within family relationships. It is an opportunity to address past hurts, misunderstandings, and conflicts that have divided generations. Through fasting and prayer, you seek God's healing touch to mend broken relationships, restore unity, and cultivate a spirit of forgiveness and reconciliation.

As you fast, you intercede for family members who may have been affected by generational patterns of dysfunction or discord. This spiritual discipline involves extending grace, forgiveness, and love as you seek God's intervention to heal wounds and restore unity within your family lineage.

Reflect on moments when God used fasting to bring reconciliation and healing within your family. These testimonies illustrate His power to break down walls of division and restore relationships, paving the way for unity and solidarity rooted in Christ's love.

Imagine navigating conflicts or estrangements within your family that stem from generational differences or misunderstandings. Through fasting for breaking generational curses, you humble yourself before God, seeking His wisdom and guidance to foster reconciliation, heal wounds, and build a legacy of unity and love (Ephesians 4:32).

Establishing a Legacy of Faith and Obedience

Fasting for breaking generational curses empowers you to establish a legacy of faith, obedience, and righteousness for future generations. It is an opportunity to sow seeds of spiritual inheritance that will bear fruit in the lives of your children, grandchildren, and beyond. Through fasting, you declare your commitment to God's kingdom principles and invite His blessings to shape your family's destiny.

During a fast, you consecrate yourself and your family to God's purposes, dedicating time to pray for generational blessings and divine favor. This spiritual discipline involves investing in spiritual disciplines, such as studying Scripture, teaching your children about God's faithfulness, and modeling a life of faith and obedience.

Consider the impact of generational blessings and spiritual inheritance you desire to pass on to future generations. Through fasting for breaking generational curses, you sow seeds of faithfulness, stewardship, and generosity, trusting in God to establish a lasting legacy of His goodness and grace.

Picture yourself laying a foundation of faith and obedience that contrasts with negative generational patterns of disobedience or spiritual apathy. Through fasting, you partner with God to build a legacy rooted in His promises, ensuring that future generations inherit blessings and walk in His divine favor (Psalm 103:17-18).

Releasing God's Promises and Walking in Authority

Fasting for breaking generational curses releases God's promises and empowers you to walk in authority over the enemy's schemes. It is a declaration of God's victory over generational strongholds and an assertion of your identity as a child of God, equipped with spiritual armor and authority to overcome every obstacle.

As you fast, you declare God's promises of freedom, deliverance, and blessing over your life and family. This spiritual discipline involves standing firm in your authority as a believer, resisting the enemy's attacks, and declaring victory in Jesus' name over generational curses.

Reflect on moments when fasting empowered you to confront spiritual opposition or break free from generational patterns of bondage. These testimonies illustrate God's faithfulness to fulfill His promises and empower His children to live victoriously in Christ.

Imagine facing spiritual battles or setbacks that have persisted through generations, such as financial hardship or health issues. Through fasting for breaking generational curses, you exercise your authority in Christ, commanding freedom and restoration in areas where generational curses once held sway (Luke 10:19).

Closing: Fasting for Breaking Generational Curses

Fasting for breaking generational curses is a transformative spiritual discipline that invites God's healing, restoration, and blessing into every area of your family's legacy. As you commit to fasting and prayer, may you experience divine breakthroughs, reconciliation, and a renewed sense of purpose in Christ. Rest in His faithfulness, stand on His promises, and embrace the fullness of the person He has created you to be through fasting for breaking generational curses.

10. Fasting for Overcoming Fear and Anxiety

Fasting for overcoming fear and anxiety is a transformative spiritual practice that empowers you to confront and conquer the internal battles that hinder your peace and well-being. It involves abstaining from food or other distractions while dedicating focused time to prayer, meditation, and seeking God's presence. Through fasting, you position yourself to experience God's supernatural peace, courage, and freedom from the grip of fear and anxiety.

During a fast for overcoming fear and anxiety, you commit to surrendering your worries, doubts, and insecurities to God. This spiritual discipline involves trusting in God's promises of peace and provision while seeking His wisdom and guidance to navigate life's challenges with faith and resilience.

Imagine embarking on a period of fasting and prayer to confront specific fears or anxieties that have plagued your mind and spirit. Through fasting, you cultivate a deeper dependence on God's strength and discover His ability to calm your fears and renew your mind with His truth and assurance.

Picture yourself facing a daunting situation—perhaps a job interview, a difficult conversation, or a health concern—that triggers anxiety and apprehension. Through fasting for overcoming fear and anxiety, you release your concerns to God, trusting in His unfailing love and power to provide peace that surpasses understanding (Philippians 4:6-7).

Experiencing Spiritual Growth and Renewal

Fasting for overcoming fear and anxiety fosters spiritual growth and renewal as you seek God's presence and purpose for your life. It is a journey of deepening intimacy with God, where you learn to rely on His strength and promises rather than succumbing to fear-driven thoughts and behaviors. Through fasting, you open yourself to God's transformative work in your heart, renewing your mind and spirit with His peace and courage.

As you fast, you engage in spiritual disciplines such as prayer, worship, and Scripture meditation to nurture your relationship with God. This spiritual discipline involves surrendering your fears and anxieties at His feet while embracing His truth and promises as the foundation of your faith.

Reflect on moments when fasting enabled you to experience breakthroughs in your spiritual journey, such as overcoming deep-seated fears of failure, rejection, or uncertainty. These testimonies illustrate God's faithfulness in guiding you through seasons of doubt and empowering you to walk in His freedom and purpose.

Envision a time when fear and anxiety threatened to overwhelm your sense of peace and purpose. Through fasting for overcoming fear and anxiety, you seek God's presence and guidance, allowing His peace to guard your heart and mind, enabling you to face challenges with renewed confidence and assurance (Isaiah 41:10).

Breaking the Cycle of Negative Thought Patterns

Fasting for overcoming fear and anxiety empowers you to break free from negative thought patterns and destructive behaviors that perpetuate anxiety. It is an opportunity to renew your mind with God's truth and replace fear-driven thoughts with His promises of hope, strength, and security. Through fasting, you cultivate a mindset of faith and resilience, enabling you to confront fear head-on and embrace God's peace that transcends circumstances.

During a fast, you intentionally confront and renounce negative thought patterns, such as worry, fear of the future, or fear of inadequacy, by declaring God's truth over your life. This spiritual discipline involves aligning your thoughts with His Word and allowing His Spirit to transform your mindset from fear to faith.

Consider instances when fasting empowered you to break free from cycles of anxiety and worry, enabling you to trust in God's provision and sovereignty. These experiences demonstrate God's ability to renew your mind and equip you with His peace and strength to navigate life's challenges victoriously.

Picture yourself encountering recurring thoughts of fear or anxiety that threaten your peace and confidence. Through fasting for overcoming fear and anxiety, you confront these thoughts with God's promises, trusting in His faithfulness to calm your fears and equip you with His strength to face each day with courage and resilience (2 Timothy 1:7).

Walking in God's Freedom and Purpose

Fasting for overcoming fear and anxiety empowers you to walk in God's freedom and fulfill His purpose for your life. It is a declaration of faith in His ability to heal, restore, and guide you through every season of uncertainty and challenge. Through fasting, you embrace God's invitation to live abundantly in His peace, joy, and assurance of His perfect plan for your life.

As you fast, you surrender your fears and anxieties to God, embracing His promise to give you a future filled with hope and purpose. This spiritual discipline involves seeking His will and direction, trusting that He has plans to prosper you and not to harm you, plans to give you hope and a future (Jeremiah 29:11).

Reflect on moments when fasting led to breakthroughs in your faith journey, enabling you to step into new opportunities and overcome obstacles with God's strength. These testimonies illustrate God's faithfulness in guiding you toward His purposes and fulfilling His promises of abundant life.

Imagine pursuing God's calling on your life, despite fears of inadequacy or uncertainty about the future. Through fasting for overcoming fear and anxiety, you align your desires with God's will, trusting in His provision and guidance to lead you into a life marked by His peace, purpose, and fulfillment (Psalm 32:8).

In summary, fasting for overcoming fear and anxiety is a transformative spiritual discipline that empowers you to confront fear, renew your mind with God's truth, and walk in His freedom and purpose. As you commit to fasting and prayer, may you experience God's peace that surpasses understanding and discover all the great things He has created you to become. Trust in His promises, lean on His strength, and embrace His invitation to live fearlessly in His love and grace.

11. A Pathway to Victory in Your Court Case

Fasting has long been recognized not only as a spiritual discipline but also as a practice that can bring profound benefits in times of need and adversity. When facing a daunting court case, whether it involves legal disputes, personal challenges, or injustices, fasting can serve as a powerful tool to seek divine intervention, clarity of mind, and favor in the eyes of the law. By committing to fasting, you begin a sojourn of spiritual alignment, resilience, and unwavering faith in God's ability to intervene and bring about justice.

Fasting for the purpose of winning a court case involves abstaining from food or other distractions while dedicating focused time to prayer, meditation, and seeking God's guidance. This spiritual discipline is rooted in the belief that by humbling oneself before God and seeking His will fervently, one can receive clarity, wisdom, and divine favor to navigate legal challenges successfully.

Consider a scenario where an individual is facing a complex legal battle, such as a custody dispute or a civil lawsuit. Through fasting, this person seeks spiritual clarity and guidance, believing that God's wisdom and favor will influence the outcome of the court proceedings. This commitment to fasting not only demonstrates faith but also empowers the individual to approach the case with a renewed sense of confidence and trust in God's sovereignty.

Circumstances:

1. **Seeking Divine Favor**: Imagine preparing for a court case where the odds seem stacked against you. By fasting, you align your heart and mind with God's purpose, trusting that His favor will open doors and sway decisions in your favor. This spiritual alignment empowers you to face legal challenges with courage and perseverance.
2. **Clarity of Mind and Spirit**: During a fast, you experience heightened clarity of mind and spirit, enabling you to articulate your case effectively and make sound decisions under pressure. This mental clarity is essential in navigating legal complexities and presenting your arguments persuasively before the court.
3. **Strength in Adversity**: Fasting strengthens your resilience and fortitude in the face of adversity. It equips you with the spiritual and emotional strength to endure prolonged legal battles, setbacks, or challenges that may arise during the court proceedings.
4. **Divine Intervention**: Through fasting, you invite divine intervention into your legal situation, believing that God's justice will prevail, and His righteousness will be established. This faith-driven approach instills hope and confidence, knowing that God is fighting on your behalf.

Embracing Spiritual Discipline and Trust in God's Plan

Fasting for the purpose of winning a court case is more than a religious ritual; it is a profound act of faith and trust in God's plan for your life. It involves surrendering your fears, anxieties, and uncertainties to God while placing your legal matters in His capable hands. By fasting, you demonstrate a willingness to seek God's wisdom, discernment, and direction, believing that He will guide you through the legal process and bring about a just resolution.

The discipline of fasting requires a steadfast commitment to abstain from food or other comforts, accompanied by fervent prayer and meditation on God's Word. This spiritual discipline not only strengthens your relationship with God but also deepens your reliance on His providence and sovereignty in all aspects of your life, including legal challenges.

Reflect on individuals throughout history who have turned to fasting during times of legal turmoil or persecution. Their unwavering faith and commitment to seeking God's intervention serve as powerful examples of how fasting can influence outcomes and bring about miraculous interventions in legal proceedings.

Situations:

1. **Crisis Resolution**: Imagine facing a crisis where legal action is necessary to protect your rights or seek justice. Through fasting, you align your priorities with God's will, trusting that He will intervene on your behalf and bring about a favorable resolution to the legal dispute.
2. **Personal Transformation**: Fasting fosters personal transformation and spiritual growth, equipping you with the inner strength and resilience to face legal challenges with grace and integrity. It empowers you to embody God's principles of justice, mercy, and righteousness throughout the legal process.
3. **Victory and Testimony**: As you commit to fasting for the purpose of winning a court case, you anticipate victory not only in the courtroom but also in your spiritual journey. Your testimony of God's faithfulness and provision through fasting serves as a beacon of hope and inspiration to others facing similar legal battles.

Inference: Trusting in God's Timing and Providence

In inference, fasting for the purpose of winning a court case is a profound expression of faith and reliance on God's divine intervention and justice. It involves aligning your heart, mind, and spirit with God's will, trusting that His timing and providence will prevail in all legal matters. As you embark on this spiritual journey of fasting, may you experience God's peace, wisdom, and favor, knowing that He is faithful to guide you through every legal challenge and lead you to victory according to His perfect plan.

12. Finding Freedom from Addictions Through Fasting

Aa Fasting is not just a physical act of abstaining from food; it is a spiritual discipline that can bring profound liberation from the grip of addiction. Whether struggling with substance abuse, unhealthy behaviors, or compulsive habits, fasting provides a pathway to healing, renewal, and spiritual breakthrough. By committing to fasting, you head off on an exploration of self-discovery, surrender, and empowerment through God's transformative grace.

Fasting for freedom from addictions involves intentionally abstaining from food or certain activities while dedicating focused time to prayer, meditation, and seeking God's guidance. This spiritual discipline aims to weaken the hold of addiction, cleanse the body and mind, and open the door to God's healing and restoration.

Consider an individual battling with alcohol addiction. Through fasting, this person sets aside time to seek God's intervention and strength, believing that God's power can break the chains of addiction and restore wholeness. This commitment to fasting not only detoxifies the body but also purifies the soul, paving the way for lasting freedom from destructive behaviors.

Circumstances:

1. **Spiritual Awakening**: Imagine someone caught in a cycle of addiction, feeling powerless and trapped. Through fasting, they experience a spiritual awakening, recognizing their need for God's intervention and surrendering their struggles to Him. This transformative encounter with God's presence ignites hope and fuels their determination to break free from addiction.
2. **Renewed Mind and Spirit**: During a fast for freedom from addictions, individuals often experience a renewed sense of clarity, peace, and purpose. As they detoxify physically and spiritually, they gain clarity of mind to confront the root causes of addiction and embrace healthier, God-honoring choices.
3. **Breaking Chains of Bondage**: Fasting serves as a catalyst for breaking the chains of bondage that addiction imposes. It empowers individuals to confront triggers, temptations, and unhealthy patterns with spiritual resilience and reliance on God's strength.
4. **Healing and Restoration**: Through fasting, individuals open themselves to God's healing and restoration, both physically and emotionally. They experience His unconditional love and forgiveness, enabling them to forgive themselves and others impacted by their addiction.

Embracing God's Transformative Grace and Purpose

Fasting for freedom from addictions is a journey of faith, courage, and perseverance. It requires a willingness to surrender control and trust in God's ability to bring about healing and transformation. By aligning your desires with God's will and seeking His guidance through fasting, you embark on a path toward a life of freedom, purpose, and fulfillment.

The discipline of fasting involves sacrificially setting aside physical comforts to pursue spiritual breakthrough and intimacy with God. It is an act of humility and faith, acknowledging your dependence on God's strength and grace to overcome addiction and live abundantly in His truth.

Reflect on individuals who have experienced freedom from addictions through fasting and prayer. Their testimonies illustrate God's faithfulness in breaking chains of bondage, restoring relationships, and empowering them to live victoriously over addiction.

Situations:

1. **Personal Transformation**: Imagine someone struggling with a gambling addiction who commits to fasting and prayer. Through this spiritual discipline, they confront their addiction with God's strength, experience inner healing, and develop healthier habits rooted in God's truth and grace.
2. **Family and Community Impact**: Fasting for freedom from addictions not only transforms individuals but also impacts families and communities. As individuals experience healing and restoration, they become catalysts for positive change and advocates for others seeking freedom from addiction.
3. **Walking in Freedom**: Through fasting, individuals gain the courage and resilience to resist temptation, overcome setbacks, and embrace God's plan for their lives. They discover their identity and purpose in Christ, empowered to live authentically and serve others with compassion and grace.

Closing: Embracing God's Promise of Freedom and Abundant Life

In closing, fasting for freedom from addictions is a transformative journey of faith, surrender, and spiritual renewal. It empowers individuals to break free from the bondage of addiction, experience God's healing and restoration, and embrace a life of purpose and fulfillment. As you commit to fasting and prayer, may you encounter God's transformative grace, discover all the great things He has created you to become, and walk in the freedom and abundant life found in Christ.

13. The Power of Fasting to Resolve Spiritual Hindrances

Fasting is a powerful spiritual discipline that not only nourishes the soul but also breaks down barriers that hinder your spiritual growth and connection with God. Whether you're facing spiritual obstacles, unresolved conflicts, or seeking deeper intimacy with God, fasting offers a pathway to clarity, renewal, and transformation. By committing to fasting, you enter an odyssey of faith, surrender, and empowerment to overcome spiritual hindrances and embrace the abundant life God intended for you.

Fasting for resolving spiritual hindrances involves intentionally abstaining from food or other distractions while dedicating focused time to prayer, meditation, and seeking God's guidance. This spiritual discipline aims to purify the heart, strengthen spiritual discernment, and align your life with God's will and purpose.

Consider an individual struggling with persistent doubt, spiritual dryness, or emotional wounds. Through fasting, this person sets aside time to seek God's intervention and healing, believing that fasting can break through spiritual barriers and renew their faith. This commitment not only cleanses the spirit but also opens the door to divine revelation and guidance.

Situations:

1. **Seeking Spiritual Clarity**: Imagine facing a season of confusion or uncertainty in your spiritual journey. Through fasting, you seek clarity of God's direction, wisdom, and discernment. This spiritual discipline helps you align your thoughts and actions with God's purpose, enabling you to navigate challenges and make decisions rooted in faith.
2. **Overcoming Spiritual Dryness**: During a fast, you experience a deepening of spiritual intimacy and connection with God. This period of fasting allows you to break free from spiritual complacency or apathy, renewing your passion and zeal for God's presence and Word.
3. **Healing Emotional Wounds**: Fasting serves as a catalyst for emotional healing and restoration. It enables you to release past hurts, bitterness, or unforgiveness, allowing God's grace to bring healing and reconciliation in relationships and inner peace.
4. **Spiritual Warfare and Victory**: Through fasting, you engage in spiritual warfare against forces of darkness or spiritual attacks. By surrendering to God's strength and protection, fasting empowers you to overcome temptation, resist evil influences, and walk in victory over spiritual hindrances.

Accepting God's Promises and Transformative Power

Fasting for resolving spiritual hindrances is more than a religious practice; it is a profound act of faith and surrender to God's transformative power in your life. It requires humility, perseverance, and a willingness to trust God's timing and purposes for your spiritual growth and breakthrough.

The discipline of fasting involves sacrificially setting aside physical comforts to pursue spiritual breakthrough and intimacy with God. It is an expression of your desire to seek God's will, guidance, and transformation in every area of your life.

Reflect on individuals who have experienced spiritual breakthroughs through fasting and prayer. Their testimonies serve as powerful reminders of God's faithfulness in overcoming obstacles, renewing faith, and restoring hope in His promises.

Consequences:

1. **Personal Transformation**: Imagine someone facing persistent spiritual obstacles, such as doubt, fear, or unresolved sin. Through fasting, they confront these hindrances with faith and perseverance, trusting God to remove barriers and restore spiritual vitality.
2. **Community and Ministry Impact**: Fasting for resolving spiritual hindrances not only transforms individual lives but also impacts families, communities, and ministries. As individuals experience breakthroughs and renewed passion for God, they become agents of change and instruments of His love and grace.
3. **Revival and Spiritual Awakening**: Through fasting, individuals participate in spiritual revival and awakening. This spiritual discipline ignites a hunger for God's presence, revival of hearts, and transformation of communities, leading to renewed commitment to prayer, worship, and obedience.

Ending: Adopting God's Transformative Work

In inference, fasting for resolving spiritual hindrances is a transformative journey of faith, surrender, and spiritual renewal. It empowers you to break through barriers, experience God's healing and restoration, and embrace His promises of abundant life and purpose. As you commit to fasting and prayer, may you encounter God's transformative grace, discover all the great things He has created you to become, and walk in the freedom and spiritual breakthrough found in Christ.

14. The Power of Family Fasting

Family fasting is a transformative spiritual practice that fosters unity, strengthens bonds, and deepens faith within households. It involves intentional periods of abstaining from food or other distractions while dedicating time to prayer, worship, and seeking God's guidance together as a family. This sacred discipline not only nurtures individual spiritual growth but also cultivates a shared journey of faith, encouraging each family member to discover the abundant blessings and purposes God has in store.

Family fasting is a sacred commitment where each member voluntarily participates in abstaining from meals or certain activities as an act of devotion and seeking God's presence. It aims to strengthen spiritual resilience, deepen relational connections, and align the family's heart with God's will and purposes.

Consider a family facing challenges such as discord, lack of spiritual intimacy, or struggles with individual issues. Through family fasting, they set aside designated times to collectively seek God's intervention and guidance. This shared experience not only unites their hearts in prayer but also strengthens their faith and trust in God's transformative power to heal, restore, and guide their lives.

Circumstances:

1. **Building Spiritual Resilience**: Imagine a family navigating through a season of uncertainty or adversity. By engaging in family fasting, they cultivate spiritual resilience and courage to face challenges together. This shared commitment deepens their trust in God's faithfulness and strengthens their resolve to overcome obstacles as a united front.
2. **Strengthening Family Bonds**: Family fasting fosters deeper relational connections and mutual support among members. As they prioritize spiritual growth and seek God's wisdom together, they experience a heightened sense of unity, empathy, and compassion within the family unit.
3. **Cultivating Spiritual Disciplines**: Through family fasting, children learn valuable lessons in faith, humility, and dependence on God. Parents serve as role models in demonstrating the importance of prioritizing spiritual disciplines and seeking God's guidance in all aspects of life.
4. **Encountering God's Provision**: Family fasting provides opportunities for each member to witness God's provision, guidance, and transformative work in their lives. As they commit to fasting and prayer, they experience divine interventions, breakthroughs in relationships, and clarity in decision-making aligned with God's purposes.

Acceptance of God's Promises and Family Legacy

Family fasting is more than a religious practice; it is a sacred journey of faith, obedience, and surrender to God's transformative work within each family member's life. It requires humility, perseverance, and a shared commitment to grow in faith and obedience to God's will.

The discipline of family fasting involves sacrificially setting aside physical comforts to pursue spiritual breakthrough, unity, and growth as a family. It is an act of obedience and trust in God's promises to bless and guide families who seek His presence and direction together.

Reflect on families who have experienced spiritual revival, healing from past wounds, or strengthened relationships through family fasting and prayer. Their testimonies serve as powerful reminders of God's faithfulness and provision in uniting families and fulfilling His purposes in their lives.

Situations:

1. **Transforming Family Dynamics**: Family fasting leads to transformational shifts in attitudes, communication patterns, and relational dynamics within the household. As each member commits to seeking God's wisdom and grace, they experience reconciliation, forgiveness, and renewed love that transcend past conflicts or misunderstandings.
2. **Impacting Future Generations**: Family fasting establishes a legacy of faith, obedience, and dependence on God's guidance for future generations. Children witness firsthand the importance of prioritizing spiritual disciplines, seeking God's will, and experiencing His transformative power in their family's journey.
3. **Community and Ministry Outreach**: Families engaged in fasting often become catalysts for positive change and spiritual revival within their communities and ministries. Their unified commitment to seek God's kingdom leads to acts of service, compassion, and evangelism that impact lives and glorify God's name.

Conclusion: Accepting Unity, Growth, and Divine Purpose

In winding up, family fasting is a sacred journey that fosters unity, strengthens bonds, and cultivates spiritual growth within households. It empowers families to align their hearts with God's will, experience His transformative power, and fulfill His purposes together. As you commit to family fasting and prayer, may you encounter God's presence, discover all the great things He has created your family to become, and walk in the fullness of His blessings and promises.

15. Literary Fasting

Literary fasting involves abstaining from certain genres of literature or media consumption, often for spiritual or intellectual enrichment.

Benefits:

- **Enhanced Focus**: By limiting exposure to entertainment media, literary fasting promotes intellectual focus, concentration, and critical thinking.
- **Spiritual Enrichment**: It fosters deeper spiritual insights, contemplation, and connection by directing attention to sacred texts, philosophical works, or educational materials.

16. Spiritual Fasting

Spiritual fasting involves abstaining from food or certain types of food for spiritual purposes, often practiced in various religions and belief systems worldwide.

Benefits:

- **Deepened Divine Link**: Spiritual fasting enhances spiritual awareness, devotion, and connection to higher consciousness or divine principles.
- **Discipline and Self-Control**: It cultivates discipline, self-control, and mindfulness in daily practices, promoting inner peace and harmony.
- **Community and Unity**: Participating in communal fasting rituals fosters community bonds, solidarity, and shared spiritual experiences.

17. Social Media Fasting

Social media fasting refers to limiting or abstaining from social media platforms for a period to reduce screen time, digital distractions, and promote mental well-being.

Benefits:

- **Improved Mental Health**: Reduces anxiety, stress, and feelings of comparison or inadequacy associated with social media use.
- **Enhanced Focus and Productivity**: Increases productivity, creativity, and focus on meaningful activities or personal goals.
- **Deeper Connections**: Strengthens real-life relationships, communication skills, and face-to-face interactions with others.

18. Environmental Fasting

Environmental fasting encourages mindful consumption, waste reduction, and ecological stewardship to support environmental sustainability.

Benefits:

- **Reduced Carbon Footprint**: Minimizes personal impact on the environment through conscious lifestyle choices and consumption habits.
- **Promotes Eco-Friendly Practices**: Supports conservation efforts, recycling initiatives, and sustainable living practices for a cleaner, healthier planet.

- **Educational and Advocacy Opportunities**: Raises awareness, inspires others, and advocates for environmental protection and global sustainability.

19. Time-Restricted Eating

Time-restricted eating (TRE) involves consuming all daily calories within a specific time window, typically 8-12 hours, with fasting periods in between.

Benefits:

- **Weight Management**: Helps regulate appetite, reduce calorie intake, and promote weight loss or maintenance without strict dietary restrictions.
- **Enhanced Digestive Health**: Improves digestion, gut health, and nutrient absorption by allowing adequate fasting periods for metabolic rest and repair.
- **Metabolic Benefits**: Enhances insulin sensitivity, regulates blood sugar levels, and supports metabolic flexibility for optimal health and longevity.

20. Hybrid Fasting Approaches

Hybrid fasting approaches combine elements of different fasting methods or integrate fasting with other health practices for personalized benefits.

Benefits:

- **Customized Health Goals**: Tailors fasting protocols to individual needs, preferences, and health conditions for maximum efficacy and sustainability.
- **Comprehensive Wellness**: Addresses multiple aspects of health, including physical fitness, mental clarity, emotional well-being, and spiritual growth.
- **Long-Term Sustainability**: Promotes long-term adherence to fasting practices by incorporating diverse strategies, nutritional support, and lifestyle modifications.

Deduction

Each type of fasting offers unique benefits that contribute to overall health, well-being, and personal growth. Whether you're seeking physical rejuvenation through water fasting, spiritual enrichment through spiritual fasting, or environmental stewardship through eco-friendly practices, fasting can be adapted to suit diverse lifestyles and goals.

By embracing fasting as a holistic practice, individuals can cultivate resilience, discipline, and a deeper connection to themselves and their surroundings. Integrating fasting with mindful eating, regular physical activity, and self-care practices enhances its transformative power and supports long-term wellness.

As you explore and incorporate fasting into your life, remember to prioritize safety, listen to your body's signals, and seek guidance from healthcare professionals or experts when necessary. Embrace the journey of self-discovery, renewal, and empowerment that fasting can offer, leading to a healthier, more vibrant life.

21. Therapeutic Fasting

Fasting as a therapeutic intervention used under medical supervision to treat specific health conditions or support healing processes.

Benefits:

- **Inflammatory Conditions**: Fasting can reduce inflammation markers and symptoms associated with chronic inflammatory diseases like rheumatoid arthritis and inflammatory bowel disease.
- **Metabolic Disorders**: It helps regulate blood sugar levels, improve insulin sensitivity, and manage conditions like type 2 diabetes and metabolic syndrome.
- **Autoimmune Disorders**: Fasting may modulate immune responses and alleviate symptoms in autoimmune conditions by promoting immune system rebalancing and reducing autoimmune activity.

22. Fasting for Longevity and Anti-Aging Benefits

Fasting strategies aimed at extending lifespan, promoting cellular longevity, and delaying age-related decline.

Benefits:

- **Cellular Repair**: Fasting induces autophagy, a cellular cleaning process that removes damaged cells and organelles, promoting cellular rejuvenation and longevity.
- **Mitochondrial Health**: It enhances mitochondrial function and efficiency, supporting energy production, metabolic health, and overall vitality.
- **Anti-Aging Effects**: Fasting may reduce oxidative stress, inflammation, and DNA damage, contributing to anti-aging effects and extending health span.

23. Cultural and Religious Significance of Fasting

Fasting practices are deeply rooted in cultural traditions, religious rituals, and spiritual disciplines.

Benefits:

- **Spiritual Growth**: Fasting fosters spiritual discipline, devotion, and connection to divine principles, enhancing religious observance and community solidarity.
- **Cultural Identity**: It preserves cultural heritage, traditions, and values, promoting a sense of belonging and cultural continuity within communities.
- **Shared Experience**: Participating in communal fasting rituals fosters empathy, compassion, and collective spiritual growth among individuals and communities.

Deduction

Each type of fasting offers distinct benefits that contribute to physical health, mental clarity, emotional well-being, spiritual growth, and overall longevity. Whether practiced for weight management, cognitive enhancement, therapeutic purposes, or spiritual devotion, fasting can be adapted to individual needs, preferences, and cultural contexts.

As you explore different fasting methods and their benefits, consider integrating fasting into a holistic approach to health and well-being. Seek guidance from healthcare professionals or experts to ensure safety, especially when considering therapeutic fasting for specific health conditions.

Accept the true power of fasting as a pathway to personal growth, resilience, and enhanced vitality. Whether embarking on intermittent fasting for metabolic health or spiritual fasting for deeper connection, may your fasting journey be guided by mindfulness, self-awareness, and a commitment to holistic wellness.

24. Fasting for Gut Health

Fasting methods that support digestive health, gut microbiome balance, and overall gastrointestinal function.

Benefits:

- **Digestive Rest**: Fasting periods allow the digestive system to rest, heal, and recover from daily processing of food, promoting optimal gut function.

- **Microbiome Balance**: Fasting can positively influence gut microbiota composition, supporting diversity and beneficial bacteria growth.
- **Reduced Inflammation**: It may reduce gut inflammation markers and symptoms associated with digestive disorders like irritable bowel syndrome (IBS) or leaky gut syndrome.

25. Fasting for Athletic Performance

Fasting strategies used by athletes to optimize performance, recovery, and metabolic efficiency.

Benefits:

- **Fat Adaptation**: Fasting promotes metabolic flexibility, encouraging the body to use stored fat for energy, which can enhance endurance and stamina during prolonged physical activity.
- **Muscle Preservation**: Controlled fasting periods may preserve lean muscle mass while promoting fat loss, optimizing body composition for athletes.
- **Enhanced Recovery**: Fasting may support post-exercise recovery processes, including inflammation reduction and muscle repair mechanisms.

26. Fasting as a Lifestyle Practice

Incorporating fasting into daily routines as a sustainable lifestyle choice for long-term health benefits.

Benefits:

- **Sustainable Weight Management**: Fasting can facilitate weight loss, weight maintenance, and metabolic regulation without constant calorie restriction.
- **Longevity Promotion**: It promotes cellular repair, oxidative stress reduction, and inflammation management, potentially extending lifespan and health span.
- **Holistic Wellness**: Integrating fasting with nutritious eating, regular exercise, and adequate sleep supports holistic wellness, vitality, and disease prevention.

27. Fasting for Personal Growth and Spiritual Renewal

Utilizing fasting as a tool for personal development, spiritual exploration, and inner transformation.

Benefits:

- **Self-Discovery**: Fasting fosters introspection, mindfulness, and self-awareness, facilitating personal growth, clarity of purpose, and alignment with values.
- **Soulful Bond**: It deepens spiritual practices, rituals, and connections to higher consciousness, enhancing spiritual fulfillment and meaning in life.
- **Civic Participation**: Engaging in communal fasting traditions fosters solidarity, empathy, and shared experiences among members of religious or cultural communities. It strengthens bonds and deepens connections through collective participation in spiritual practices.

Deduction

Fasting encompasses a broad spectrum of practices with diverse benefits that extend beyond physical health to encompass mental acuity, emotional resilience, spiritual depth, and overall well-being. Whether approached for weight management, cognitive enhancement, athletic performance, or spiritual devotion, fasting can be tailored to individual needs and goals.

By embracing fasting as a lifestyle practice and integrating it with other health-promoting behaviors, individuals can harness its transformative potential for sustained vitality, resilience, and personal fulfillment. Remember to approach fasting mindfully, seek guidance when needed, and listen to your body's signals to optimize health outcomes and enjoy the journey of self-discovery and holistic wellness.

May your exploration of fasting be guided by curiosity, intentionality, and a commitment to lifelong health and happiness.

28. Fasting for Hormonal Balance

How fasting influences hormonal regulation, endocrine function, and reproductive health.

Benefits:

- **Insulin Sensitivity**: Fasting improves insulin sensitivity, lowers insulin levels, and enhances glucose metabolism, reducing the risk of type 2 diabetes and metabolic syndrome.
- **Hormone Optimization**: It may regulate hormones such as growth hormone (GH), cortisol, and leptin, supporting overall hormonal balance and metabolic efficiency.

- **Fertility Support**: Fasting can promote reproductive health by reducing inflammation, balancing sex hormones, and supporting menstrual regularity in women.

29. Fasting for Cardiovascular Health

How fasting practices contribute to cardiovascular function, heart health, and disease prevention.

Benefits:

- **Heart Disease Prevention**: Fasting may lower blood pressure, improve lipid profiles (cholesterol and triglycerides), and reduce cardiovascular risk factors like inflammation and oxidative stress.
- **Blood Vessel Health**: It supports endothelial function, arterial elasticity, and blood flow regulation, promoting cardiovascular resilience and longevity.
- **Stroke and Heart Attack Prevention**: Fasting may reduce the risk of ischemic events by improving vascular health, metabolic efficiency, and inflammatory markers.

30. Fasting and Cancer Prevention

The potential role of fasting in cancer prevention, treatment support, and metabolic therapy.

Benefits:

- **Cellular Protection**: Fasting induces autophagy and apoptosis in cancer cells, promoting cellular detoxification and reducing tumor growth potential.
- **Metabolic Therapy**: It may enhance the efficacy of cancer treatments like chemotherapy and radiation therapy by sensitizing cancer cells to treatment and protecting healthy cells.
- **Reduced Cancer Risk**: Fasting supports immune function, reduces inflammation, and may lower the risk of certain cancers by inhibiting tumor initiation and progression pathways.

31. Fasting for Immune System Function

How fasting influences immune response, immune cell regeneration, and overall immune system function.

Benefits:

- **Immune Cell Renewal**: Fasting triggers stem cell regeneration of immune cells, rejuvenating the immune system and enhancing defense against infections and diseases.
- **Inflammatory Modulation**: It may reduce chronic inflammation markers, autoimmune responses, and inflammatory conditions by promoting immune system rebalancing.
- **Antimicrobial Defense**: Fasting supports antimicrobial defense mechanisms, enhancing immune surveillance, and response to pathogens.

Petitions for Financial Freedom Through Types of Fasting

Water Fast:

Heavenly Father, as I embark on this water fast, I seek Your guidance and provision in every area of my life, especially my finances. Grant me clarity of mind and spirit to discern Your will clearly. I declare that through this fast, You will open doors of financial opportunity and prosperity according to Your riches in glory. (Philippians 4:19)

Partial Fast:

Lord God, during this partial fast, I humbly come before You, acknowledging my dependence on Your provision. As I deny myself, I ask for Your wisdom to manage my finances wisely and to recognize opportunities for increase. Let this fast be a catalyst for financial breakthroughs and stability in my life. (James 1:5)

Daniel Fast:

Gracious Father, like Daniel and his companions, I commit to this Daniel fast, seeking Your favor and blessing upon my finances. Strengthen me physically and spiritually as I abstain from certain foods. I pray for divine insight into financial matters and supernatural provision beyond my expectations. (Daniel 1:12)

Intermittent Fast:

Lord Jesus, during this intermittent fast, I surrender my financial concerns into Your hands. Help me to discipline my eating habits and use this time of fasting to draw closer to You. I ask for Your guidance in making wise financial decisions and for doors of opportunity to open that lead to financial abundance. (Matthew 6:33)

Extended Fast:

Eternal God, as I embark on this extended fast, I seek Your face earnestly for breakthroughs in my finances. Grant me perseverance and strength throughout this time of consecration. I declare Your promises of provision and prosperity over my life, trusting in Your faithfulness to fulfill them. (Isaiah 58:11)

Scripture References:

- **Philippians 4:19** - "And my God will supply every need of yours according to his riches in glory in Christ Jesus."

- **James 1:5** - "If any of you lacks wisdom, let him ask God, who gives generously to all without reproach, and it will be given him."

- **Daniel 1:12** - "Test your servants for ten days; let us be given vegetables to eat and water to drink."

- **Isaiah 58:11** - "And the LORD will guide you continually and satisfy your desire in scorched places and make your bones strong; and you shall be like a watered garden, like a spring of water, whose waters do not fail."

3-Day Fast:

Heavenly Father, as I begin on this 3-day fast, I surrender my financial worries and concerns into Your hands. Grant me clarity of mind and spirit during this time of consecration. I seek Your divine favor and blessing over my finances, believing that through this fast, You will release financial breakthroughs and provision according to Your will. (Psalm 34:10)

7-Day Fast:

Lord God, as I commit to this 7-day fast, I humbly come before You, acknowledging Your sovereignty over my life and finances. Strengthen me physically, emotionally, and spiritually throughout this period of fasting. I pray for Your divine wisdom to manage my finances wisely and to discern opportunities for financial increase. Let this fast be a catalyst for prosperity and abundance in every area of my life. (Proverbs 3:9-10)

21-Day Fast:

Gracious Father, during this 21-day fast, I dedicate myself to seeking Your face diligently. I surrender all financial struggles and challenges to You, knowing that You are my giver and my supporter. I declare Your promises of provision and prosperity over my life, believing that as I seek You first, all things, including financial stability and breakthroughs, will be added unto me. (Matthew 6:31-33)

40-Day Fast:

Lord Jesus, as I embark on this 40-day fast, I commit my entire being to You. I surrender my desires and ambitions, trusting in Your perfect plan for my life. I declare Your Word that man shall not live by bread alone but by every word that comes from Your mouth. Grant me the strength and perseverance to endure this extended fast, and I believe for unprecedented financial blessings and favor as a result of my obedience and faith in You. (Deuteronomy 8:3)

Scripture References:

- **Psalm 34:10** - "The young lions suffer want and hunger; but those who seek the LORD lack no good thing."

- **Proverbs 3:9-10** - "Honor the LORD with your wealth and with the first fruits of all your produce; then your barns will be filled with plenty, and your vats will be bursting with wine."

- **Matthew 6:31-33** - "Therefore do not be anxious, saying, 'What shall we eat?' or 'What shall we drink?' or 'What shall we wear?' For the Gentiles seek after all these things, and your heavenly Father knows that you need them all. But seek first the kingdom of God and his righteousness, and all these things will be added to you."

- **Deuteronomy 8:3** - "And he humbled you and let you hunger and fed you with manna, which you did not know, nor did your fathers know, that he might make you know that man does not live by bread alone, but man lives by every word that comes from the mouth of the LORD."

Prayer for Debt Freedom:

Lord God, I come to You burdened with debt, seeking Your mercy and grace. I ask for Your supernatural provision and wisdom to break free from financial bondage. Help me to honor You with my finances and to walk in financial freedom, trusting in Your provision and guidance. (Psalm 37:21)

Affirmations for Economic Success Through Types of Fasting and Their Benefits

Water Fast:

I affirm that as I cleanse my body through water fasting, I am also cleansing my financial life, releasing old patterns and welcoming new abundance. (Isaiah 58:8)

I affirm that my clarity of mind and spirit during this water fast allows me to receive divine inspiration for financial breakthroughs. (Philippians 4:7)

I affirm that God's provision flows abundantly to me as I trust in Him during this water fast, opening doors of financial opportunity. (Philippians 4:19)

Partial Fast:

I affirm that through my partial fast, I exercise discipline over my physical appetites, aligning myself with God's plan for financial abundance. (1 Corinthians 9:27)

I affirm that as I seek God diligently in this partial fast, He reveals strategies and ideas for financial success beyond my imagination. (Jeremiah 33:3)

I affirm that my partial fast strengthens my faith, enabling me to walk boldly into the financial promises God has for me. (Hebrews 11:6)

Daniel Fast:

I affirm that during my Daniel fast, I surrender my desires to align with God's will, inviting His favor and blessings into my financial endeavors. (Daniel 1:12)

I affirm that God's wisdom guides me in making sound financial decisions as I honor Him through my Daniel fast. (James 1:5)

I affirm that my Daniel fast empowers me to break financial strongholds and step into a season of unprecedented provision. (Isaiah 58:9-11)

Intermittent Fast:

I affirm that my intermittent fast cultivates discipline and self-control, essential qualities for achieving financial success. (Galatians 5:22-23)

I affirm that as I practice intermittent fasting, I am reminded of my dependence on God, who abundantly supplies all my needs. (Philippians 4:13)

I affirm that my intermittent fast strengthens my resolve to pursue God's financial blessings with faith and perseverance. (Hebrews 10:35)

Positive Affirmations for Financial Stability:

I affirm that God's promises of prosperity and abundance are mine to claim as I commit to fasting and seeking His face. (Deuteronomy 8:18)

I affirm that through fasting, I am positioned to receive divine strategies and solutions for overcoming financial challenges. (Isaiah 40:31)

I affirm that God's grace and favor surround me, opening doors of financial opportunity that no one can shut. (Psalm 84:11)

Affirmations for Financial Stability:

I affirm that I am a wise steward of the financial resources entrusted to me, multiplying them for God's kingdom purposes. (Matthew 25:21)

I affirm that God's provision is more than enough to meet all my financial needs and bless others through me. (2 Corinthians 9:8)

I affirm that I walk in God's divine order and peace concerning my finances, free from anxiety and fear. (Philippians 4:6-7)

Affirmations for Generosity and Impact:

I affirm that God blesses me abundantly so that I may be a blessing to others, sowing seeds of generosity and reaping a harvest of financial blessings. (Luke 6:38)

I affirm that my financial success glorifies God and testifies to His faithfulness and provision in my life. (1 Corinthians 10:31)

3-Day Fast:

I affirm that as I dedicate myself to this 3-day fast, I am positioning myself to receive divine clarity and direction for financial breakthroughs. (James 4:8)

I affirm that during this 3-day fast, God is opening my eyes to see opportunities for financial increase and prosperity that align with His will. (Psalm 119:18)

I affirm that my commitment to seek God through this 3-day fast is paving the way for unexpected financial blessings and favor. (Isaiah 30:18)

7-Day Fast:

I affirm that as I embark on this 7-day fast, I am surrendering my financial worries and anxieties to God, trusting in His provision and care. (Matthew 6:25-26)

I affirm that God's promises of abundance and prosperity are manifesting in my life as I seek Him diligently through this 7-day fast. (Jeremiah 29:13)

I affirm that my faithfulness in this 7-day fast is aligning me with divine opportunities and connections that will lead to financial success. (Proverbs 3:5-6)

21-Day Fast:

I affirm that during this 21-day fast, I am renewing my mind and spirit, preparing myself to receive God's supernatural provision and blessings in my finances. (Romans 12:2)

I affirm that as I commit to this 21-day fast, God is breaking every chain of financial bondage and releasing me into a season of unprecedented abundance. (Isaiah 58:6-11)

I affirm that my endurance and perseverance in this 21-day fast are positioning me to inherit God's promises of financial prosperity. (Hebrews 10:36)

40-Day Fast:

I affirm that as I embark on this 40-day fast, I am consecrating myself to God's purposes and opening myself up to His supernatural provision and favor. (Matthew 4:4)

I affirm that God's promises of prosperity and success are my portion as I seek Him wholeheartedly through this 40-day fast. (Joshua 1:8)

I affirm that my commitment to this 40-day fast is releasing divine strategies and solutions for financial breakthroughs that will impact generations. (Isaiah 58:9-12)

Additional Financial Mastery Affirmations:

Affirmations for Financial Stability:

I affirm that God is my provider, and His faithfulness ensures my financial stability in all circumstances. (Philippians 4:19)

I affirm that I am a wise steward of the resources entrusted to me, multiplying them for God's kingdom purposes. (Matthew 25:21)

I affirm that God's wisdom guides me in making sound financial decisions that lead to prosperity and success. (James 1:5)

Affirmations for Generosity and Impact:

I affirm that my generosity opens doors of opportunity and favor that lead to greater financial abundance. (Luke 6:38)

Prayers:

Prayer for Spiritual Strength

Heavenly Father, in this journey of fasting, I come before You with a heart filled with reverence and expectation. Grant me, O Lord, the strength to persevere through this time of fasting. As I deny myself physical nourishment, may Your Spirit nourish my soul. Help me to rely on Your strength and not on my own understanding. Let Your presence be my sustenance, filling me with spiritual vigor and resolve. Psalm 28:7 reminds me that "The Lord is my strength and my shield; my heart trusts in him, and he helps me."

Prayer for Spiritual Insight

O God, Your Word brightens my walk and shows me the way (Psalm 119:105). During this period of fasting, open my eyes to see the truths hidden in Your word. Illuminate my mind with Your wisdom and understanding. As I seek Your face in prayer and fasting, reveal Your will for my life. Let Your Holy Spirit guide me into all truth, leading me in paths of righteousness for Your name's sake.

Prayer for Emotional Healing

Loving Father, You are the healer of our broken hearts and wounded spirits. As I fast before You, I bring my emotional burdens and pains. Heal the hurts that linger within me. Pour out Your comfort and peace upon my soul. Help me to forgive others as You have forgiven me, releasing bitterness and resentment. May Your love overflow in my heart, filling me with joy unspeakable and full of glory.

Prayer for Physical Strength

Gracious God, You are the giver of life and health. During this time of fasting, I present my body as a living sacrifice, holy and pleasing to You (Romans 12:1). Strengthen my physical body as I abstain from food. Renew my energy and vitality. Grant me restful sleep and rejuvenate my weary limbs. May Your healing touch be upon me, restoring every cell and fiber of my being.

Prayer for Family and Relationships

Heavenly Father, I lift up my family and relationships before You during this time of fasting. Strengthen the bonds of love and unity among us. Heal any rifts or misunderstandings. May Your peace reign in our homes and hearts. Help us to love one another with Your unconditional love. Protect us from harm and danger. May our lives be a testimony of Your grace and mercy.

Prayer for Spiritual Revival

O Lord, stir within me a hunger and thirst for righteousness (Matthew 5:6). Revive my spirit as I seek Your face in fasting and prayer. Awaken within me a passion for Your kingdom and Your righteousness. Renew my zeal for Your glory. Use me as a vessel of Your love and grace in this world. Let Your kingdom come, and Your will be done in my life and in the lives of those around me.

Prayer for Humility and Surrender

Gracious God, during this time of fasting, I humble myself before You. Strip away any pride or self-reliance. Teach me the beauty of surrendering to Your will. Mold me and shape me according to Your purposes. May my life bring honor and glory to Your name. Help me to walk in humility, considering others better than myself. Fill me with Your Spirit of gentleness and meekness.

Prayer for the Nations and Leaders

Lord, Your word instructs us to pray for all people, for kings and all those in authority (1 Timothy 2:1-2). I lift up the nations of the world and their leaders before You. Grant them wisdom and discernment. Guide them in decisions that promote justice, peace, and righteousness. May Your kingdom come and Your will be done on earth as it is in heaven. Use Your church to be a light and salt in every nation.

Fasting continues to demonstrate multifaceted benefits that span physical health, mental clarity, emotional resilience, spiritual growth, and ethical considerations. Whether adopted for hormonal balance, cardiovascular health, cancer prevention, immune system function, or ethical eating practices, fasting offers diverse pathways to personal and planetary well-being.

By integrating fasting with holistic lifestyle practices, nutritional education, and community engagement, individuals can optimize health outcomes, cultivate sustainable habits, and contribute to global health and environmental stewardship. Embrace the transformative potential of fasting as a journey of self-discovery, empowerment, and holistic wellness, ensuring each fasting practice aligns with personal values, health goals, and ethical principles.

Chapter 13:

Praying for Financial Breakthrough: Seeking Yahweh's Provision

Prayer is a powerful conduit for seeking Yahweh's provision and experiencing financial breakthrough. This chapter explores the transformative impact of prayer in aligning your financial goals with Yahweh's divine plan. By cultivating a heart of gratitude, surrender, and faith through prayer, you open yourself to Yahweh's abundant blessings and provision. Embrace prayer as a cornerstone of your financial journey, believing in Yahweh's promise to supply all your needs according to His riches in glory.

Yahweh desires to bless you abundantly in every area of your life, including your finances. As you commit your financial aspirations and challenges to Yahweh through prayer, trust in His faithfulness and provision to guide you toward financial abundance and stewardship. Embrace prayer as a sacred dialogue with Yahweh, inviting His wisdom, favor, and breakthrough into your financial circumstances. Align your heart with Yahweh's will and timing, knowing that He delights in blessing His children with prosperity and peace.

In our journey of faith, seeking a financial breakthrough is a pivotal moment where we align our desires with God's will for our lives. This breakthrough signifies a profound change and divine intervention in our financial circumstances. Whether facing job loss, medical challenges, or other financial pressures, we come to Yahweh, acknowledging His sovereignty over all creation and every aspect of our lives (Psalm 24:1).

Yahweh, the Eternal One, owns everything in the heavens and the earth (Haggai 2:8). His ownership extends beyond material wealth to encompass wisdom, provision, and blessings. As we approach Him in prayer, we recognize that all our needs are met through His abundant grace and provision (Philippians 4:19).

In this comprehensive section, we explore the spiritual discipline of fasting to seek financial breakthroughs. Fasting, throughout history, has been practiced by various religious and spiritual traditions to deepen one's connection with the divine and align oneself with spiritual truths that can bring about transformative change, including in the realm of finances.

Names of Yahweh: Understanding His Provision and Blessing

Yahweh-Jireh: The Lord Will Provide

Yahweh-Jireh, meaning "The Lord Will Provide," signifies God's faithfulness in meeting our needs. This name was revealed when Abraham, in obedience, prepared to sacrifice Isaac, and God provided a ram as a substitute (Genesis 22:14). When we pray for financial breakthrough, we trust in Yahweh-Jireh's promise to provide abundantly according to His will (Matthew 6:31-32).

Prayer and Affirmation:

"Yahweh-Jireh, thank you for your promise to provide for all my needs. As I seek your guidance and trust in your provision, I declare that you are my provider in every circumstance. Help me manage my resources wisely and glorify you with my financial stewardship. Amen."

Yahweh-Rapha: The Lord Who Heals

Yahweh-Rapha, meaning "The Lord Who Heals," reveals God's ability to heal not only physical ailments but also financial wounds and uncertainties. This name emphasizes restoration and renewal, aligning our financial situations with God's divine healing power (Jeremiah 30:17).

Prayer and Affirmation:

"Yahweh-Rapha, I come to you with my financial struggles, seeking your healing touch upon my finances. Heal the brokenness and uncertainties and guide me in making wise financial decisions that honor you. I trust in your promise to restore and renew every area of my life. Amen."

Yahweh-Nissi: The Lord Is My Banner

Yahweh-Nissi, meaning "The Lord Is My Banner," signifies victory and protection. This name was proclaimed by Moses after defeating the Amalekites, symbolizing God's presence and triumph in our battles (Exodus 17:15). When praying for financial breakthrough, we declare Yahweh-Nissi's victory over financial challenges and trust in His guidance and protection.

Prayer and Affirmation:

"Yahweh-Nissi, I lift my financial struggles to you, knowing that you are my banner of victory. Protect me from financial harm and guide me toward financial stability and prosperity. I declare your victory over every financial challenge I face. Thank you for being my refuge and strength. Amen."

Trusting in Yahweh's Promises

In our pursuit of financial breakthrough, we are reminded of Yahweh's promises throughout Scripture. Each name of God reveals His character and assures us of His unwavering presence and provision in our lives. As we pray and meditate on these truths, we are encouraged to align our hearts with God's will, knowing that He desires to bless us abundantly (Matthew 6:33).

Let us hold fast to the assurance that Yahweh hears our prayers for financial breakthrough. Through His names and promises, we find strength and hope in navigating financial challenges. Let us continue to seek Yahweh's wisdom, provision, and guidance, trusting in His unfailing love and care for us (Psalm 37:25).

You are uniquely endowed with the divine potential to manifest greatness in every aspect of your life. Yahweh, the provider of all things, has ordained you not to merely survive but to thrive abundantly. Your financial journey is not just about accumulating wealth but about aligning your spirit with Yahweh's purposeful plan for your life. Through prayer and fasting, you tap into a realm where barriers are shattered, and blessings overflow.

Exploring Yahweh's Provisions Through Prayer

At the core of your financial breakthrough lies the practice of fervent prayer. Prayer is your direct line of communication with Yahweh, where petitions are transformed into manifestations of His grace and favor. As you embark on this journey, remember that Yahweh's promises are steadfast, and His provision knows no bounds. Each prayer you utter is a declaration of faith, a steppingstone towards the abundance that awaits.

Detailing the Power of Affirmations

Affirmations are powerful tools that align your thoughts and words with the promises of Yahweh. They serve as daily reminders of His faithfulness and your unwavering belief in His provision. By speaking affirmations of financial breakthrough, you invite Yahweh's blessings to permeate every aspect of your life, creating a fertile ground for prosperity and success.

Psalms for Protection: Shielding Your Journey

While seeking financial prosperity, protection is paramount. The Psalms serve as a shield of divine protection, enveloping you in Yahweh's unfailing love and guarding your path against adversity. Incorporating Psalms of protection into your prayers fortifies your spirit and ensures that your journey towards financial breakthrough is guided by Yahweh's sovereign hand.

Psalms for Financial Breakthrough: Declaring Abundance

Yahweh delights in your prosperity and longs to bless you abundantly. The Psalms resonate with declarations of financial abundance, affirming Yahweh's promise to provide for His children beyond measure. By meditating on and proclaiming these Psalms, you align your heart with Yahweh's will, inviting His overflowing blessings into your financial endeavors.

Scripture References: Anchoring Your Faith

Throughout this chapter, you will find scripture references that underscore Yahweh's faithfulness in providing for His people. These references serve as anchors for your faith, reminding you of Yahweh's enduring promises and His commitment to bless those who seek Him wholeheartedly.

Prayers of Supplications for Wealth Creation

Prayer for Financial Wisdom

Lord Yahweh, grant me the wisdom of Solomon to make sound financial decisions (James 1:5). Help me to be diligent in my work and faithful in managing the resources You have entrusted to me (Luke 16:10). May Your wisdom guide me in investments, savings, and spending, so that I may honor You with my financial stewardship.

Prayer for Debt Freedom

Yahweh, I lift up my financial burdens before You. Your Word promises that the borrower is servant to the lender (Proverbs 22:7), but You have the power to release me from bondage. Grant me the discipline to manage my finances responsibly and the perseverance to break free from debt. Provide opportunities and strategies for me to become debt-free, that I may glorify You with my financial freedom.

Prayer for Financial Increase and Abundance

Yahweh, You are the God of abundance who desires to bless Your children exceedingly and abundantly above all that we ask or think (Ephesians 3:20). I pray for supernatural financial increase and overflow in my life, according to Your will and purpose. May Your blessings pour out upon me and my household, that we may be a testimony of Your goodness and provision (Malachi 3:10).

Prayer for Wisdom in Giving and Saving

Lord Yahweh, grant me discernment and wisdom in how I give and how I save. Help me to be a cheerful giver, knowing that You love a cheerful giver who gives generously (2 Corinthians 9:7). Teach me to save diligently for the future, understanding that You provide for both my present needs and my future security (Proverbs 21:20).

Prayer for Protection from Financial Hardship

Heavenly Father, shield me and my family from financial hardship and unexpected expenses. Your Word assures me that You are my refuge and strength, a very present help in trouble (Psalm 46:1). Protect us from financial crises and grant us Your peace that surpasses all understanding (Philippians 4:7).

Prayer for Thankfulness and Gratitude

Yahweh, I thank You for Your faithfulness and provision in my life. Help me to cultivate a heart of gratitude and thanksgiving, knowing that every good and perfect gift comes from You (James 1:17). May my life be a continual offering of praise to Your holy name, for You alone are worthy of all honor and glory (Revelation 4:11).

Prayer for Contentment and Trust

Heavenly Father, teach me to find contentment in You alone, knowing that godliness with contentment is great gain (1 Timothy 6:6). Help me to trust in Your provision and to seek Your kingdom above all else, confident that You will supply all my needs according to Your riches in glory (Matthew 6:33; Philippians 4:19).

Prayer for Guidance in Investments

Yahweh, I seek Your guidance in financial investments. Grant me discernment to make wise choices and to honor You with the resources You have entrusted to me (Proverbs 3:9-10). May my investments bring glory to Your name and bear fruit that blesses others and advances Your kingdom (Luke 12:33).

Prayer for a Prosperous Household

Lord Yahweh, I lift up my household before You. Bless our finances and establish us as a testimony of Your provision and faithfulness (Psalm 128:1-2). Strengthen the bonds of love and unity within my family, that we may steward our resources wisely and honor You in all that we do (Proverbs 15:27).

Prayer for Open Doors of Opportunity

Heavenly Father, open doors of opportunity for financial prosperity and advancement in my career/business. Your Word declares that You open doors that no one can shut and shut doors that no one can open (Revelation 3:8). I trust in Your perfect timing and divine orchestration of my life's journey (Isaiah 22:22).

Prayer for Generational Blessings

Yahweh, I pray for generational blessings upon my descendants. May Your favor rest upon them, and may they continue to walk in Your ways and experience Your provision throughout their lives (Psalm 103:17). Grant me wisdom to lay a foundation of faithfulness and stewardship that extends to future generations (Proverbs 13:22).

Prayer for a Spirit of Excellence

Lord Yahweh, I commit my work and endeavors to You. Grant me a spirit of excellence and integrity in all my financial dealings (Daniel 6:3). May my commitment to honor You through my work attract Your favor and blessings, setting me apart for Your purposes (Proverbs 22:29).

Prayer for Supernatural Breakthrough

Heavenly Father, I pray for supernatural breakthrough in my financial situation. You are the God of miracles who makes a way where there seems to be no way (Isaiah 43:19). Remove every obstacle and hindrance that stands in the way of Your blessings and provision in my life (Psalm 18:29).

Prayer for God's Favor and Blessing

Yahweh, I seek Your favor and blessing upon my financial endeavors. Your Word promises that the blessing of the Lord makes rich, and You add no sorrow with it (Proverbs 10:22). Let Your favor surround me like a shield, opening doors of opportunity and prosperity that come only from You (Psalm 5:12).

Prayer for Restoring What is Lost

Lord Yahweh, I surrender to You the areas of my life where financial loss has occurred. Your Word assures me that You are a God of restoration who can redeem what the enemy has stolen (Joel 2:25-26). Restore unto me the years that the locusts have eaten and bless me with abundance beyond measure (Job 42:10).

Prayer for Continued Faithfulness

Heavenly Father, thank You for Your faithfulness throughout my financial journey. As I continue to seek Your provision and guidance, strengthen my faith and renew my trust in Your promises (Hebrews 10:23). Help me to walk in obedience and surrender to Your will, cognizant that You are combining all things for my growth (Romans 8:28).

Prayer for Humility and Gratitude

Heavenly Father, I come before You with a heart of humility and gratitude. You have blessed me abundantly, and I acknowledge that every good and perfect gift comes from You (James 1:17). Help me to steward Your blessings with humility, gratitude, and a heart that seeks to glorify Your name in all circumstances (Colossians 3:17).

Prayer for Diligence and Hard Work

Lord Yahweh, I commit to working diligently and with excellence in all that I do. Your Word encourages me to work heartily unto You, knowing that my labor in the Lord is not in vain (Colossians 3:23-24). Grant me strength and perseverance to pursue my goals with integrity and diligence, trusting in Your provision and guidance (Proverbs 14:23).

Prayer for Overcoming Financial Fear and Anxiety

Yahweh, I surrender my fears and anxieties about finances into Your hands. Your Word assures me that You have not given me a spirit of fear, but of power, love, and a sound mind (2 Timothy 1:7). Grant me peace and confidence in Your provision, knowing that You are my provider and protector (Philippians 4:6-7).

Prayer for Wisdom in Financial Planning

Heavenly Father, grant me wisdom and discernment in financial planning and decision-making. Your Word instructs me to plan diligently and seek counsel, knowing that with wise guidance, plans succeed (Proverbs 15:22; Proverbs 21:5). Guide me in setting goals that align with Your purposes and stewarding resources wisely for Your glory (1 Corinthians 10:31).

Prayer for Supernatural Increase and Abundance

Yahweh, I pray for supernatural increase and abundance in my financial life. Your Word promises that You are able to do exceedingly abundantly above all that we ask or think, according to the power that works in us (Ephesians 3:20). I declare Your blessings of prosperity and overflow over every area of my finances, trusting in Your provision and grace (Malachi 3:10).

Prayer for Favor in Financial Negotiations

Lord Yahweh, I seek Your favor and guidance in all financial negotiations and transactions. Your Word assures me that You bless the work of my hands and establish the plans of my heart (Psalm 90:17). Grant me favor and wisdom as I navigate financial agreements and contracts, that Your will may be done in all things (Proverbs 3:5-6).

Wealth Building Affirmations

Affirmation of Trust in Yahweh's Provision

I trust in Yahweh with all my heart and lean not on my own understanding. In all my ways, I acknowledge Him, and He directs my paths. (Proverbs 3:5-6)

Affirmation of Abundance and Overflow

The blessing of Yahweh makes rich, and He adds no sorrow with it. I walk in His abundance and overflow in every area of my life. (Proverbs 10:22)

Affirmation of Wisdom and Discernment

Yahweh grants me wisdom generously when I ask, and He guides my financial decisions with His discernment. (James 1:5)

Affirmation of Prosperity and Success

Yahweh delights in my prosperity and success. I am blessed to be a blessing, and His favor rests upon me in all that I do. (Psalm 1:3)

Affirmation of Generosity and Blessing Others

I am a cheerful giver, and Yahweh blesses me abundantly so that I can be a blessing to others. My generosity opens doors of opportunity and favor. (2 Corinthians 9:7-8)

Affirmation of God's Abundant Provision

Yahweh supplies all my needs according to His riches in glory. I lack nothing, for He is my provider and sustainer. (Philippians 4:19)

Affirmation of Security in Yahweh's Care

I am rooted and established in Yahweh's love and provision. My finances are secure under His divine protection. (Psalm 16:5-6)

Affirmation of Supernatural Increase and Prosperity

Yahweh blesses the work of my hands and causes me to prosper. I walk in supernatural increase and prosperity in all my endeavors. (Deuteronomy 28:8)

Affirmation of Divine Guidance and Direction

Yahweh guides my steps and directs my path. I walk in His divine guidance, leading to financial breakthroughs and prosperity. (Proverbs 3:6)

Affirmation of Fearlessness in Financial Challenges

I am fearless in the face of financial challenges, for Yahweh is with me. He strengthens and upholds me with His righteous right hand. (Isaiah 41:10)

Affirmation of Open Doors and Divine Opportunities

Divine doors of opportunity and favor open before me. Yahweh's favor surrounds me like a shield, leading to greater financial blessings. (Psalm 5:12)

Affirmation of Confidence in Yahweh's Provision

I am confident in Yahweh's provision for my life. He is my provider and sustainer, and I rest in His unfailing love and care. (Psalm 55:22)

Affirmation of Financial Increase and Harvest

Yahweh brings increase and harvest into my life. I sow seeds of faith and generosity, reaping a bountiful harvest of blessings and provision. (Galatians 6:9)

Affirmation of Peace and Contentment in Yahweh

Yahweh's peace guards my heart and mind in Christ Jesus. I am content in His presence, knowing that He supplies all my needs according to His riches. (Philippians 4:7-19)

Affirmation of Supernatural Debt Cancellation

Yahweh cancels my debts and releases me from financial bondage. I walk in freedom and abundance, trusting in His miraculous provision. (Isaiah 43:25)

Affirmation of Victory and Success

I am more than a conqueror through Yahweh who loves me. I walk in victory over financial challenges, knowing that He fights for me." (Romans 8:37)

Affirmation of Gratitude and Thankfulness

I am grateful for Yahweh's abundant blessings in my life. I give thanks in all circumstances, knowing that He works all things together for my good. (1 Thessalonians 5:18)

Affirmation of Faith in Yahweh's Promises

I stand on Yahweh's promises of provision and blessing. His word is my foundation, and I declare His faithfulness over my financial future. (Psalm 119:105)

Affirmation of Trusting God's Timing

I trust in Yahweh's perfect timing for my financial breakthrough. He makes all things beautiful in His time. (Ecclesiastes 3:11)

Affirmation of Walking in God's Favor

Yahweh's favor surrounds me like a shield, and doors of opportunity and blessing open before me. I walk in His favor and grace. (Psalm 84:11)

Affirmation of Supernatural Provision

Yahweh is my provider, and His provision surpasses all understanding. I trust in His abundant supply for every area of my life. (Philippians 4:7)

Affirmation of Wisdom and Discernment

Yahweh grants me wisdom and discernment in financial matters. I make wise decisions that honor Him and lead to prosperity. (Proverbs 3:13)

Affirmation of Abundant Blessings

Yahweh blesses me abundantly and makes me a channel of His blessings to others. I walk in His favor and generosity. (Ephesians 1:3)

Affirmation of Trusting in Yahweh's Care

I cast all my cares upon Yahweh, for He cares for me. I rest in His provision and trust in His unfailing love. (1 Peter 5:7)

Affirmation of Divine Favor and Blessing

Yahweh's favor is upon me, and His blessings overtake me. I am blessed to be a blessing, walking in His abundance and grace." (Psalm 23:6)

Affirmation of Confidence in Yahweh's Promises

I am confident in Yahweh's promises of provision and blessing. He is faithful, and His word never fails. (Hebrews 10:23)

Affirmation of Gratitude and Thankfulness

I am grateful for Yahweh's provision and blessings in my life. I give thanks in all circumstances, knowing that He is working for my good. (Romans 8:28)

Affirmation of Security in Yahweh's Love

Yahweh's love surrounds me, and His provision sustains me. I am secure in His care and confident in His provision for my life. (Psalm 91:4)

Affirmation of Supernatural Favor in Business

Yahweh's favor rests upon my business endeavors. Doors of opportunity open, and I walk in supernatural favor and success. (Psalm 90:17)

Affirmation of Financial Strength and Stability

I am strong and courageous in Yahweh's strength. He establishes my finances on a firm foundation, securing my future. (Psalm 18:32-34)

Affirmation of Wisdom in Financial Planning

Yahweh grants me wisdom in financial planning. I steward His resources faithfully, honoring Him in all financial decisions. (Proverbs 16:3)

Affirmation of Prosperity in Adversity

Even in times of adversity, Yahweh blesses me with prosperity. I am resilient and thrive under His divine provision. (Isaiah 58:11)

Declaration of Bountiful Yield and Increase

Yahweh blesses the work of my hands with abundant harvest and increase. I am fruitful and multiply in His provision. (Genesis 1:28)

Affirmation of God's Faithfulness in Provision

Yahweh is faithful to provide for all my needs. His promises endure forever, and His provision sustains me. (Psalm 145:13)

Affirmation of Courage in Financial Challenges

I face financial challenges with courage and faith. Yahweh is my strength and shield, and I overcome obstacles in His power. (Psalm 28:7)

Affirmation of Overflowing Blessings

Yahweh showers me with overflowing blessings. I receive His abundance and share His goodness with others. (Malachi 3:10)

Affirmation of Steadfast Trust in Yahweh

My trust in Yahweh remains steadfast. He is my rock and fortress, providing security and stability in all circumstances. (Psalm 62:6)

Affirmation of Abundance in Yahweh's Kingdom

Yahweh's kingdom is marked by abundance and prosperity. I am a citizen of His kingdom, receiving His blessings and favor. (Matthew 6:33)

Affirmation of God's Provision in Times of Need

Yahweh provides for me abundantly in times of need. His grace is sufficient, and I lack nothing in His provision. (2 Corinthians 9:8)

Affirmation of Victory Over Financial Challenges

I am victorious over every financial challenge. Yahweh fights for me, and I walk in His victory and triumph. (Exodus 14:14)

Affirmation of Abundant Provision in Yahweh's Presence

In Yahweh's presence, there is fullness of joy and provision. I dwell in His presence, receiving His abundant blessings. (Psalm 16:11)

Affirmation of God's Promises in Financial Challenges

I stand on Yahweh's promises in times of financial challenge. His words sustain me, and His provision never fails. (Isaiah 41:10)

Affirmation of Trusting Yahweh's Timing

Yahweh's timing is perfect for my financial breakthrough. I wait upon Him with patience, knowing He makes all things beautiful in His time. (Ecclesiastes 3:11)

Psalm 55:22 (NIV):

Cast your cares on the LORD and he will sustain you; he will never let the righteous be shaken.

This verse encourages believers to trust in God's provision and care. By relying on Him, especially during times of financial difficulty or uncertainty, you can find strength and stability.

Luke 6:38 (NIV):

Give, and it will be given to you. A good measure, pressed down, shaken together and running over, will be poured into your lap. For with the measure you use, it will be measured to you.

This verse emphasizes the principle of generosity and giving. When you give freely and generously, not only in financial terms but also in kindness and love, God promises abundant blessings in return.

Matthew 6:19-21 (NIV):

Do not store up for yourselves treasures on earth, where moths and vermin destroy, and where thieves break in and steal. But store up for yourselves treasures in heaven, where moths and vermin do not destroy, and where thieves do not break in and steal. For where your treasure is, there your heart will be also.

These verses teach the importance of prioritizing spiritual wealth over material possessions. By focusing on eternal treasures and investing in God's kingdom, you align your heart and priorities with God's will, which leads to lasting fulfillment and blessings.

Philippians 4:6-7 (NIV):

Do not be anxious about anything, but in every situation, by prayer and petition, with thanksgiving, present your requests to God. And the peace of God, which transcends all understanding, will guard your hearts and your minds in Christ Jesus.

These verses offer reassurance and guidance on dealing with financial worries and anxieties. Instead of dwelling on concerns, turn to prayer, trusting that God hears your requests and will provide according to His perfect will. This passage promises peace that surpasses human understanding, guarding your heart and mind in Christ Jesus.

These powerful Bible verses on financial breakthrough serve as a source of strength, encouragement, and guidance for anyone seeking stability and blessings in their financial life. By studying and applying these scriptures, you can deepen your faith, align your priorities with God's kingdom, and experience the peace and provision that comes from trusting in Him.

As you meditate on these verses, consider how you can incorporate their teachings into your daily life. Whether you're facing financial challenges, seeking to grow in generosity, or striving to align your heart with God's will, these scriptures provide timeless wisdom and promises from God's Word.

2 Corinthians 9:6-8 (NIV):

Remember this: Whoever sows sparingly will also reap sparingly, and whoever sows generously will also reap generously. Each of you should give what you have decided in your heart to give, not reluctantly or under compulsion, for God loves a cheerful giver. And God is able to bless you abundantly, so that in all things at all times, having all that you need, you will abound in every good work.

These verses highlight the principle of sowing and reaping in generosity. When you give joyfully and generously, relinquishing to God's abundance, He promises to bless you abundantly, enabling you to continue being a blessing to others.

Proverbs 22:9 (NIV):

The generous will themselves be blessed, for they share their food with the poor.

Generosity is not only about financial giving but also extends to sharing resources and blessings with those in need. This verse underscores the reciprocal blessing that comes from a generous heart.

1 Timothy 6:17-19 (NIV):

Command those who are rich in this present world not to be arrogant nor to put their hope in wealth, which is so uncertain, but to put their hope in God, who richly provides us with everything for our enjoyment. Command them to do good, to be rich in good deeds, and to be generous and willing to share. In this way, they will lay up treasure for themselves as a firm foundation for the coming age, so that they may take hold of the life that is truly life.

These verses provide guidance for those who possess wealth and resources. Instead of trusting in wealth alone, they are encouraged to trust in God, use their wealth for good deeds and generosity, thereby storing up eternal treasures and securing a meaningful life in God's kingdom.

These additional Bible verses for financial breakthrough underscore the importance of trust, generosity, and prioritizing God in our financial lives. By aligning our actions with God's principles and trusting in His provision, we invite His blessings and experience His faithfulness in every aspect of our lives, including finances.

As you reflect on these scriptures, consider how you can apply their teachings to your own financial journey. Whether you are facing challenges, seeking to grow in generosity, or striving to honor God with your resources, these verses offer timeless wisdom and promises from God's Word.

May these scriptures inspire and encourage you to trust in God's provision, live generously, and experience His abundant blessings in your financial life and beyond. Remember, God is faithful, and He delights in blessing His children according to His riches and purposes.

Psalm 37:25 (NIV):

I was young and now I am old, yet I have never seen the righteous forsaken or their children begging bread.

This verse speaks to God's faithfulness in providing for His people. Throughout their lives, those who trust in Him are not abandoned or left in want. It's a comforting reminder that God cares for His children and meets their needs.

Psalm 34:10 (NIV):

The lions may grow weak and hungry, but those who seek the LORD lack no good thing.

This verse illustrates that those who seek God and His ways will lack nothing good. It's a reassurance that God's provision extends beyond mere material needs to encompass everything that is good for His children.

Reflection and Application

These Bible verses offer profound insights and promises regarding financial provision and God's faithfulness. They encourage us to trust in God's provision, prioritize His kingdom, and live generously towards others. Here are a few ways to reflect and apply these teachings:

- **Trust in God's Provision:** Reflect on times when God has provided for you and your family. Trust that He will continue to meet your needs according to His riches.
- **Generosity:** Consider how you can be more generous with your finances, time, and resources. Giving opens the way for God's blessings to flow into your life.

- **Seeking God's Kingdom:** Make it a priority to seek God's kingdom and righteousness in your daily life. Trust that as you prioritize Him, He will take care of your needs.
- **Freedom from Worry:** Release any anxieties about finances into God's hands. He knows your needs and promises to provide abundantly for those who trust in Him.

As you meditate on these scriptures and apply their principles in your life, may you experience God's faithfulness and provision in profound ways. His promises are true, and His blessings are abundant for those who seek Him wholeheartedly.

- **Stewardship:** Reflect on how you manage your finances. Are you being a good steward of the resources God has entrusted to you? Seek wisdom in financial decisions and strive to honor God with your financial choices.
- **Faith in God's Timing:** Sometimes, God's provision may not come immediately or in the way we expect. Trust in His perfect timing and remain steadfast in faith. He knows what you need and will provide according to His will.
- **Gratitude and Thanksgiving:** Cultivate a heart of gratitude for God's provision, both past and present. Express thanksgiving regularly, acknowledging God's faithfulness in providing for your needs.
- **Seeking Wisdom:** Continually seek wisdom and knowledge in financial matters. Educate yourself about budgeting, saving, investing, and stewardship principles that align with biblical values.
- **Service and Giving:** Look for opportunities to serve others and give generously. God blesses a cheerful giver (2 Corinthians 9:7), and your generosity can impact lives and further God's kingdom.

Petition Prayer for Economic Advancement:

Let's conclude with a prayer based on these reflections:

"Heavenly Father, I come before You with gratitude for Your faithfulness and provision in my life. Thank You for promising to meet all my needs according to Your glorious riches in Christ Jesus. Help me to trust in Your timing and to seek Your kingdom above all else. Grant me wisdom to steward my finances wisely and to honor You in all my financial decisions.

Lord, I release any worries or anxieties about my financial situation into Your hands. You know my needs, and I trust in Your perfect provision. Unlock new avenues of opportunity and favor the labor of my hands, so that I may thrive and bring blessings to others. Teach me to be generous and to give cheerfully, knowing that You bless those who give freely.

Thank You, Lord, for Your promises in Scripture that assure me of Your provision and care. May Your peace guard my heart and mind as I navigate financial challenges. In Jesus' name, Amen."

Yahweh-Jireh: The Lord Will Provide

Yahweh-Jireh, the God who provides abundantly for His people, I come before you with a heart full of gratitude. You are the source of all wealth and provision. Your Word declares in Philippians 4:19, "And my God will supply every need of yours according to his riches in glory in Christ Jesus." I claim this promise over my life today, trusting in your unfailing provision.

Father, I bring before you my financial needs and challenges. You know the burdens I carry and the uncertainties I face. I ask for your wisdom to manage my finances with diligence and integrity. Grant me the wisdom to oversee your entrusted blessings with integrity. Open doors of opportunity for income and financial growth. Provide me with creative ideas and opportunities to increase my income and overcome financial obstacles.

Lord, I declare your Word from Psalm 37:25, "I have been young, and now am old, yet I have not seen the righteous forsaken or his children begging for bread." I rely on your steadfastness to meet every one of my needs from your boundless abundance. Thank you, Yahweh-Jireh, for your provision that goes beyond my understanding and sustains me in every season of life.

Affirmation Prayers for Yahweh-Jireh

1. **Declaration of Trust**: Heavenly Father, I trust in your provision. You are Yahweh-Jireh, my provider. I declare that my needs are met abundantly through your grace and power.
2. **Confidence in Provision**: Lord, I believe that you supply all my needs according to your riches in glory. I receive your provision with thanksgiving and trust in your perfect timing.
3. **Wisdom in Stewardship**: Father, grant me wisdom to manage my finances wisely. Help me to honor you with my wealth and to steward resources faithfully for your kingdom's sake.

4. **Open Doors of Opportunity**: Yahweh-Jireh, open doors of opportunity for financial increase and prosperity. Lead me to avenues where I can use my skills and talents to generate income and bless others.
5. **Faith in Your Promises**: Thank you, Lord, for your promises of provision. I stand on your Word and declare that you are faithful to fulfill all that you have promised concerning my financial well-being.
6. **Gratitude for Provision**: Heavenly Father, I am grateful for your daily provision in my life. You provide abundantly, and I praise you for your faithfulness and love.
7. **Confidence in Your Timing**: Lord, I trust in your perfect timing for financial breakthroughs. Help me to wait patiently and expectantly for your provision to manifest in my life.
8. **Generosity and Sharing**: Father, teach me to be generous and willing to share as you have commanded. May I use the blessings you provide to bless others and advance your kingdom on earth.
9. **Freedom from Anxiety**: Yahweh-Jireh, I surrender my worries and anxieties about finances into your hands. Replace my fears with faith in your provision and peace that surpasses all understanding.
10. **Continued Trust and Dependence**: Lord, I commit my financial future into your hands. I choose to trust in you and depend on your unfailing provision each day.

These prayers and affirmations are designed to align your heart with God's promises for financial breakthrough and provision. May they strengthen your faith and bring you closer to experiencing the abundance that Yahweh-Jireh desires for His children.

Yahweh-Jireh: The Lord Will Provide

Heavenly Father, Yahweh-Jireh, I come before you with a heart full of gratitude and expectation. Your Word declares in Matthew 6:31-33, "Therefore do not be anxious, saying, 'What shall we eat?' or 'What shall we drink?' or 'What shall we wear?' For the Gentiles seek after all these things, and your heavenly Father knows that you need them all. But seek first the kingdom of God and his righteousness, and all these things will be added to you." I choose to seek your kingdom first, trusting in your promise to provide for all my needs.

Lord, I bring before you my financial situation. You know my desires and the challenges I face. Grant me wisdom to make sound financial decisions and to honor you with my finances. Open doors of opportunity for new streams of income and financial increase. Guide me to resources and connections that will help me achieve financial stability and abundance.

Father, I declare your Word from Psalm 23:1, "The Lord is my shepherd; I shall not want." I believe in your provision that exceeds my expectations and sustains me in every season of life. Thank you, Yahweh-Jireh, for your faithfulness and provision that never fails.

Affirmation Prayers for Divine Guidance

1. **Guidance in Decision-Making**: Heavenly Father, guide me in making wise financial decisions. Grant me clarity of mind and discernment to choose paths that align with your will and purpose for my life.
2. **Stewardship and Responsibility**: Father, I commit to being a faithful steward of the resources you have entrusted to me. Grant me wisdom to manage my finances responsibly and to honor you with my financial decisions.
3. **Faith in Abundance**: Yahweh-Jireh, I declare your promises of abundance and provision over my life. I believe that you are able to do immeasurably more than all I ask or imagine, according to your power that is at work within me (Ephesians 3:20).
4. **Peace Amidst Challenges**: Lord, in times of financial difficulty, grant me peace that surpasses all understanding. Help me to fix my eyes on you and to trust that you will supply all my needs according to your glorious riches in Christ Jesus (Philippians 4:19).
5. **Blessing Others**: Father, make me a channel of your blessings. May I be generous in sharing what you have blessed me with, knowing that it is more blessed to give than to receive (Acts 20:35).
6. **Boldness in Faith**: Lord, strengthen my faith to believe in your promises for my financial well-being. Help me to boldly declare your Word and to stand firm in the assurance of your provision.
7. **Victory Over Fear**: Heavenly Father, I renounce all fear and anxiety about finances. Fill me with your peace and assurance that you are my provider and protector.
8. **Gratitude in Abundance**: Yahweh-Jireh, thank you for your abundant blessings in my life. I am grateful for your faithfulness and goodness that sustain me each day.
9. **Continued Trust**: Lord, I surrender my financial worries and burdens to you. I choose to trust in your unfailing love and provision, aware that You are maneuvering all things for my betterment (Romans 8:28).

These prayers and affirmations are crafted to deepen your faith, align your heart with God's promises, and empower you to walk confidently in His provision.

Lord, I surrender my fears and anxieties to you. Grant me the strength to overcome challenges and the faith to trust in your provision and guidance.

Affirmation Prayers for Trust and Guidance

1. **Strength in Adversity**: Father, I thank you for being my strength in times of weakness. I declare that through Christ's fortification, I have the ability to succeed in all endeavors (Philippians 4:13).
2. **Wisdom and Discernment**: Lord, grant me wisdom and discernment to make decisions that honor you. Help me to seek your guidance in all aspects of my life, including my finances and relationships.
3. **Peace in Uncertainty**: Yahweh-Shalom, I accept Your peace that goes beyond all comprehension. Guard my heart and mind in Christ Jesus, especially in moments of uncertainty and doubt (Philippians 4:7).
4. **Courage to Step Out in Faith**: Father, strengthen my faith to step out in obedience to your Word. Help me to trust in your promises and to walk boldly in the path you have set before me.
5. **Victory Over Doubt**: Lord, I reject every doubt and negative thought that seeks to undermine my faith. I declare that I am more than a conqueror through him who loved us (Romans 8:37).
6. **Gratitude and Thanksgiving**: Heavenly Father, I praise you for your goodness and faithfulness in my life. Thank you for providing for all my needs according to your riches in glory in Christ Jesus (Philippians 4:19).
7. **Protection and Provision**: Yahweh-Jireh, I trust in your provision for my life. You are my provider, and I rest in the assurance that you will never leave me nor forsake me (Hebrews 13:5).
8. **Restoration and Renewal**: Lord, I surrender my past mistakes and failures to you. Thank you for your promise of restoration and renewal in my life (Joel 2:25-26).
9. **Faithfulness in Prayer**: Father, teach me to pray according to your will and to persevere in prayer with faith and expectancy. Help me to align my desires with your purposes for my life.
10. **Hope and Assurance**: Heavenly Father, I anchor my hope in you alone. You are my rock and my fortress, my deliverer in whom I trust (Psalm 18:2).

These prayers and affirmations are designed to strengthen your faith, deepen your trust in God's provision, and encourage you to seek His guidance in all areas of your life.

Surrender and Trust

1. **Surrendering to God's Will**: Heavenly Father, I surrender my will to yours. Help me to trust in your perfect plan for my life and to walk in obedience to your Word.
2. **Trusting in God's Timing**: Lord, I trust that your timing is perfect. Give me patience and perseverance as I wait on you for answers and direction (Psalm 27:14).
3. **Letting Go of Anxiety**: Yahweh, I cast all my anxieties on you because you care for me (1 Peter 5:7). Help me to replace worry with trust in your provision and care.
4. **Walking in Faith**: Father, increase my faith to believe in your promises. Help me to step out in faith, knowing that you are with me every step of the way (Hebrews 11:1).
5. **Strength in Weakness**: Lord, your Word says that your grace is sufficient for me, and your power is made perfect in weakness (2 Corinthians 12:9). I rely on your strength to carry me through challenges.

Affirmation Prayers for Spiritual Strength and Courage

1. **Spiritual Armor**: I put on the full armor of God— the belt of truth, the breastplate of righteousness, the shoes of the gospel of peace, the shield of faith, the helmet of salvation, and the sword of the Spirit, which is the Word of God (Ephesians 6:13-17).
2. **Renewed Mind**: Lord, transform my mind by renewing it with your Word. Help me to think thoughts that are pleasing to you and to align my mind with your truth (Romans 12:2).
3. **Peace Amidst Trials**: Father, I receive Your peace that surpasses all human understanding. Guard my heart and mind in Christ Jesus, especially in times of trials and uncertainty (Philippians 4:7).
4. **Confidence in Prayer**: Lord, I approach your throne of grace with confidence, knowing that you hear my prayers and answer according to your will (Hebrews 4:16).
5. **Walking in Love**: Help me, Lord, to walk in love towards others as you have loved me. Enable me to show kindness, patience, and forgiveness to those around me (Ephesians 4:32).

Gratitude and Hope

1. **Gratitude for Blessings**: Heavenly Father, I thank you for the blessings in my life— both big and small. Help me to have a heart of gratitude and to acknowledge your goodness each day.
2. **Hope in Christ**: Lord, you are my hope and my salvation. I place my trust in you alone, knowing that you hold my future and that your plans for me are good (Jeremiah 29:11).
3. **Victory Over Fear**: Father, I reject the spirit of fear and embrace your spirit of power, love, and sound mind (2 Timothy 1:7). I walk in victory, knowing that you are with me.
4. **Faithful Stewardship**: Lord, help me to be a faithful steward of all that you have entrusted to me— my time, talents, resources, and relationships. May I use them for your glory and kingdom purposes.
5. **Perseverance in Faith**: Father, give me endurance and steadfastness in my faith journey. Help me to run the race set before me with perseverance, keeping my eyes fixed on Jesus (Hebrews 12:1-2).

These prayers and affirmations are intended to strengthen your faith, encourage spiritual growth, and deepen your relationship with God.

Trust and Faith

1. **Trusting God's Guidance**: Heavenly Father, I trust in your guidance and wisdom. Lead me on the path of righteousness and illuminate my steps according to your Word (Psalm 119:105).
2. **Faith in Difficult Times**: Lord, increase my faith to believe in your promises, especially when circumstances seem overwhelming. Help me to remember that with you, all things are possible (Mark 9:23).
3. **Confidence in Prayer**: Father, I approach you with confidence, knowing that you hear my prayers and answer according to your will. Thank you for the privilege of communing with you (1 John 5:14).
4. **Strength in Weakness**: Lord, your Word says that your strength is made perfect in my weakness. I surrender my weaknesses to you, trusting in your power to sustain me (2 Corinthians 12:9-10).
5. **Peace in Decision-Making**: Holy Spirit, grant me peace and clarity as I make decisions. Guide my thoughts and actions according to your heavenly assignment and plan for my life (Proverbs 3:5-6).

Affirmation Prayers for Inner Strength and Renewal

1. **Renewed Mind**: Lord, transform my mind daily by the renewing of your Word. Help me to think thoughts that are pure, noble, and pleasing to you (Romans 12:2).
2. **Spiritual Armor**: I put on the full armor of God every day— the belt of truth, breastplate of righteousness, shoes of the gospel of peace, shield of faith, helmet of salvation, and sword of the Spirit (Ephesians 6:13-18).
3. **Courage in Adversity**: Father, grant me courage and boldness to face challenges with faith and perseverance. Let your strength be my refuge and fortress in times of trouble (Psalm 46:1-3).
4. **Gratitude and Contentment**: Lord, I thank you for your abundant blessings in my life. Assist me in developing a mindset of appreciation and peace, regardless of circumstances (1 Thessalonians 5:18).
5. **Victory Over Fear**: Father, I reject the spirit of fear and embrace your spirit of power, love, and sound mind. I walk in victory, knowing that you are with me always (2 Timothy 1:7).

Hope and Endurance

1. **Hope in Christ**: Heavenly Father, you are my hope and salvation. I place my trust in you, knowing that your plans for me are good and filled with hope for the future (Jeremiah 29:11).
2. **Perseverance in Faith**: Lord, give me endurance and steadfastness in my faith journey. Help me to run with perseverance the race marked out for me, fixing my eyes on Jesus (Hebrews 12:1-2).
3. **Trust in Provision**: Father, I trust in your provision for my needs— physically, emotionally, and spiritually. Thank you for supplying all that I require according to your riches in glory (Philippians 4:19).
4. **Restoration and Healing**: Lord, I pray for restoration and healing in every area of my life— body, mind, and spirit. May your peace and wholeness reign in me (Isaiah 53:5).
5. **Faithfulness and Obedience**: Father, help me to be faithful and obedient to your Word. May my life reflect your love and grace to others, drawing them closer to you (John 15:10-11).

These prayers and affirmations are meant to inspire and strengthen your spiritual journey, fostering a deeper connection with God and His promises. Feel free to use them as part of your daily devotions or whenever you seek encouragement and spiritual upliftment.

Prayers for Business Success:

Heavenly Father, I come before You seeking Your guidance and blessing upon my business endeavors. Grant me wisdom and discernment to make sound decisions that lead to prosperity. (Proverbs 3:5-6)

Lord, I commit my business plans into Your hands. May they align with Your will and bring glory to Your name. Bless the work of my hands and cause my business to flourish. (Deuteronomy 8:18)

Father, I declare that every obstacle to the growth and success of my business is removed in Jesus' name. Grant me favor with clients, partners, and stakeholders. (Psalm 90:17)

Prayers for Debt Freedom:

Heavenly Father, I surrender my financial burdens to You. Grant me wisdom to manage my finances wisely and discipline to eliminate debt. (Romans 13:8)

Lord, I declare freedom from the bondage of debt. Provide opportunities for financial increase and supernatural debt cancellation. (Philippians 4:19)

Father, I trust in Your provision to meet all my needs according to Your riches in glory. Grant me peace and assurance as I seek financial freedom. (Matthew 6:25-26)

Prayers for Generosity and Stewardship:

Heavenly Father, teach me to be a good steward of the resources You have entrusted to me. Help me to use my finances wisely for Your kingdom and to bless others. (Luke 6:38)

Lord, give me a heart of generosity and compassion towards those in need. Use me as a channel of Your blessings to impact lives and glorify Your name. (2 Corinthians 9:6-8)

Father, I commit to honoring You with my finances. May my giving reflect my trust and obedience to Your word. (Malachi 3:10)

Prayer for Financial Wisdom:

Heavenly Father, I seek Your wisdom in managing my finances. Grant me discernment to make wise decisions that honor You and benefit my financial well-being. (James 1:5)

Lord, guide me in budgeting, investing, and planning for my future. Help me to prioritize my spending and to be diligent in saving. (Proverbs 21:5)

Father, I surrender my financial worries to You and trust in Your provision. Thank You for Your faithfulness and for always being my provider. In Jesus' name, amen.

Prayer for Increased Income:

Heavenly Father, I lift up my financial needs to You. I pray for opportunities to increase my income and improve my financial situation. (Psalm 118:25)

Lord, open doors of employment, promotion, and entrepreneurship that align with Your will for my life. Grant me favor and success in all my endeavors. (Proverbs 16:3)

Father, I trust in Your timing and provision. Thank You for blessing the work of my hands and for Your abundant grace in my life. In Jesus' name, amen.

These prayers are constructed to align with biblical principles and can be personalized according to individual circumstances and needs. Incorporating these prayers into daily devotions and fasting periods can deepen spiritual growth and align personal goals with God's promises for financial breakthrough and success.

Chapter 14:
Importance of Using Proper Herbs When Fasting

Herbs have been integral to fasting practices throughout history, offering spiritual and physical benefits. This chapter explores the significance of using proper herbs during fasting, enhancing detoxification, promoting healing, and supporting overall well-being. By incorporating Yahweh's creation into your fasting journey, you amplify its transformative power and align your body with His divine healing and restoration. Embrace the holistic benefits of herbs as Yahweh's provision for nourishment and vitality during your fasting experience.

Yahweh has provided herbs as a gift for your nourishment and healing during fasting. As you incorporate these natural blessings into your fasting regimen, invite Yahweh's presence to infuse each herb with His divine healing and renewal. Embrace the opportunity to connect with Yahweh's creation in enhancing your spiritual and physical well-being, trusting in His wisdom and provision to guide you toward wholeness and vitality. Let Yahweh's abundant grace and blessings flow through every herb, restoring and rejuvenating your body, mind, and spirit.

Sunday - Herbs of the Sun (Fire Element):

On Sundays, herbs associated with the Sun and the Fire element, such as cinnamon and ginger, are commonly used. These herbs are known for their invigorating properties, providing warmth and energy to kickstart the week of fasting. They promote vitality and enthusiasm, essential for maintaining stamina and focus in spiritual practices.

Sunday Herbs with Fire Element:

1. **Basil (Ocimum basilicum)**
    - **Element:** Fire

- Basil is associated with the fire element due to its warm and invigorating properties.
- Basil is a fragrant herb commonly used in Mediterranean and Asian cuisines. It is known for its fresh, peppery flavor and is often used in salads, pasta dishes, and as a garnish.

2. **Cinnamon (Cinnamomum verum)**
    - **Element:** Fire
    - Cinnamon's warming and spicy nature align it with the fire element.
    - Cinnamon is a popular spice derived from the bark of trees. It adds a sweet and aromatic flavor to both sweet and savory dishes, as well as beverages.
3. **Rosemary (Rosmarinus officinalis)**
    - **Element:** Fire
    - Rosemary's strong aroma and flavor make it a fire element herb.
    - Rosemary is an evergreen herb used in cooking to add a robust, pine-like fragrance to dishes like roasted meats, potatoes, and bread.
4. **Chili Pepper (Capsicum spp.)**
    - **Element:** Fire
    - Chili peppers are known for their spicy, heating qualities, making them a representation of the fire element.
    - Chili peppers come in various shapes and heat levels. They are used worldwide to add heat and flavor to foods.
5. **Ginger (Zingiber officinale)**
    - **Element:** Fire
    - Ginger's pungent and warming nature aligns it with the fire element.
    - Ginger is a versatile herb used in both culinary and medicinal applications. It adds a spicy, zesty flavor to dishes and beverages.

Sunday Herbs with Sun Element:

1. **St. John's Wort (Hypericum perforatum)**
    - **Element:** Sun
    - St. John's Wort's bright yellow flowers and traditional use in uplifting mood align it with the Sun element, symbolizing vitality and joy.
    - St. John's Wort is used in herbal remedies, particularly for its potential to support emotional well-being.
2. **Calendula (Calendula officinalis)**
    - **Element:** Sun
    - Calendula's vibrant orange and yellow blooms connect it with the Sun element, symbolizing energy and healing.

- Calendula flowers are used in herbal remedies and skincare products for their potential benefits and vibrant color.

3. **Sunflower (Helianthus annuus)**
   - **Element:** Sun
   - Sunflower's towering presence and affinity for following the sun align it with the Sun element, symbolizing growth and positivity.
   - Sunflower seeds are consumed as snacks and used in cooking and baking.

4. **Cinnamon (Cinnamomum verum)**
   - **Element:** Sun
   - Cinnamon's warm and spicy flavor connects it with the Sun element, symbolizing vitality and warmth.
   - Cinnamon bark is used as a spice in various culinary dishes and desserts.

5. **Marigold (Tagetes spp.)**
   - **Element:** Sun
   - Marigold's bright and cheerful appearance aligns it with the Sun element, symbolizing energy and protection.
   - Marigold flowers are used in herbal remedies, skincare products, and as ornamental plants.

6. **Chamomile (Matricaria chamomilla)**
   - **Element:** Sun
   - Chamomile's soothing and calming nature connects it with the Sun element, symbolizing vitality and tranquility.
   - Chamomile flowers are used in herbal teas and skincare products for their soothing and floral flavor.

7. **Lemongrass (Cymbopogon citratus)**
   - **Element:** Sun
   - Lemongrass' zesty and refreshing aroma aligns it with the Sun element, symbolizing energy and clarity.
   - Lemongrass leaves are used in culinary dishes and herbal teas for their lemony flavor.

8. **Goldenseal (Hydrastis canadensis)**
   - **Element:** Sun
   - Goldenseal's vibrant yellow root and traditional use in health align it with the Sun element, symbolizing vitality and healing.
   - Goldenseal root is used in herbal remedies for its potential benefits.

9. **Angelica (Angelica archangelica)**
   - **Element:** Sun
   - Angelica's towering and aromatic presence connects it with the Sun element, symbolizing energy and protection.

- Angelica root and seeds are used in herbal remedies and culinary creations.

10. **Lavender (Lavandula angustifolia)**
    - **Element:** Sun
    - Lavender's soothing and floral aroma aligns it with the Sun element, symbolizing vitality and relaxation.
    - Lavender flowers are used in aromatherapy, teas, and skincare products for their calming properties.

11. **Arnica (Arnica montana)**
    - **Element:** Sun
    - Arnica's bright yellow flowers and use in healing balms align it with the Sun element, symbolizing vitality and recovery.
    - Arnica is used topically in creams and ointments for its potential benefits for bruises and sore muscles.

12. **Mistletoe (Viscum album)**
    - **Element:** Sun
    - Mistletoe's evergreen nature and traditional use in celebrations connect it with the Sun element, symbolizing vitality and renewal.
    - Mistletoe is used in festive decorations and has cultural significance.

13. **Lemon Balm (Melissa officinalis)**
    - **Element:** Sun
    - Lemon Balm's citrusy aroma and soothing properties align it with the Sun element, symbolizing vitality and comfort.
    - Lemon Balm leaves are used in herbal teas and culinary creations for their lemony flavor.

14. **Saffron (Crocus sativus)**
    - **Element:** Sun
    - Saffron's vibrant red stigmas and use in culinary dishes connect it with the Sun element, symbolizing vitality and luxury.
    - Saffron is one of the most expensive spices and is used to flavor and color various dishes.

15. **Ginger (Zingiber officinale)**
    - **Element:** Sun
    - Ginger's spicy and warming flavor aligns it with the Sun element, symbolizing vitality and energy.
    - Ginger root is used in culinary dishes, teas, and traditional medicine for its potential health benefits.

Monday - Herbs of the Moon (Water Element):

Herbs aligned with the Moon and the Water element, such as chamomile and jasmine, are ideal for Mondays. These herbs foster emotional balance and tranquility, helping to soothe the soul and alleviate any emotional turbulence that fasting may bring. They promote a sense of inner peace and receptivity to spiritual insights.

Monday Herbs with Water Element:

1. **Mint (Mentha spp.)**
   - **Element:** Water
   - Mint's cooling and refreshing qualities align it with the water element.
   - Mint leaves are commonly used in teas, desserts, and cocktails for their invigorating and soothing flavor.
2. **Lemongrass (Cymbopogon citratus)**
   - **Element:** Water
   - Lemongrass's citrusy and refreshing aroma connects it with the water element.
   - Lemongrass is used in Asian cuisine and herbal teas, imparting a lemony, herbal flavor.
3. **Cucumber (Cucumis sativus)**
   - **Element:** Water
   - Cucumbers have a high-water content and a hydrating quality, making them a representation of the water element.
   - Cucumbers are crisp and mild-flavored vegetables often eaten raw in salads and sandwiches.
4. **Chamomile (Matricaria chamomilla)**
   - **Element:** Water
   - Chamomile's calming and soothing properties align it with the water element.
   - Chamomile is a gentle herb commonly used in herbal teas and remedies to promote relaxation and ease digestion.
5. **Lavender (Lavandula spp.)**
   - **Element:** Water
   - Lavender's aromatic and calming nature associates it with the water element.
   - Lavender is known for its fragrant flowers, often used in teas, culinary dishes, and aromatherapy for its relaxing aroma.
6. **Calendula (Calendula officinalis)**
   - **Element:** Water
   - Calendula's soothing and healing properties align it with the water element.

- Calendula flowers are used in herbal remedies, salves, and skincare products for their potential skin-soothing benefits.

7. **Coriander (Coriandrum sativum)**
   - **Element:** Water
   - Coriander's fresh and citrusy flavor connects it with the water element.
   - Coriander leaves (cilantro) and seeds are used in various cuisines to add a bright, herbal note to dishes.

8. **Sage (Salvia officinalis)**
   - **Element:** Water
   - Sage's wisdom and grounding qualities make it a representation of the water element.
   - Sage is an aromatic herb used to flavor dishes like stuffing, sausages, and poultry.

9. **Parsley (Petroselinum crispum)**
   - **Element:** Water
   - Parsley's fresh and vibrant green appearance aligns it with the growth and abundance associated with water.
   - Parsley is a versatile herb used as a garnish and to enhance the flavor of various dishes, including salads, soups, and sauces.

10. **Dandelion (Taraxacum officinale)**
    - **Element:** Water
    - Dandelion's resilience and nourishing nature connect it with the water element.
    - Dandelion greens are edible and can be used in salads, while dandelion root is often used in herbal remedies.

11. **Lemon Balm (Melissa officinalis)**
    - **Element:** Water
    - Lemon Balm's citrusy and calming properties align it with the water element.
    - Lemon Balm is used in herbal teas and remedies for its potential to promote relaxation and ease stress.

12. **Dill (Anethum graveolens)**
    - **Element:** Water
    - Dill's fresh and aromatic nature connects it with the water element.
    - Dill leaves and seeds are used in culinary dishes, particularly in pickles, sauces, and seafood.

13. **Evening Primrose (Oenothera biennis)**
    - **Element:** Water
    - Evening Primrose's resilience and soothing properties align it with the water element.

- Evening Primrose oil is used in supplements and skincare products for its potential benefits, especially for skin health.

14. **Chervil (Anthriscus cerefolium)**
    - **Element:** Water
    - Chervil's delicate and mild flavor connects it with the water element.
    - Chervil leaves are used as a culinary herb, adding a subtle anise-like note to dishes.

15. **Watercress (Nasturtium officinale)**
    - **Element:** Water
    - Watercress's preference for watery habitats makes it a representation of the water element.
    - Watercress is a peppery leafy green used in salads, sandwiches, and as a garnish.

16. **Fennel (Foeniculum vulgare)**
    - **Element:** Water
    - Fennel's crisp and aromatic nature aligns it with the water element.
    - Fennel bulb, seeds, and fronds are used in culinary dishes, adding a mild licorice-like flavor.

17. **Angelica (Angelica archangelica)**
    - **Element:** Water
    - Angelica's resilience and association with waterways make it a representation of the water element.
    - Angelica root is used in herbal remedies, particularly in digestive and respiratory blends.

18. **Lovage (Levisticum officinale)**
    - **Element:** Water
    - Lovage's robust and celery-like flavor connects it with the water element.
    - Lovage leaves and stems are used as a culinary herb to enhance soups, stews, and savory dishes.

19. **Marshmallow (Althaea officinalis)**
    - **Element:** Water
    - Marshmallow's soothing and mucilaginous properties align it with the water element.
    - Marshmallow root is used in herbal remedies to support the respiratory and digestive systems.

20. **Plantain (Plantago spp.)**
    - **Element:** Water
    - Plantain's ability to thrive in damp environments connects it with the water element.

- Plantain leaves are used in herbal remedies for their potential benefits, particularly for skin and mucous membrane health.

21. **Watermelon (Citrullus lanatus)**
    - **Element:** Water
    - Watermelon's high water content and hydrating nature make it a representation of the water element.
    - Watermelon is a juicy fruit enjoyed fresh, especially in hot weather, for its refreshing taste.

22. **Chicory (Cichorium intybus)**
    - **Element:** Water
    - Chicory's ability to grow near water sources aligns it with the water element.
    - Chicory leaves are used in salads, and chicory root is roasted and used as a coffee substitute.

23. **Irish Moss (Chondrus crispus)**
    - **Element:** Water
    - Irish Moss's oceanic habitat and mucilaginous quality connect it with the water element.
    - Irish Moss is used as a thickening agent in culinary dishes and as an ingredient in skincare products.

24. **Pennyroyal (Mentha pulegium)**
    - **Element:** Water
    - Pennyroyal's association with wetlands and its aromatic nature align it with the water element.
    - Pennyroyal has been used traditionally in herbal teas but should be used with caution due to its potency.

25. **Water Lily (Nymphaea spp.)**
    - **Element:** Water
    - Water lilies' growth in aquatic environments makes them a representation of the water element.
    - Water lily flowers have cultural significance and may be used decoratively.

Tuesday - Herbs of Mars (Fire Element):

Tuesday, associated with Mars and the Fire element, calls for herbs like cayenne and garlic. These herbs stimulate courage, determination, and physical vitality, assisting in overcoming challenges and obstacles encountered during fasting. They empower individuals with strength and resilience, ensuring steadfastness in spiritual commitment.

Tuesday Herbs with Mars Element:

1. **Garlic (Allium sativum)**
   - **Element:** Mars
   - Garlic's pungent and bold flavor aligns it with the Mars element, symbolizing strength and vitality.
   - Garlic is a staple in various cuisines and is known for its strong, aromatic taste. It is used in a wide range of savory dishes.
2. **Onion (Allium cepa)**
   - **Element:** Mars
   - Onions, with their sharp and assertive flavor, are associated with the Mars element.
   - Onions are used as a base ingredient in many recipes, contributing a savory and slightly sweet taste.
3. **Thyme (Thymus vulgaris)**
   - **Element:** Mars
   - Thyme's strong and earthy aroma makes it a representation of the Mars element.
   - Thyme is a fragrant herb used to season various dishes, particularly roasted meats, soups, and stews.
4. **Horseradish (Armoracia rusticana)**
   - **Element:** Mars
   - Horseradish's intense and spicy flavor aligns it with the Mars element.
   - Horseradish is known for its pungent taste and is often used as a condiment to add heat to dishes.
5. **Nettle (Urtica dioica)**
   - **Element:** Mars
   - Nettle's sharp stinging quality and robust presence connect it with the Mars element.
   - Nettle is used in herbal teas and as a culinary ingredient, offering a unique earthy taste.
6. **Red Pepper (Capsicum annuum)**
   - **Element:** Mars
   - Red pepper's fiery and spicy nature aligns it with Mars, symbolizing energy and heat.
   - Red peppers are used in various cuisines to add spice and flavor to dishes.
7. **Cayenne Pepper (Capsicum annuum)**
   - **Element:** Mars
   - Cayenne pepper's intense heat and stimulating properties connect it with the Mars element.

- Cayenne pepper is known for its fiery taste and is often used to add a kick to recipes.

8. **Ginger (Zingiber officinale)**
   - **Element:** Mars
   - Ginger's spicy and warming qualities align it with Mars, symbolizing energy and vigor.
   - Ginger is used in culinary dishes, teas, and remedies for its unique flavor and potential health benefits.

9. **Rosemary (Rosmarinus officinalis)**
   - **Element:** Mars
   - Rosemary's bold aroma and robust flavor make it a representation of the Mars element.
   - Rosemary is used to season various dishes, especially those featuring poultry and roasted meats.

10. **Black Pepper (Piper nigrum)**
    - **Element:** Mars
    - Black pepper's pungent and warming properties align it with Mars, symbolizing boldness and energy.
    - Black pepper is a common spice used to enhance the flavor of a wide range of dishes.

11. **Basil (Ocimum basilicum)**
    - **Element:** Mars
    - Basil's bold and aromatic nature connects it with the Mars element.
    - Basil leaves are used in various cuisines, particularly Italian, for their sweet and slightly peppery flavor.

12. **Mustard (Brassica spp.)**
    - **Element:** Mars
    - Mustard's spicy and intense flavor aligns it with the Mars element.
    - Mustard seeds and condiments are used in a wide range of dishes and condiments for their sharp taste.

13. **Chili Pepper (Capsicum spp.)**
    - **Element:** Mars
    - Chili peppers' fiery heat and invigorating qualities make them a representation of the Mars element.
    - Chili peppers are used to add heat and flavor to many dishes, especially in spicy cuisines.

14. **Clove (Syzygium aromaticum)**
    - **Element:** Mars
    - Clove's intense and warming aroma aligns it with the Mars element.

- Cloves are used as a spice and in various recipes for their strong, sweet, and spicy flavor.

15. **Dragon's Blood (Daemonorops spp.)**
    - **Element:** Mars
    - Dragon's Blood's vibrant red resin and association with protection connect it with the Mars element.
    - Dragon's Blood resin is used in incense, rituals, and traditional practices for its symbolism and scent.

16. **Arnica (Arnica montana)**
    - **Element:** Mars
    - Arnica's vibrant yellow flowers and use in healing salves align it with the Mars element.
    - Arnica is used topically in creams and ointments for its potential benefits in relieving muscle soreness and bruising.

17. **Tarragon (Artemisia dracunculus)**
    - **Element:** Mars
    - Tarragon's assertive and bittersweet flavor connects it with the Mars element.
    - Tarragon leaves are used as a culinary herb, adding a distinctive anise-like taste to dishes.

18. **Feverfew (Tanacetum parthenium)**
    - **Element:** Mars
    - Feverfew's resilient nature and traditional use in remedies align it with the Mars element.
    - Feverfew leaves are used in herbal remedies for their potential benefits, especially for migraine relief.

19. **Agrimony (Agrimonia eupatoria)**
    - **Element:** Mars
    - Agrimony's association with protection and banishing connects it with the Mars element.
    - Agrimony is used in herbal remedies for its potential benefits, particularly for digestive health.

20. **Bergamot (Citrus bergamia)**
    - **Element:** Mars
    - Bergamot's invigorating and citrusy scent aligns it with the Mars element.
    - Bergamot essential oil is used in aromatherapy and skincare products for its uplifting aroma.

21. **Borage (Borago officinalis)**
    - **Element:** Mars

- Borage's vibrant blue flowers and invigorating properties align it with the Mars element.
- Borage leaves and flowers are used in culinary dishes and herbal teas for their mild cucumber-like flavor.

22. **Cumin (Cuminum cyminum)**
    - **Element:** Mars
    - Cumin's warm and earthy flavor connects it with the Mars element.
    - Cumin seeds are used as a spice in various cuisines, adding a distinct nutty and spicy taste.
23. **Corallorhiza Orchid (Corallorhiza spp.)**
    - **Element:** Mars
    - Corallorhiza orchids' unique appearance and adaptation to forest habitats make them a representation of the Mars element.
    - These orchids are not used for culinary or medicinal purposes but are admired for their beauty.
24. **Cassia (Cinnamomum cassia)**
    - **Element:** Mars
    - Cassia's strong and spicy aroma aligns it with the Mars element.
    - Cassia is a type of cinnamon used as a spice in baking and cooking, known for its sweet and fiery flavor.
25. **Ginseng (Panax ginseng)**
    - **Element:** Mars
    - Ginseng's adaptogenic and stimulating properties connect it with the Mars element.
    - Ginseng root is used in herbal remedies and supplements for its potential benefits, including energy and vitality.
26. **Wednesday - Herbs of Mercury (Air Element):**
27. Mercury and the Air element guide the herb choices for Wednesday, such as lavender and lemongrass. These herbs enhance mental clarity, communication, and adaptability, facilitating clear thought and effective prayer during fasting. They support intellectual pursuits and spiritual discernment, aiding in making decisions aligned with divine guidance.
28. **Thursday - Herbs of Jupiter (Earth Element):**
29. Jupiter and the Earth element influence Thursday's herb selections, such as sage and juniper. These herbs promote wisdom, abundance, and growth, fostering spiritual expansion and prosperity during fasting. They encourage generosity of spirit and a deeper connection with divine providence, enhancing gratitude and trust in divine provision.
30. **Friday - Herbs of Venus (Water Element):**

31. Friday, associated with Venus and the Water element, invites the use of herbs like rose and hibiscus. These herbs cultivate love, harmony, and compassion, nurturing relationships and self-care practices during fasting. They support emotional healing and renewal, fostering a sense of beauty and grace in spiritual disciplines.
32. **Saturday - Herbs of Saturn (Earth Element):**
33. Saturday's herbs, aligned with Saturn and the Earth element, include patchouli and comfrey. These herbs promote discipline, introspection, and grounding, facilitating inner strength and resilience in spiritual practices. They encourage patience and perseverance, guiding individuals through the challenges and lessons of fasting with steadfastness.

Wednesday - Herbs of Mercury (Air Element):

Mercury and the Air element guide the herb choices for Wednesday, such as lavender and lemongrass. These herbs enhance mental clarity, communication, and adaptability, facilitating clear thought and effective prayer during fasting. They support intellectual pursuits and spiritual discernment, aiding in making decisions aligned with divine guidance.

Wednesday Herbs with Mercury Element:

1. **Lavender (Lavandula angustifolia)**
    - **Element:** Mercury
    - Lavender's versatile and communicative qualities align it with the Mercury element, symbolizing adaptability and clarity.
    - Lavender flowers are used in aromatherapy, teas, and skincare products for their calming properties.
2. **Peppermint (Mentha x piperita)**
    - **Element:** Mercury
    - Peppermint's invigorating and stimulating aroma connects it with the Mercury element, symbolizing communication and alertness.
    - Peppermint leaves are used in herbal teas and culinary creations for their refreshing flavor.
3. **Chamomile (Matricaria chamomilla)**
    - **Element:** Mercury
    - Chamomile's gentle and calming nature aligns it with the Mercury element, symbolizing communication and tranquility.
    - Chamomile flowers are used in herbal teas and skincare products for their soothing and floral flavor.

4. **Thyme (Thymus vulgaris)**
   - **Element:** Mercury
   - Thyme's adaptable growth and culinary uses connect it with the Mercury element, symbolizing communication and versatility.
   - Thyme leaves are used as a culinary herb, adding a savory flavor to dishes.
5. **Lemon Balm (Melissa officinalis)**
   - **Element:** Mercury
   - Lemon Balm's citrusy aroma and soothing properties align it with the Mercury element, symbolizing communication and comfort.
   - Lemon Balm leaves are used in herbal teas and culinary creations for their lemony flavor.
6. **Dill (Anethum graveolens)**
   - **Element:** Mercury
   - Dill's feathery leaves and culinary uses connect it with the Mercury element, symbolizing communication and flavor.
   - Dill leaves and seeds are used in pickles, sauces, and salads for their distinctive flavor.
7. **Rosemary (Rosmarinus officinalis)**
   - **Element:** Mercury
   - Rosemary's fragrant and adaptable nature aligns it with the Mercury element, symbolizing communication and memory.
   - Rosemary leaves are used as a culinary herb and in herbal remedies for their piney flavor.
8. **Fennel (Foeniculum vulgare)**
   - **Element:** Mercury
   - Fennel's feathery fronds and culinary uses connect it with the Mercury element, symbolizing communication and digestion.
   - Fennel bulb and seeds are used in culinary dishes for their anise-like flavor.
9. **Marjoram (Origanum majorana)**
   - **Element:** Mercury
   - Marjoram's aromatic leaves and culinary uses align it with the Mercury element, symbolizing communication and warmth.
   - Marjoram leaves are used as a culinary herb, adding a sweet and floral flavor to dishes.
10. **Valerian (Valeriana officinalis)**
    - **Element:** Mercury
    - Valerian's calming and sedative properties connect it with the Mercury element, symbolizing communication and relaxation.
    - Valerian root is used in herbal remedies, particularly for its potential benefits related to sleep and anxiety.

11. **Sage (Salvia officinalis)**
    - **Element:** Mercury
    - Sage's wisdom and versatility in culinary and herbal applications align it with the Mercury element, symbolizing communication and discernment.
    - Sage leaves are used as a culinary herb, known for their earthy and savory flavor.
12. **Coriander (Coriandrum sativum)**
    - **Element:** Mercury
    - Coriander's aromatic seeds and culinary uses connect it with the Mercury element, symbolizing communication and flavor.
    - Coriander seeds are used in spice blends and culinary dishes, offering a citrusy and warm taste.
13. **Lemon Verbena (Aloysia citrodora)**
    - **Element:** Mercury
    - Lemon Verbena's lemony aroma and use in herbal teas align it with the Mercury element, symbolizing communication and clarity.
    - Lemon Verbena leaves are used in herbal teas and as a flavoring agent for their refreshing flavor.
14. **Basil (Ocimum basilicum)**
    - **Element:** Mercury
    - Basil's aromatic leaves and culinary uses connect it with the Mercury element, symbolizing communication and flavor.
    - Basil leaves are used in various cuisines, particularly Italian, for their sweet and slightly peppery flavor.
15. **Caraway (Carum carvi)**
    - **Element:** Mercury
    - Caraway's versatile seeds and culinary uses align it with the Mercury element, symbolizing communication and flavor.
    - Caraway seeds are used in bread, pastries, and spice blends for their earthy and slightly sweet taste.
16. **Parsley (Petroselinum crispum)**
    - **Element:** Mercury
    - Parsley's vibrant green leaves and culinary uses align it with the Mercury element, symbolizing communication and freshness.
    - Parsley is used as a garnish and in culinary dishes for its mild and fresh flavor.
17. **Dandelion (Taraxacum officinale)**
    - **Element:** Mercury
    - Dandelion's persistence and use in herbal remedies connect it with the Mercury element, symbolizing communication and detoxification.

- Dandelion leaves and roots are used in herbal teas and supplements for potential health benefits.

18. **Borage (Borago officinalis)**
    - **Element:** Mercury
    - Borage's bright blue flowers and traditional use in mood enhancement align it with the Mercury element, symbolizing communication and courage.
    - Borage flowers are used in culinary dishes and beverages for their mild cucumber-like flavor.

19. **Lovage (Levisticum officinale)**
    - **Element:** Mercury
    - Lovage's aromatic leaves and culinary uses connect it with the Mercury element, symbolizing communication and boldness.
    - Lovage leaves are used as a culinary herb, known for their intense celery-like flavor.

20. **Hyssop (Hyssopus officinalis)**
    - **Element:** Mercury
    - Hyssop's aromatic leaves and historical use in rituals align it with the Mercury element, symbolizing communication and purification.
    - Hyssop is used in culinary dishes and has cultural and spiritual significance.

21. **Marigold (Calendula officinalis)**
    - **Element:** Mercury
    - Marigold's vibrant orange and yellow blooms connect it with the Mercury element, symbolizing communication and vitality.
    - Marigold flowers are used in herbal remedies, skincare products, and as ornamental plants.

22. **Pennyroyal (Mentha pulegium)**
    - **Element:** Mercury
    - Pennyroyal's aromatic leaves and historical use in herbal remedies align it with the Mercury element, symbolizing communication and protection.
    - Pennyroyal leaves have been used traditionally in herbal remedies, but caution is advised due to potential toxicity.

23. **Tarragon (Artemisia dracunculus)**
    - **Element:** Mercury
    - Tarragon's aromatic leaves and culinary uses connect it with the Mercury element, symbolizing communication and flavor.
    - Tarragon leaves are used in culinary dishes, particularly for their anise-like flavor.

24. **Chervil (Anthriscus cerefolium)**
    - **Element:** Mercury

- Chervil's delicate leaves and culinary uses align it with the Mercury element, symbolizing communication and finesse.
- Chervil leaves are used in culinary dishes, adding a mild and slightly sweet flavor.

25. **Comfrey (Symphytum officinale)**
    - **Element:** Mercury
    - Comfrey's robust growth and traditional use in healing connect it with the Mercury element, symbolizing communication and stability.
    - Comfrey leaves are used in herbal remedies, particularly for their potential benefits for skin and bone health.

Thursday - Herbs of Jupiter (Earth Element):

Jupiter and the Earth element influence Thursday's herb selections, such as sage and juniper. These herbs promote wisdom, abundance, and growth, fostering spiritual expansion and prosperity during fasting. They encourage generosity of spirit and a deeper connection with divine providence, enhancing gratitude and trust in divine provision.

Thursday Herbs with Jupiter Element:

1. **Basil (Ocimum basilicum)**
    - **Element:** Jupiter
    - Basil's vibrant and expansive aroma connects it with the Jupiter element, symbolizing growth and abundance.
    - Basil leaves are used in various cuisines, particularly Italian, for their sweet and slightly peppery flavor.
2. **Cinnamon (Cinnamomum verum)**
    - **Element:** Jupiter
    - Cinnamon's warm and uplifting scent aligns it with the Jupiter element, symbolizing expansion and positivity.
    - Cinnamon is a spice used in both sweet and savory dishes, known for its sweet and spicy flavor.
3. **Dandelion (Taraxacum officinale)**
    - **Element:** Jupiter
    - Dandelion's resilience and abundance in the wild connect it with the Jupiter element, symbolizing growth and vitality.
    - Dandelion greens are edible and can be used in salads, while dandelion root is often used in herbal remedies.
4. **Fennel (Foeniculum vulgare)**

- **Element:** Jupiter
- Fennel's sweet and expansive aroma aligns it with the Jupiter element, symbolizing growth and optimism.
- Fennel bulb, seeds, and fronds are used in culinary dishes, adding a mild licorice-like flavor.

5. **Jasmine (Jasminum spp.)**
    - **Element:** Jupiter
    - Jasmine's fragrant and uplifting flowers connect it with the Jupiter element, symbolizing expansion and grace.
    - Jasmine flowers are used in teas, perfumes, and aromatherapy for their enchanting scent.

6. **Mullein (Verbascum thapsus)**
    - **Element:** Jupiter
    - Mullein's tall and robust growth in various environments align it with the Jupiter element, symbolizing abundance and healing.
    - Mullein leaves and flowers are used in herbal remedies, particularly for respiratory support.

7. **Sage (Salvia officinalis)**
    - **Element:** Jupiter
    - Sage's wisdom and expansive nature make it a representation of the Jupiter element, symbolizing growth and knowledge.
    - Sage is an aromatic herb used to flavor dishes like stuffing, sausages, and poultry.

8. **Mugwort (Artemisia vulgaris)**
    - **Element:** Jupiter
    - Mugwort's resilience and associations with protection connect it with the Jupiter element, symbolizing growth and shielding.
    - Mugwort is used in herbal remedies, particularly for its potential benefits related to sleep and dreams.

9. **Peppermint (Mentha x piperita)**
    - **Element:** Jupiter
    - Peppermint's refreshing and expansive aroma aligns it with the Jupiter element, symbolizing growth and vitality.
    - Peppermint leaves are used in herbal teas and culinary dishes for their invigorating and cooling flavor.

10. **Rose (Rosa spp.)**
    - **Element:** Jupiter
    - Rose's exquisite and expansive flowers connect it with the Jupiter element, symbolizing growth and love.

- Rose petals are used in teas, culinary creations, perfumes, and skincare products for their captivating scent.

11. **Chervil (Anthriscus cerefolium)**
    - **Element:** Jupiter
    - Chervil's delicate and mild flavor aligns it with the Jupiter element, symbolizing growth and harmony.
    - Chervil leaves are used as a culinary herb, adding a subtle anise-like note to dishes.

12. **Saffron (Crocus sativus)**
    - **Element:** Jupiter
    - Saffron's precious and aromatic stigma connect it with the Jupiter element, symbolizing expansion and luxury.
    - Saffron threads are used as a spice and food coloring, adding a distinct flavor and color to dishes.

13. **Lemon Balm (Melissa officinalis)**
    - **Element:** Jupiter
    - Lemon Balm's citrusy and calming properties align it with the Jupiter element, symbolizing growth and relaxation.
    - Lemon Balm is used in herbal teas and remedies for its potential to promote relaxation and ease stress.

14. **Hawthorn (Crataegus spp.)**
    - **Element:** Jupiter
    - Hawthorn's abundance of berries and traditional associations with protection connect it with the Jupiter element, symbolizing growth and resilience.
    - Hawthorn berries and flowers are used in herbal remedies, particularly for heart health.

15. **Hyssop (Hyssopus officinalis)**
    - **Element:** Jupiter
    - Hyssop's aromatic nature and historical use in purification rituals align it with the Jupiter element, symbolizing growth and clarity.
    - Hyssop leaves and flowers are used in culinary dishes and herbal remedies.

16. **Mint (Mentha spp.)**
    - **Element:** Jupiter
    - Mint's refreshing and expansive aroma aligns it with the Jupiter element, symbolizing growth and vitality.
    - Mint leaves are used in culinary dishes, herbal teas, and desserts for their cool and invigorating flavor.

17. **Borage (Borago officinalis)**
    - **Element:** Jupiter

- Borage's vibrant blue flowers and invigorating properties connect it with the Jupiter element, symbolizing growth and courage.
- Borage leaves and flowers are used in culinary creations and herbal teas for their mild cucumber-like flavor.

18. **Chamomile (Matricaria chamomilla)**
    - **Element:** Jupiter
    - Chamomile's soothing and calming nature aligns it with the Jupiter element, symbolizing growth and relaxation.
    - Chamomile flowers are used in herbal teas and skincare products for their gentle and floral flavor.

19. **Bee Balm (Monarda didyma)**
    - **Element:** Jupiter
    - Bee Balm's vibrant red flowers and use by Native Americans connect it with the Jupiter element, symbolizing growth and wisdom.
    - Bee Balm leaves and flowers are used in culinary dishes and herbal remedies.

20. **Anise (Pimpinella anisum)**
    - **Element:** Jupiter
    - Anise's sweet and aromatic flavor aligns it with the Jupiter element, symbolizing growth and delight.
    - Anise seeds are used as a spice and flavoring agent, often in baked goods and liqueurs.

21. **Calendula (Calendula officinalis)**
    - **Element:** Jupiter
    - Calendula's bright and sunny appearance aligns it with the Jupiter element, symbolizing growth and healing.
    - Calendula flowers are used in herbal remedies and skincare products for their potential benefits and vibrant color.

22. **Oregano (Origanum vulgare)**
    - **Element:** Jupiter
    - Oregano's robust and aromatic flavor connects it with the Jupiter element, symbolizing growth and abundance.
    - Oregano leaves are used as a culinary herb, enhancing the taste of Italian and Mediterranean dishes.

23. **Yellow Dock (Rumex crispus)**
    - **Element:** Jupiter
    - Yellow Dock's hardy growth and traditional use in tonics align it with the Jupiter element, symbolizing growth and vitality.
    - Yellow Dock root is used in herbal remedies, particularly for digestive and skin health.

24. **Lemon Verbena (Aloysia citrodora)**
    - **Element:** Jupiter
    - Lemon Verbena's citrusy and uplifting scent aligns it with the Jupiter element, symbolizing growth and joy.
    - Lemon Verbena leaves are used in teas and culinary creations for their lemony flavor.
25. **Bergamot (Monarda didyma)**
    - **Element:** Jupiter
    - Bergamot's vibrant red flowers and use by Native Americans connect it with the Jupiter element, symbolizing growth and wisdom.
    - Bergamot leaves and flowers are used in teas and culinary dishes, imparting a citrusy and floral flavor.

Friday - Herbs of Venus (Water Element):

Friday, associated with Venus and the Water element, invites the use of herbs like rose and hibiscus. These herbs cultivate love, harmony, and compassion, nurturing relationships and self-care practices during fasting. They support emotional healing and renewal, fostering a sense of beauty and grace in spiritual disciplines.

Friday Herbs with Venus Element:

1. **Rose (Rosa spp.)**
    - **Element:** Venus
    - Rose's exquisite and romantic fragrance connects it with the Venus element, symbolizing love and beauty.
    - Rose petals are used in teas, culinary creations, perfumes, and skincare products for their captivating scent.
2. **Lavender (Lavandula angustifolia)**
    - **Element:** Venus
    - Lavender's soothing and floral aroma aligns it with the Venus element, symbolizing love and relaxation.
    - Lavender flowers are used in aromatherapy, teas, and skincare products for their calming properties.
3. **Chamomile (Matricaria chamomilla)**
    - **Element:** Venus
    - Chamomile's gentle and calming nature connects it with the Venus element, symbolizing love and tranquility.
    - Chamomile flowers are used in herbal teas and skincare products for their soothing and floral flavor.

4. **Jasmine (Jasminum spp.)**
   - **Element:** Venus
   - Jasmine's sweet and romantic fragrance aligns it with the Venus element, symbolizing love and sensuality.
   - Jasmine flowers are used in teas, perfumes, and aromatherapy for their enchanting scent.
5. **Cardamom (Elettaria cardamomum)**
   - **Element:** Venus
   - Cardamom's warm and exotic flavor connects it with the Venus element, symbolizing love and indulgence.
   - Cardamom seeds are used as a spice in various culinary dishes and desserts.
6. **Vanilla (Vanilla planifolia)**
   - **Element:** Venus
   - Vanilla's sweet and comforting scent aligns it with the Venus element, symbolizing love and pleasure.
   - Vanilla is used to flavor desserts, beverages, and baked goods for its rich and sweet flavor.
7. **Passionflower (Passiflora incarnata)**
   - **Element:** Venus
   - Passionflower's intricate and alluring appearance connects it with the Venus element, symbolizing love and fascination.
   - Passionflower is used in herbal remedies for its potential calming effects.
8. **Lemon Verbena (Aloysia citrodora)**
   - **Element:** Venus
   - Lemon Verbena's citrusy and uplifting scent aligns it with the Venus element, symbolizing love and joy.
   - Lemon Verbena leaves are used in teas and culinary creations for their lemony flavor.
9. **Cherry (Prunus avium)**
   - **Element:** Venus
   - Cherries' sweet and luscious taste connects them with the Venus element, symbolizing love and indulgence.
   - Cherries are enjoyed fresh, in desserts, and as a flavoring in various products.
10. **Hibiscus (Hibiscus sabdariffa)**
    - **Element:** Venus
    - Hibiscus' vibrant and seductive appearance aligns it with the Venus element, symbolizing love and attraction.

- Hibiscus flowers are used in herbal teas and beverages for their tart and refreshing flavor.

11. **Damiana (Turnera diffusa)**
    - **Element:** Venus
    - Damiana's historical use as an aphrodisiac connects it with the Venus element, symbolizing love and passion.
    - Damiana leaves are used in herbal remedies and herbal teas for their potential aphrodisiac properties.

12. **Patchouli (Pogostemon cablin)**
    - **Element:** Venus
    - Patchouli's earthy and sensual scent aligns it with the Venus element, symbolizing love and sensuality.
    - Patchouli essential oil is used in perfumes, aromatherapy, and skincare products for its distinctive aroma.

13. **Strawberry (Fragaria x ananassa)**
    - **Element:** Venus
    - Strawberries' sweet and juicy flavor connects them with the Venus element, symbolizing love and sweetness.
    - Strawberries are enjoyed fresh, in desserts, and as a flavoring in various products.

14. **Rosemary (Rosmarinus officinalis)**
    - **Element:** Venus
    - Rosemary's fragrant and romantic nature aligns it with the Venus element, symbolizing love and memory.
    - Rosemary leaves are used as a culinary herb and in herbal remedies for their piney flavor.

15. **Sweet Woodruff (Galium odoratum)**
    - **Element:** Venus
    - Sweet Woodruff's delicate white flowers and sweet aroma connect it with the Venus element, symbolizing love and charm.
    - Sweet Woodruff is used to flavor beverages, especially May wine, and desserts.

16. **Raspberry (Rubus idaeus)**
    - **Element:** Venus
    - Raspberries' sweet and juicy nature connects them with the Venus element, symbolizing love and indulgence.
    - Raspberries are enjoyed fresh, in jams, desserts, and as a flavoring in various products.

17. **Yarrow (Achillea millefolium)**
    - **Element:** Venus

- Yarrow's delicate and feathery appearance aligns it with the Venus element, symbolizing love and healing.
- Yarrow leaves and flowers are used in herbal remedies for various potential benefits.

18. **Violet (Viola odorata)**
    - **Element:** Venus
    - Violets' charming and fragrant flowers connect them with the Venus element, symbolizing love and innocence.
    - Violet flowers are used in herbal teas, culinary creations, and confectionery for their sweet scent and taste.

19. **Strawflower (Helichrysum bracteatum)**
    - **Element:** Venus
    - Strawflower's everlasting blooms and use in crafts align it with the Venus element, symbolizing love and endurance.
    - Strawflowers are often used in dried flower arrangements and decorations.

20. **Periwinkle (Vinca minor)**
    - **Element:** Venus
    - Periwinkle's charming blue flowers and ground-covering growth connect it with the Venus element, symbolizing love and protection.
    - Periwinkle is used in landscaping and has a history of medicinal use.

Saturday - Herbs of Saturn (Earth Element):

Saturday's herbs, aligned with Saturn and the Earth element, include patchouli and comfrey. These herbs promote discipline, introspection, and grounding, facilitating inner strength and resilience in spiritual practices. They encourage patience and perseverance, guiding individuals through the challenges and lessons of fasting with steadfastness.

Saturday Herbs with Saturn Element:

1. **Sage (Salvia officinalis)**
    - **Element:** Saturn
    - Sage's wisdom and grounding qualities connect it with the Saturn element, symbolizing discipline and structure.
    - Sage is an aromatic herb used to flavor dishes like stuffing, sausages, and poultry.
2. **Thyme (Thymus vulgaris)**
    - **Element:** Saturn
    - Thyme's earthy and enduring nature aligns it with Saturn's stability and structure.

- Thyme is a fragrant herb used to season various dishes, particularly roasted meats, soups, and stews.

3. **Mugwort (Artemisia vulgaris)**
   - **Element:** Saturn
   - Mugwort's resilience and connection to dreams and divination make it a representation of the Saturn element.
   - Mugwort is used in herbal teas and spiritual practices for its calming effects and dream-enhancing properties.

4. **Comfrey (Symphytum officinale)**
   - **Element:** Saturn
   - Comfrey's ability to support healing and regeneration aligns it with Saturn's restorative energy.
   - Comfrey leaves and roots are used in topical ointments and teas to promote skin and bone health.

5. **Black Walnut (Juglans nigra)**
   - **Element:** Saturn
   - Black walnut's strong and enduring shell represents the Saturn element, symbolizing protection and boundaries.
   - Black walnut is used for its flavorful nuts and the tannin-rich hulls in herbal remedies.

6. **Yarrow (Achillea millefolium)**
   - **Element:** Saturn
   - Yarrow's resilience and ability to thrive in harsh conditions align it with the Saturn element, symbolizing endurance.
   - Yarrow is used in herbal remedies for its potential health benefits, including digestive support and wound healing.

7. **Wormwood (Artemisia absinthium)**
   - **Element:** Saturn
   - Wormwood's bitter and strong presence connects it with Saturn's power and boundaries.
   - Wormwood is used sparingly due to its intense bitterness and is an essential ingredient in absinthe liqueur.

8. **Burdock (Arctium lappa)**
   - **Element:** Saturn
   - Burdock's deep roots and grounding qualities make it a representation of the Saturn element, symbolizing stability.
   - Burdock roots are used in culinary dishes and herbal remedies for their potential health benefits, particularly in supporting skin health.

9. **Horehound (Marrubium vulgare)**
   - **Element:** Saturn

- Horehound's resilience and traditional use in cough remedies align it with Saturn's enduring energy.
- Horehound is used in herbal teas and lozenges for its potential benefits in soothing respiratory discomfort.

10. **Black Cohosh (Actaea racemosa)**
    - **Element:** Saturn
    - Black Cohosh's deep-rooted nature and traditional medicinal use connect it with Saturn's grounding influence.
    - Black Cohosh is used in herbal remedies, particularly for women's health support during menopause.

11. **Hyssop (Hyssopus officinalis)**
    - **Element:** Saturn
    - Hyssop's durability and historical use in purification rituals align it with Saturn's cleansing energy.
    - Hyssop is used in culinary dishes and herbal teas for its aromatic and slightly bitter flavor.

12. **Juniper (Juniperus communis)**
    - **Element:** Saturn
    - Juniper's hardy nature and association with protection make it a representation of the Saturn element.
    - Juniper berries are used to flavor gin and various dishes, offering a unique, pine-like taste.

13. **Valerian (Valeriana officinalis)**
    - **Element:** Saturn
    - Valerian's grounding and calming properties align it with Saturn's influence over peace and stability.
    - Valerian root is used in herbal remedies to promote relaxation and improve sleep quality.

14. **Hawthorn (Crataegus spp.)**
    - **Element:** Saturn
    - Hawthorn's sturdy branches and folklore associations with protection connect it with Saturn's grounding energy.
    - Hawthorn berries, leaves, and flowers are used in herbal remedies to support heart health.

15. **Bistort (Polygonum bistorta)**
    - **Element:** Saturn
    - Bistort's ability to grow in challenging environments aligns it with Saturn's resilience.
    - Bistort root has been used in traditional herbal medicine for its potential astringent and digestive benefits.

16. **Blessed Thistle (Cnicus benedictus)**
    - **Element:** Saturn
    - Blessed Thistle's historical use in protective and healing rituals aligns it with Saturn's energy.
    - Blessed Thistle is sometimes used in herbal teas and remedies for its potential digestive and stimulating properties.
17. **Sandalwood (Santalum album)**
    - **Element:** Saturn
    - Sandalwood's sacred and grounding qualities connect it with Saturn's spiritual aspects.
    - Sandalwood is often used in incense, perfumes, and skincare for its aromatic and calming properties.
18. **Patchouli (Pogostemon cablin)**
    - **Element:** Saturn
    - Patchouli's earthy and grounding scent makes it a representation of Saturn's stability.
    - Patchouli is used in perfumes, aromatherapy, and skincare for its unique and enduring aroma.
19. **Hemlock (Conium maculatum)**
    - **Element:** Saturn
    - Hemlock's toxicity and historical associations with banishment align it with Saturn's boundaries.
    - Hemlock is a poisonous plant and should not be consumed or used in any way.
20. **Wolfsbane (Aconitum spp.)**
    - **Element:** Saturn
    - Wolfsbane's toxic nature and use in protection rituals connect it with Saturn's cautionary energy.
    - Wolfsbane is extremely poisonous and should not be handled or ingested.

Incorporating herbs aligned with their corresponding days of the week and elemental influences enhances the fasting experience holistically. These herbs not only support physical health and well-being but also deepen spiritual awareness and emotional resilience. By consciously selecting herbs that resonate with each day's elemental qualities, individuals engaging in fasting can enrich their spiritual journey, foster balance, and align more closely with divine guidance and purpose. This practice underscores the holistic approach to fasting, integrating natural remedies that support the body, mind, and spirit throughout the fasting week.

Enhanced Elemental Alignment: Aligning herbs with specific days and their elemental influences enhances the energetic resonance and effectiveness of fasting practices. This alignment supports a holistic approach by harmonizing physical, emotional, and spiritual energies throughout the fasting week.

Spiritual Focus and Clarity: Using herbs corresponding to each day's elemental qualities fosters spiritual focus and clarity. This aids in deepening meditation, prayer, and reflection during fasting, facilitating a heightened sense of connection with divine guidance and purpose.

Emotional Stability and Resilience:

Herbs associated with elemental energies contribute to emotional stability and resilience throughout the fasting period. They help manage stress, anxiety, and emotional fluctuations, promoting inner peace and strength amidst spiritual disciplines.

Physical Vitality and Well-being:

Utilizing herbs aligned with elemental influences supports physical vitality and well-being during fasting. For instance, herbs of the Sun (Fire element) on Sunday, such as ginger and cinnamon, provide energy and warmth, aiding in physical stamina and digestion.

Emotional Nurturing and Support:

Herbs like chamomile and jasmine, associated with the Moon (Water element) on Monday, offer emotional nurturing and support. They calm the mind, soothe emotions, and enhance receptivity to spiritual insights, fostering emotional balance and tranquility.

Mental Clarity and Focus:

Wednesday's herbs of Mercury (Air element), such as lavender and lemongrass, promote mental clarity and focus. They aid in clear thinking, communication, and decision-making during fasting, supporting intellectual pursuits and spiritual discernment.

Scriptural Basis

- **Psalm 19:14:** "May these words of my mouth and this meditation of my heart be pleasing in your sight, Lord, my Rock and my Redeemer."
- **Psalm 119:105:** "Your word is a lamp for my feet, a light on my path."

- **Proverbs 3:5-6:** "Trust in the Lord with all your heart and lean not on your own understanding; in all your ways submit to him, and he will make your paths straight."

Incorporating herbs aligned with their corresponding elemental influences throughout the fasting week enriches the spiritual journey by supporting physical health, emotional balance, and spiritual alignment. This holistic approach enhances the effectiveness of fasting practices, facilitating deeper connections with divine wisdom, peace, and guidance.

By consciously selecting and utilizing herbs that resonate with each day's elemental qualities, individuals engaging in fasting can cultivate a harmonious integration of body, mind, and spirit. This intentional practice not only enhances the overall fasting experience but also fosters personal growth, resilience, and spiritual enrichment.

Spiritual Growth and Transformation:

The use of herbs aligned with elemental energies supports spiritual growth and transformation throughout the fasting period. Each day's herbs facilitate a deeper connection with divine wisdom, helping individuals align their spiritual practices with their personal and communal intentions.

Holistic Healing and Wellness:

Incorporating herbs that resonate with specific elemental qualities promotes holistic healing and wellness. From physical rejuvenation to emotional balance and mental clarity, these herbs contribute to overall well-being during fasting, fostering a harmonious integration of body, mind, and spirit.

Community and Ritual:

Using herbs according to their elemental associations enhances communal and ritualistic aspects of fasting. It strengthens the collective spiritual journey, fostering unity and shared experiences among individuals or groups engaging in fasting practices together.

Practical Application and Integration

Neighborhood Interaction:

When fasting together in community or as a group, aligning herbs with elemental influences can enrich collective spiritual practices. This promotes unity and a shared sense of purpose, encouraging mutual support and camaraderie among participants.

Personal Reflection and Introspection:

Herbs corresponding to each day's elemental qualities aid in personal reflection and introspection during fasting. They create a conducive environment for inner exploration, self-discovery, and spiritual discernment, allowing individuals to deepen their connection with their inner selves and with the divine.

Environmental Connection:

Recognizing the elemental associations of herbs also fosters a deeper connection with the natural world. It encourages mindfulness of the earth's resources and cycles, promoting gratitude and stewardship in relation to the plants and elements that sustain and support life.

Scriptural Basis

- **Psalm 139:23-24:** "Search me, God, and know my heart; test me and know my anxious thoughts. See if there is any offensive way in me, and lead me in the way everlasting."
- **Colossians 3:17:** "And whatever you do, whether in word or deed, do it all in the name of the Lord Jesus, giving thanks to God the Father through him."

Using Sunday through Saturday herbs with their elemental associations enriches the fasting experience by aligning physical, emotional, and spiritual energies with divine intentions. This intentional practice supports holistic healing, personal growth, and community engagement, fostering a deeper connection with God and the natural world.

By integrating herbs that resonate with each day's elemental qualities, individuals embarking on fasting journeys can enhance their spiritual practices, cultivate inner peace, and seek divine guidance with clarity and purpose. This holistic approach not only strengthens faith and resilience but also deepens appreciation for the sacred rhythms of life and creation.

Enhanced Spiritual Discipline:

Incorporating herbs aligned with elemental energies enhances spiritual discipline during fasting. These herbs serve as aids in maintaining focus, dedication, and perseverance in spiritual practices, supporting a deeper connection with divine presence and guidance.

Emotional Resilience and Stability:

Herbs corresponding to each day's elemental qualities contribute to emotional resilience and stability. They help individuals manage stress, anxiety, and emotional fluctuations that may arise during fasting, promoting inner peace and emotional well-being.

Physical Detoxification and Vitality:

Utilizing herbs known for their cleansing and revitalizing properties supports physical detoxification and vitality. These herbs aid in purifying the body, boosting immune function, and enhancing overall physical health during the fasting period.

Ritualistic Practices:

Engaging in ritualistic practices with herbs aligned to elemental energies enriches the fasting experience. It deepens the ceremonial aspect of fasting, fostering reverence, mindfulness, and spiritual alignment with divine purpose and intention.

Personalized Spiritual Journey:

Selecting herbs based on their elemental associations allows for a personalized spiritual journey during fasting. It encourages individuals to tailor their practices according to their unique spiritual needs, preferences, and intentions, promoting authenticity and deeper spiritual growth.

Seasonal and Environmental Awareness:

Recognizing the elemental influences of herbs cultivates awareness of seasonal and environmental rhythms. It encourages gratitude and stewardship toward the natural world, fostering a deeper connection with creation and its role in sustaining spiritual and physical well-being.

Scriptural Basis

- **Psalm 51:10:** "Create in me a pure heart, O God, and renew a steadfast spirit within me."

- **Galatians 5:22-23:** "But the fruit of the Spirit is love, joy, peace, forbearance, kindness, goodness, faithfulness, gentleness, and self-control."

Nutritional Support:

Herbs such as dandelion and nettle offer vitamins and minerals crucial for maintaining health during fasting periods when solid foods are restricted. They can be consumed in teas or as supplements to complement liquid diets commonly adopted during fasts.

Detoxification:

Many herbs possess detoxifying properties that assist the body in eliminating toxins accumulated from environmental pollutants and processed foods. This cleansing effect is beneficial during fasting as it supports the liver and kidneys, essential organs in toxin removal.

Energy and Vitality:

Adaptogenic herbs like ashwagandha and ginseng may help mitigate fatigue and promote resilience to stress, which can be heightened during fasting. This allows individuals to maintain energy levels and mental clarity throughout the fasting period.

Spiritual and Emotional Balance:

Herbs like lavender and chamomile are known for their calming effects on the nervous system, aiding in emotional stability and promoting a tranquil state conducive to prayer and meditation during fasting.

Scriptural Basis

- **Psalm 104:14:** "He causes the grass to grow for the cattle, and vegetation for the service of man, that he may bring forth food from the earth."
- **Genesis 1:29:** "And God said, 'See, I have given you every herb that yields seed which is on the face of all the earth, and every tree whose fruit yields seed; to you it shall be for food.'"

During this time of fasting, strengthen my faith and increase my dependence on you alone. Help me to seek you earnestly, knowing that you are a rewarder of those who diligently seek you. May this fasting period be a time of spiritual breakthrough and financial blessing in my life, to the glory of your name.

The practice of incorporating prayers and affirmations into fasting for spiritual sensitivity and clarity is grounded in the belief that God desires intimacy and communication with His children. It is a journey of deepening relationship, where fasting becomes not merely a physical discipline but a spiritual gateway to hearing God's voice and discerning His will. By aligning prayers with scriptural promises and affirming faith in God's guidance, individuals can experience profound spiritual growth and clarity during their fasting journey.

Incorporating prayers and affirmations into fasting for emotional balance and stability is rooted in the belief that God desires wholeness and peace for His children. It is a journey of surrendering anxieties and fears, trusting in God's promises, and experiencing His peace that transcends understanding. By aligning prayers with scriptural truths and affirming faith in God's provision, individuals cultivate resilience and emotional strength during their fasting journey.

The integration of prayers and affirmations into fasting practices for emotional balance and stability enhances the spiritual experience and deepens intimacy with God. Through heartfelt prayers and declarations rooted in scripture, believers cultivate a responsive heart to God's peace and resilience in facing emotional challenges. This spiritual discipline of fasting combined with prayerful affirmation invites divine comfort and strength, transforming individuals into vessels of God's peace and stability.

The journey of fasting, prayer, and using herbs for financial breakthrough, physical health, and wellness is a deeply spiritual and transformative experience. It involves seeking God's guidance, trusting in His provision, and affirming His promises over your life. Through this journey, individuals can experience not only physical benefits such as detoxification and vitality but also spiritual growth, emotional healing, and a strengthened relationship with God.

In summary, incorporating the use of proper herbs during fasting enhances the spiritual, physical, and emotional aspects of the experience. It supports health and vitality, aids in detoxification, and contributes to a focused and spiritually attuned mindset. Coupled with prayers and affirmation prayers rooted in scripture, this holistic approach fosters a deeper connection with God, promotes personal growth, and invites divine intervention in areas of financial need and overall well-being. As you begin on this journey, may you find strength, clarity, and abundant blessings as you seek God's will and His presence in your life.